T0022538

Teddy Spha Palasthira was born in London. He has served in the Thai diplomatic service, completed a long career in advertising, was a visiting professor at the Missouri School of Journalism, and is an honorary Barrister-at-Law at Lambs Chambers, Middle Temple, London, from where he graduated a long time ago. A recipient of the Italian Order of Merit, Grand Officer of the Republic, Teddy is now into his fourth career as a writer. He has written two books on advertising in the last century, and has since written *Addresses* in 2010, *The Last Siamese* in 2013, *The Siamese Trail of Ho Chi Minh* in 2016, and *Ode to Manuela of Trento* in 2018. He lives in Thailand with his wife and family.

SIAMESE ANGLOPHILE

BY THE SAME AUTHOR

A Print Point of View

The Rise of Asian Advertising

Addresses

The Last Siamese

The Siamese Trail of Ho Chi Minh

Ode to Manuela

SIAMESE ANGLOPHILE

50s British Schoolboy to
90s American Adman

My Life of Jobs

Teddy Spha Palasthira

TALISMAN

First published in 2022 by

Talisman Publishing Pte Ltd
talisman@apdsing.com

www.talismanpublishing.com

ISBN: 978-981-18-4816-2
Copyright © 2022 Teddy Spha Palasthira

Cover inspired by Artist Graham Byfield

All rights reserved. No part of this publication may be
reproduced in any form or by any means, electronic or
mechanical, including photocopying, recording, or any
information storage and retrieval system, without the
prior written permission of the copyright owners.

To my wife Patricia

CONTENTS

AUTHOR'S NOTE

Reader be warned.

The events described in the first eight chapters of this book happened more than sixty years ago, and the last two chapters from the seventies to the mid-nineties of the twentieth century. They were different eras, and I write about the way things were. In doing so, I was required to make a difficult choice. Was I going to tone down the language to describe certain people's discriminatory words and behaviour that were prevalent at the time, and couch my narrative in the euphemisms of modern political correctness? Or even censor them completely? Or should I tell my stories the way they actually happened? After much deliberation and soul-searching, I chose to report the speech and the mores of those times even if it makes us a little uncomfortable today.

It is not easy trying to apply 21st century moral standards to political issues such as race, sexual orientation, ageism, inclusivity and diversity when describing real life events of a different century.

I have attempted to record these events to the best of my own recollection, and apologise in advance if by presenting the plain truth I have caused any offence.

I was much encouraged by Miguel de Cervantes who wisely said four centuries ago: 'Honesty is the best policy.'

INTRODUCTION

Work is a nuisance and jobs a bothersome business.

This is a memoir of my adventures in working at a great many jobs beginning in 1950s Britain.

Work is what some of us don't really like doing very much, while others love it, and can't stop doing it. For most of us, in its simplest form, work is what we need to do to put food on the table. But however tedious it is to execute, and however appealing it is to the workaholic, it is generally unavoidable.

Long ago as a student in London, I wanted to take my girlfriend out to dinner at Wiltons, my favourite restaurant, so I did some work. I needed the extra 10 UK pounds to splurge on some delicious Dover sole. The work was temporary and after I had completed the job, I went back to my other work, and that was to cram for my law exams.

And then there are those who suffer from ergophobia, a curious word to describe an aversion to work. Avoiding work is quite a skill of its own, and people like Bertie Wooster of Jeeves-the-butler fame worked very hard at it.

The hardest work of all for school children who are described by their teachers as 'lazy' is simply to sit down at their desks and just do their assigned homework. But when they go out to play with their friends, they too, really work hard at it.

The two biggest barriers in getting work done, for me at any rate, are time and its limited availability, and procrastination which is, paradoxically, a waste of time. A century ago, Jerome K. Jerome, the British humorist, elegantly echoed my sentiments on procrastination: 'I like work, it fascinates me. I can sit and look at it for hours.'

Isn't it curious that anyone, children and adults alike, can fall into the trap of doing any amount of work, provided it is not the work he or she is supposed to be doing at that moment?

And then there are people who over exert themselves in activities that they don't really consider work at all; as in the classic case of a man who is hopelessly in love and works ceaselessly to win his lady's favours, even though the poor man knows his efforts could result in unrequited love. Or the amateur gardener who works tirelessly at tending her flower beds purely for pleasure and recreation. Or culture vultures who work hard at visiting as many museums in London as they can in a week. I won't even go into the hard work some of my friends do to improve their golf handicap.

It was Henry More, the philosopher, who observed as far back as the mid-1600s, that people who live only to amuse themselves work harder at the task than most people do in earning their living.

One of the most admirable forms of work is for those who play a game to win, especially Olympic hopefuls, unless of course they are soccer players who are highly paid, and get paid even when they lose.

Then there are mega-rich billionaires who work for the sheer pleasure of it, with the single-minded objective in life of making money – more than they will ever need.

The most enjoyable work for many must surely be the art of preparing appetizing food. For many others it is taking the dog out for a walk.

For myself, I enjoy working at my writing even though the returns are meagre.

For most of us, though, it is a choice. The most boring work can be interesting, even rewarding, if we are able to connect the task at hand with its ultimate purpose.

Everything one does in one's daily life, it seems, is work.

But having a job is much more challenging.

While work consists of our general efforts and activities that we do to accomplish a goal, a job is a specific paid-for task. And that's often where the poor young high-school leaver cannot tell the difference.

In my teens I was continually and annoyingly bombarded by well-meaning adults with unhelpful questions like: 'What are you going to do when you grow up?'

Invariably I would give an equally unhelpful answer: 'I don't know yet. I'm going to look for a job and go to work.'

This then, is what this book is partly all about. Looking for a job after leaving school and then doing the work.

Chapters one to eight are a series of retrospective essays, looking back at post-war Britain, and half a chapter on Germany, when there was always work to be found, in an era when there was little unemployment.

Chapters nine and ten cover my remaining years of gainful employment around the globe.

The last chapter looks at the status of work today and what jobs may look like in the future.

In my quest to find a job that I was really good at, I would discover that they came in many forms.

Many were demanding, most were unrewarding and others just dead end ones. It took me some time to discover the high-powered ones, normally performed by the people I worked for.

As a young student in England, looking at the 'Jobs Vacant' ads in the local newspapers and the National Union of Students' bulletin boards, I discovered I was only good for an 'entry-level job'.

My biggest discovery was that in today's world, our job defines who we are. I've always believed that it is fundamentally important to know what people do for a living, before even beginning to understand that person.

I also discovered that to be good at a job requires hard work.

I'm reminded of the old Scots saying: 'hard work never killed a man.'

We were taught at school that the rewards of hard work are many: passing exams with distinction, entrance into university, praise and personal satisfaction for a job well done, career advancement, professional success, recognition of one's good work, even a decent salary. Wealth, I discovered, is not derived from hard work. We were not taught that the returns on labour are negligible when compared with the returns on capital.

Now that I have retired from the corporate and academic world, and no longer take on paid jobs, I am still doing work that is taken for granted and is just as rewarding. I still do work around the house, tending to my garden, driving and shopping, and helping my wife produce some fantastic dishes in the kitchen, and even doing the washing-up afterwards.

Perhaps the most satisfying non-paid job I have ever done was to join a volunteer group to help console and repatriate several hundred stranded Italian tourists in Thailand who had lost all their possessions, including their passports, some even their loved ones, during the Boxing Day Tsunami of 2004. The least satisfying non-paid jobs have been sitting on councils and committees, and I have been involved in many.

By far the most fulfilling job I do today is the continued pursuance of knowledge. I spend a great deal of my time reading, researching and learning, essential work for writers.

After several decades of different varieties of work, I'm still working hard at it.

Finally, a few words on the title of this book.

I was born in London when Thailand was still called 'Siam', and I continued to be called a 'Siamese' until 1949, when Thailand became the country's official name, and I was henceforth known as a 'Thai'. I was brought up as an English boy throughout most of my childhood, and together with my English legal education, I had developed a strong affinity and love for the culture, history and language of the country of my birth.

Thus *Siamese Anglophile.*

CHAPTER ONE
ELTHAMIA BLUES

It was with considerable trepidation that on a cold, grey September afternoon in 1954, I found myself dropped off by taxi at the Greek revival front portal of an austere 18th century English mansion. My heart sank and I was filled with apprehension. This brick and plaster, five-bay two-storey structure was where I would be spending the next four years of my life: Eltham College.

While many of my old English school chums look back at Eltham as the best years of their lives, for me it was pure hell. I failed to distinguish myself as a pupil, and in this cloistered boarding school I led a life of dejection. It was hard work and possibly the most strenuous kind I had ever known.

Eltham was the final school in my long, tortuous scholastic journey across six countries and thirteen institutions of learning, which had started in England in 1941, just when the air raids over London by Hitler's deadly *Luftwaffe* were at their peak, forcing my parents and me to be on a constant move to seek safety. For the next five years, I was to attend two kindergartens in Kensington, followed by three junior schools in England, (Virginia Water Junior School in Surrey, a school in Bath, and at the end of the war, Carroll School in London).

This is not meant to be a poor-mixed-up-kid narrative, but Britain in the forties and fifties was a far cry from the Swinging Sixties of the Beatles and James Bond, with exciting new developments in fashion, social attitudes and culture, and from the eighties onwards had become the world's sixth largest economy. My Eltham College days were at a time of post-war austerity, and where simple pleasures and any kind of fun were in short supply.

★ ★ ★ ★

In 1946 the family moved from London to Paris, where I found myself at the tender age of eight in *Les Abeilles,* * *huitieme classe,* a French *primaire,* where all my new friends were French. After a year I was beginning to forget how to speak and write English, so my father wisely sent me off to the American Community School in Paris, with a brief interruption in the autumn of 1948 at the International School in Geneva for one semester, where most students were also American. Many English language schools after the war were set up for American children whose parents were posted to Europe by the US government to execute the Marshall Plan, a soft loan of 17 billion dollars, to help restore the economies to Western European countries that had recently been devastated by the war. For the first time, I was exposed to a totally new version of the English language. I discovered that it was the same language spoken by some of my favourite film heroes like Laurel and Hardy, Danny Kaye and Tarzan.

My introduction to Hollywood films was in 1945, when my parents took me to see *Tarzan's New York Adventure* at our local London cinema. In one dramatic scene, an earthy Tarzan, played by Johnny Weissmuller, the Olympic swimming champion,

---

* French for bees. An appropriate name, as we were expected to work like them too.

was chased by the bad guys and to escape them, jumped off the Brooklyn Bridge into the East River, and subsequently arrested. In court, he was sworn in and directed to tell the 'truth, the whole truth, and nothing but the truth.' Clearly affronted, Tarzan said in retort: *'Tarzan never lie'*. The memory of this wonderfully naïve declaration of honesty is with me still. This cinematic experience was my baptism to the movies, which developed into a lifetime's passion for the medium.

When our family moved to Bangkok in 1949, I found myself in the midst of American evangelical teachers at the Seventh Day Adventist School, where daily readings of the Holy Bible were compulsory. After school, in the evenings and during weekends, I had private Thai language and literature tutorials.

When my Thai was halfway passable, I was plonked into a classroom of twenty-five Thai boys at Assumption College, Thailand's leading Catholic school. Among the many cultural shocks so far, this was surely the greatest. It was my tenth school to date. Paradoxically, I was secretly happy to learn my own language, difficult though it was, as well as to make friends with Thai boys for the first time.

In 1951, my father was posted to the Thai Embassy in Rome, so off I went every morning on a school bus full of American kids to the Overseas School of Rome. I had just turned thirteen. I have often wondered what would have happened if my father had sent me to an *Italian* school. Would I have married Manuela, an Italian girl, whom I was destined to meet sixteen years later?

Finally, in 1954, I was packed off to Eltham College, an English boarding school for boys. By this time I'd had enough. Which brings me back to the present.*

★ ★ ★ ★

---

* I wrote about my early life in wartime England and post-war France, Italy and Thailand, in *Addresses*, published by Post Books in 2010.

I'd always dreaded the first day of school. I dreaded making new friends and I dreaded learning a new language. Each school had its own culture and I had to get used to a whole set of new rules and regulations, not to mention the different sports that I was required to play.

And then there were the disparate uniforms: short-trousered grey flannel suits and school caps in England; itchy woollen plus fours trousers and berets like Tintin in France; your school name and number sewn above the left pocket of the regulation white school shirt in Thailand. Schools by their very composition were already a lot of hard work, let alone all the new subjects one had to learn, but nothing compared with the anguish and fear on my first day at school.

The Americans partly saved me. The atmosphere in the three American schools I attended was relaxed. The academic standards were not as rigorous. Even fourteen year old ninth-graders were still learning how to spell, and regularly held what they called 'spelling bee' contests, where I scored well. Teachers seemed to be more *democratic*. Curiously, and to my delight, there were also girls in the class. Neither were uniforms required. Jeans and t-shirts were the requisite costume.

At the American school in 1948 Paris, my drab grey English school uniform must have looked conspicuously odd amongst a sea of colourful shirts and blue jeans. My father came to my rescue by ordering a pair of Levi's from a huge Sears, Roebuck catalogue, and from then on I blended in with the class.

Looking back, trying to be the same as my peers had always been an important part of my psyche. The problem of being continually uprooted and readjusting required not just *looking* like my contemporaries, but *feeling* the culture of my new adopted country and *thinking* like my new school mates as well. These frequent cross-border changes were to result in my turning into a totally confused and mixed-up polyglot.

4

Today, when I speak Italian, I actually think in Italian. Likewise (that's the American in me), when I speak Thai, French and English I also think in those languages. When I talk to Patricia, my American wife, all the Americanisms that I had picked up at school come rushing back to me. Even the way I think about myself is confused. My mind is English, my gestures French and my belly is Italian. In my heart, I think I'm Thai. And I love wearing American jeans.

Not that Eltham College was any better or any worse than the others. It was hard to beat *Les Abeilles* in Paris for joylessness though. After a year of *devoirs* (homework) every night, spot *dictée* (dictation) at any time of the day, and the forced recitation *par coeur* of La Fontaine's fables every week, I was soon reduced to a nervous wreck. I was only nine years old. Mercifully, I had been moved to the American Community School on Boulevard Raspail, where classes were in English. (Or so I thought. I was soon required to get used to 'American English'.)

★ ★ ★ ★

It was my first night at Eltham and a mood of depression had suddenly overcome me. I was lying awake in the dormitory and the boy next to me was breathing heavily. For the first time in my life I was sleeping in the same room with a bunch of total strangers.* I was trying to fall asleep but I couldn't.

I started to reminisce about my comfortable life in Rome, where I had spent the previous two years having a wonderful time. I had been learning Italian and enjoying my food. I even won first prize at the Overseas School's pasta eating competition. The event had been reported in the social page of the *Rome Daily American,* and my name appeared in print for the

---

* Except during the night-time Blitz of 1941-43 when my parents and I sought refuge and safety in London Underground stations, camping out with hundreds of people.

first time in my life. I had started to appreciate the soft skin and long silky hair of American girls in my Freshman class, meaning that I had been in the 9th grade, and had even dated one of them. They all wore lipstick, which I found alluring. I adored my Levi's that I proudly wore every day, I had luxuriated in my expatriate lifestyle in a most beautiful country, and I had begun to love life itself.

The Overseas School of Rome is still in Via Cassia, half-an-hour drive from the Via Nomentana area where we lived. It was launched in the early fifties as an Anglo-American experiment in secular high school education, for children of parents attached to the Food and Agricultural Organisation (FAO), the diplomatic corps and multinational executives. My first girlfriend Suzie's father, Richard Spater, for example, was head of Trans World Airlines' Southern European operation. Leslie Yen, one of my closest friends, was the son of the owner of Ristorante Shanghai in Via Borgonona, Rome's first Chinese restaurant. His father was the Chinese Ambassador to Italy before he lost his position in 1948 when the Communists took over his country. And there was Carol, a delicious girl and an aspiring starlet in the 12th grade, whom all the boys drooled over, the daughter of Robert Rossen, the Hollywood film producer, who was in town to shoot *Mambo,* an Italo-American co-production starring Silvana Mangano and Michael Rennie.

I had been the only Thai kid at the Overseas School, but in this international ambience, I had been reasonably happy. I had spent my life as a foreigner in every country I lived in. Today, in the global village of the 21st century, I would have been called a TCK, a Third Culture Kid, a new demographic description of children of multinational executives and diplomats, at home everywhere. But in the 40s and 50s of the last century, children whose parents were always on the move from one country to another, particularly if they were not born in their homeland, were a rarity, forever seeking their identity. Was I English, French or Italian? During my first 28 years, I had spent only one and a half years in Thailand, so I was not even very comfortable being Thai. It never occurred to me at the time that I was suffering from an identity crisis. Now, in my ripe old age, all this upheaval has paid off. I feel at home wherever I am.

Now that I am a citizen of the world, I don't really *believe* in borders very much.

★ ★ ★ ★

But let us return to the story of my school days at Eltham. The last time I had seen England was in 1946, and my memories of London where we lived throughout the war were a landscape of bombed out houses, mounds of rubble and the smell of burning tar and wood. Wartime London is still deeply ingrained in my subconscious: nights of the Blitz, piercing air raid sirens, taking refuge in the Barons Court tube station, the distant throb of German planes, barrage balloons, anti-aircraft guns in the streets near our home, the crash of bombs and wearing stuffy gas masks, which we had to carry everywhere in a cardboard box slung over our shoulders.

It wasn't until we moved to France that I had savoured the taste of grapes, bananas and cheese for the first time, as many eggs as I wanted, and even *foie gras*. Supplies of food from the French black market were endless.

In England, *everything* had been rationed. When I came back to attend school at Eltham in 1954, not much had changed. The capital was still plagued by fog caused by coal burning fireplaces, called 'pea-soupers', and food rationing was only starting to be lifted. Britain was slowly rebuilding its economy. It was a drab country.

Transition from a cosmopolitan co-ed school in the middle of the warm Mediterranean to the stark Protestant strictures of Eltham College, a boarding school for the sons of missionaries, in the small village of Mottingham on the Kent border, was a massive jolt for a sensitive boy of fifteen. I still remember the rancid smell of freshly waxed floorboards, which permeated every classroom in the building, on the first day of the autumn term. After a happy summer holiday at home in Rome, the memory of returning to Eltham barracks, a warren full of boarders and teachers with limited personal space in the minimum cubic footage required to avert a mass 'prison' outbreak, haunts me still. The stark dining hall (not at all like Harry Potter's), the cold quadrangle – 'The Old Quad' – where boarders had to assemble every evening before dinner, the rows of hard narrow beds in the monastic dormitory, the shared washrooms and the squalid latrines – what schoolboys called the 'bog'– a tiny locker for our possessions and the total lack of privacy, were presumably a test for building the famous British character. Only I wasn't British. And I haven't even started on the food.

The worst part of my Elthamian experience was surely at mealtimes. It is a myth around the world that English food is bad. It isn't. Not many cuisines can improve on good English roasts, be it pork, beef or lamb. No one can beat a well-meuniered Dover Sole or a succulent Beef Wellington. And unique sweet delicacies like buttered crumpets, treacle tart and sticky toffee pudding can be found nowhere else in the world (although so-called 'English tearooms' in foreign hotels try to do their best).

But the food that was available when I returned to Britain in 1954 was definitely not the best. The meals at Eltham were arguably *the worst* I have ever had in my life. The preparation of good food depends on two important ingredients: the *quality of the raw materials* and the *way the food is cooked*. Eltham had neither.

Britain in the early fifties was still suffering from post-war shortages and the food rationing of essential commodities such as meat, cheese, butter, tea and sugar. It was not completely lifted until 1954, a full nine years after the end of the war. The lack of basic food in wartime Britain was so serious to the nation's existence, that it had its own name: the 'kitchen front'. With such deficiencies, even the best chefs were challenged.

I once had the misfortune to wander into the school kitchen. Apart from the malodorous boiled cabbages and the sorry sight of overcooked meat that wasn't very good to start off with, toiling away in the kitchen were the school's four cleaning ladies with dark brown aprons and scarves making a brave attempt to prepare our daily sustenance. Without wanting to sound fractious, it took a long time before my faith in English cooking was restored.

Part of the myth (and the reality) of bad British cooking can be put down to one rather ill-informed Victorian lady who left an indelible mark on generations of English cooks. Her name was Isabella Beeton whose book *Mrs Beeton's Book of Household Management* was a guide to running a household in 1861. It was a *sensible* book that taught the sensible middle-class Victorian homemaker how to dress, the correct way to look after children, how to manage servants, even how to identify poisonous foods. *Haute cuisine* was not her forte. One of her recommendations was to boil pasta for one hour and three quarters before serving. For macaroni though, she recommended a mere three quarters of an hour, just long enough 'to simmer'.

Mrs Beeton's unpalatable influence on the kitchens of the British bourgeoisie was to last well into the first half of the 20th century.

Heinz tinned spaghetti, a soft unsavoury pre-cooked preparation, was served to Manuela, my future Italian wife, by her English landlady on her first visit to London in July 1967, in a well-intentioned effort to welcome her.

'Ere you are, luv! A plyte of Ayetalian spa'ge'ee to make you feel at 'ome!'

She had boiled the contents of the can for a full ten minutes.

At Eltham, even the tea, that most iconic of British wartime sustenance, was undrinkable. Served from a giant tea urn large enough to syphon 40 cups, it was a weak, sweetened brew with hardly enough milk to hide its bitter, stewed taste. Rumour was that it was laced with bromide to keep our libidos under control, although if that was the case, it didn't seem to work.

Eltham College wasn't all bad though. It had a fine reputation for its academic record and its prowess on track and field. My father was being transferred to a new post in Asia, and needed to park me at a boarding school in England. He decided upon Eltham, in Kent, near enough to London where his colleagues at the embassy could keep a keen eye on me, and of course, because of its fine academic reputation, yet still at a fair distance away by train from the capital city's bright lights and temptations of Sodom and Gomorrah. Clearly I was sent there to study, and not to have a good time.

At least once a term, one of my father's colleagues at the embassy, Chaloke Kommarakul, the financial attaché, would invite me to stay for the weekend. As a special treat, he would take me with his family to Ley On's Chinese restaurant in Wardour Street. It was at a time when the English had got out of the habit of eating well after all the years of austerity. Ley On's was one of the oldest Chinese restaurants in London, but it wasn't very good, although it was better than eating Spam sandwiches and Swiss Rolls at the Lyon's Corner House. There were no Thai restaurants at the time.*

My latest school had been founded in 1842 for the sons of

---

* There are now around 2000 Thai restaurants in the UK, with several hundred in London alone.

missionaries in Africa, India and China, where many of my fellow boarders were born. By the 1950s, there were only about 200 missionary sons, one quarter of all Elthamians. It had also become a day school. Its nonconformist Protestant tradition involved daily attendance at Chapel, a brief morning service when uplifting hymns were sung, and where announcements were made by the headmaster, Mr Turberville. The school was originally located at Blackheath Village and relocated to Mottingham in 1912, taking over the classic building previously occupied by the Royal Naval College.

One of Eltham's most famous alumni was Eric Liddell, the British Olympic Gold Medalist runner. Born in Tiensin, China, to Scottish missionary parents, he famously won the 400 metre gold in the Paris Olympics of 1924 in the record time of 47.6 seconds. He had to withdraw from the 100 metres due to his religious beliefs that prohibited him from running on a Sunday. His rigorous Olympic training and the theological convictions that influenced him, are depicted in the Oscar winning 1981 film *Chariots of Fire*. Following his father's footsteps, he returned to China and became a teacher at an Anglo-Chinese college for wealthy students. He was interned by the invading Japanese in 1943 and died of a brain tumour on 21 February 1945, partly caused by the hardships that were inflicted on him, and sadly five months before liberation. In his memory, the Eric Liddell Sports Centre was built on the fields of Eltham College and launched on 26 June 1996. Its fitness club is open to the public.

Another famous Elthamian was George Band, who at 24, was the youngest member of the Mount Everest expedition led by Edmund Hillary and Tensing Norgay, in 1953. In 1955, Band and another climber Joe Brown, were the first to conquer Kangchenjunga, the third highest mountain in the world. Out of respect for the religious feelings of the people of Nepal and Sikkim, he stopped about three metres below the actual summit.

Like Liddell, Band was the son of Presbyterian missionaries, and born in Taiwan. He attended Eltham from 1937 to 1947 and excelled in athletics. An indoor climbing wall in the school's sports centre has been built in his honour.

★ ★ ★ ★

After an absence of 8 years I had returned to England with mixed feelings.

It was a pleasure to speak English once again. But my Englishness stopped there. I was back at work again, learning to be English. After all, I was born in England, so how difficult a job could that be?

But to be back in England and be spoken to in English by total strangers, after so many years' absence, was a bit of a cultural shock. In the streets of Rome my head would quickly spin around when I overheard English being spoken, such as American tourists talking to each other and saying something totally out of context like *'I wasn't there when Harry opened the door.'* To be able to eavesdrop on conversations and *understand every word* in a foreign country was disconcerting.

From that time, I developed the lifelong habit of eavesdropping on conversations in Thai, French or Italian in restaurants, on planes and other public places, much to the annoyance of the person I happen to be having a conversation with in English at the time. It was the same wherever I went in the world. In Thailand, I would eavesdrop on people's conversations in English, French or Italian. Once in Rome, a Thai couple was sitting next to me in a café, and I got carried away with their entire discussion. They were having a problem finding the Napoleonic museum. To their surprise and delight, I came to their rescue and pointed them in the right direction.

★ ★ ★ ★

It was now time to work hard and get a firm hold on the British matriculation system of high school education.

I had landed up at the Upper Fifth class, a year older than my English classmates. I scraped through arithmetic, algebra and geometry, worked hard at history, geography, economics, English language and literature, and sailed through French and Latin, passing all eight subjects, at what was called the Ordinary Level of Education exams. I then moved up to the Lower and Upper Sixth Forms to work hard over the next two years on three Advanced Level of Education subjects, minimum requirement for British university entrance: Economic history, modern British, European and American history (three exams that counted as one subject) and French language and literature (also one subject). I failed economic history and had to wait another year to retake it. I became known deprecatingly as a 'Third Year Sixth Former'. But at least I passed.

Was I good at school? Good English boys were good at games and sports. I was not. Thanks to my parents, I'd survived years of danger and sleepless nights during London's Blitz in the Second World War. Not getting hurt had therefore become my personal rule of survival, so I worked hard at avoiding all forms of sports that I perceived to be dangerous. Rugby was rough and dirty. It was played in the winter on the muddy fields of Eltham, and just watching opposing first fifteen house teams slog it out in the cold gave me the shivers. I was once part of a scrum, where a filthy body of boys pushed another filthy body of boys in the opposite direction for possession of the ball. Never again. If it rained, and it always did, I made sure I stayed indoors.

Although I was bad in sports, I was a good spectator. I supported the Chalmers XV, my rugby house team, and was the first to cheer them on, weather permitting.

But summer wasn't any better either. I had always been bad at ball games. I could never manage to catch the ball. I found this out when, as a boy of ten at the American school in Paris, I was given a baseball mitt to catch the ball and managed to miss all of them. I earned the moniker 'butterfingers'. It is a crime in America if you drop the ball. Cricket was much worse. The hard ball was supposed to be caught with *bare hands*. On the extremely rare occasions when I caught the ball, my palms and fingers would hurt for hours. If I continued to play this game, I thought, by the time I leave school, I wouldn't have any fingers left.

I did enjoy a good game of tennis though. I was privileged to see Lew Hoad, the Australian tennis player, win the 1957 men's singles championship on Centre Court at Wimbledon, and be presented with the silver gilt cup by the Duke of Edinburgh. Thanks to Eltham, I was able to get a ringside seat on that hot July day. It was when public schools had the kind of clout that corporations have today when it comes to booking Wimbledon.

Those eclectic years of schooling in different countries had not prepared me for any kind of academic distinction at Eltham either. Apart from French and Latin, where I got high marks, I did manage to scrape through the General Certificate Examinations in the end. I now realise, with the benefit of hindsight, that my academic performance very much depended on the friendliness and enthusiasm of the teacher.

Common to all schools, Eltham had its fair share of teachers, good and bad. They were called 'masters', and it seemed as if their main task was to 'toughen up' the schoolboys under their care.

Like me, the English writer and author of *The Day of the Jackal*, Frederick Forsyth, also went to a public school in Kent at about the same time as I did, and found that his school's philosophy was 'dedicated to bullying and the cane. Faced with that, a boy has only three choices: to capitulate and become a fawning toady, to fight back, or to withdraw into some mental carapace like a turtle in a shell. You can survive, you just don't enjoy it. I survived.'*

What really distinguished an exceptionally good master from an average one was his ability to make the subject *exciting and fun*. Better still if he had an *innate sympathy* with the problems (rare) of his pupils, rather than simply dismissing their thoughts and ideas. The average master often had a hard time empathising with his flock. The worst were those who never *ever* used an encouraging word.

The best master was the head himself. Trim, dignified and kind, Geoffrey Turburville taught Classics, but his strength lay in his ability to know the names of every single boy in school. In 1959 he retired to Samoa as a volunteer to help the poor.

The most feared master was HG Occomore, or 'Occy', the boarding school's grim housemaster. Occy ruled us boarders like a tough sergeant major. He was a pipe smoker, and he used to throw used matches and tobacco into an upside down German soldier's helmet on the floor of his office. It was whispered that he had killed the soldier in battle during the war. I was never a science student, and did not therefore attend his physics class. Fellow classmate Stephen Brown told me he kept a marble in the sleeve of his gown to use as a 'mild weapon on boys when their attention lapsed.'

After we were in our dorms and tucked in bed, we would smell the distinct aroma of Three Nuns tobacco pipe smoke, and hear the sound of canine snuffling. It was Occy on night-time patrol, making his rounds with his dachshund after lights-out, through the compound of the boarding house.

I was secretly in love with Occy's wife, who once invited a few of us spotty boys to tea. I often wondered how such a fierce man could have such a lovely wife.

---

* *The Outsider. My Life in Intrigue.* Bantam Press, 2015.

DS Moss was a wonderful French teacher. Slightly eccentric and very *simpatico,* he brought life to de Balzac's boarding house characters in *Père Goriot* and the plaintive social climber in Molière's *Le Bourgeois Gentilhomme.*

I could have performed superbly in history, my favourite subject, had 'Whoccy' Chambers been kinder to me. Unattractively overweight, thick spectacled, with a squeaky voice, he strangely wore his long, greasy tie outside his pullover; he had his favourites and clearly I was not one of them. He was also in charge of the boarders, and made caustic remarks on whatever I did.

I was fortunately assuaged by WR 'Ray' Stirling, who brought history to life, and revived my love for the subject. He was a gifted historian and an enthusiastic teacher of American history, and thanks to him I have been able to hold my own with my American friends whenever the republic's history is discussed.

Latin was another of my preferred subjects, and 'Duschie' Duchesne was an avid classics scholar, a patient teacher and an all-rounder. He was a keen sailor and proudly talked about *Moth*, his sailboat, in between tedious chapters of Caesar's *De Bello Gallico.* He was also a cricketer and an organist.

Our English teacher CAA Parkinson was so dull that he even managed to make Shakespeare boring. Try as hard as he might, he could not take the magic out of the Bard's wonderful characters and plots, although he was unable to keep me awake during long readings of Milton's *Paradise Lost.*

The most tedious was FC 'Freda' Ade, our maths teacher, already long in the tooth. During the endless silences while we were working on a written test, normally after lunch, I could hear the clock on the wall slowly ticking away the minutes, before the bell mercifully rang to end the class and save me from totally nodding off, slumped over my desk.

G McIver, the arts teacher, was by far the most empathetic.

Every piece of art we produced, good and bad, was always complimented upon. He encouraged even his most hopeless art pupils. He also taught pottery, puppetry and ran the printing club.

Despite my undistinguished performance as a *failed scholar* at Eltham, many years later I was paradoxically rated as an *exemplary teacher* by my students at the School of Journalism, when I was a Visiting Professor at the University of Missouri in America. Forty years on, it seems, I did learn something at Eltham after all.

What went wrong at Eltham? In my attempt to adapt to the culture of my latest school and make new friends, I was torn between the company of English boys and a group of rich foreign boys: one from Iraq, one from Iran and a couple of Indians born and bred in Kenya, who all *seemed* to be more cosmopolitan, and thus had more in common with me, or so I thought: Fahdli, from Baghdad, whose father was Iraqi ambassador in France; Shirazi, an Iranian Jew whose family had emigrated to England; Su-Chak and Trivedi, sons of Indian traders in Nairobi. We were known as the 'foreign legion'.

We were an unruly mob and always getting into trouble. Fahdli was often caught trying to court the village girls and invited us to join him. Trivedi and I loved the movies, so we spent our weekends at the local Odeon cinema. The problem was that all these activities outside the school were forbidden – out of bounds. Many of my misdeeds involved breaking bounds and their consequent disciplinary actions. The mere act of going out in the evening to go to the cinema, or to shop during the weekend without permission were serious offences. I was frequently gated. It was a fearful experience being severely reprimanded by Occy. How I envied the day boys who could go around whenever and wherever and with whomever they pleased.

My association with the company of foreign boys was short-lived. They all had one thing in common that I found uncomfortable. *They were all anti-British to the core.* I soon began to understand why. They came from territories that were either British colonies or former protectorates; in the fifties, over forty countries in Africa and Asia were still governed by the Colonial Office.

Their denizens were made to feel inferior in their own countries. Trivedi told me that he was brought up in a colony where it was normal to see signs outside clubs and hotels that barred entry to the indigenous population. *('Dogs and Coloured People not Allowed.')*

In July 1956, my foreign chums cheered when Nasser, the Egyptian president, seized control of the Suez Canal from the British and French. They cheered once again in 1957 when the USSR launched the Sputnik, the earth's first artificial satellite in space.

The Soviet Union was seen by the Third World as their anti-colonial champion, and the adoption of Marxist ideology by the colonised peoples served as a guide to their struggle for independence. Many Third World students in the fifties from the newly independent nations of Africa and Asia, who were to graduate from the Peoples' Friendship University of Russia,* were recruited and trained as future leaders sympathetic to Soviet ideology and anti-West values.

Coming from Thailand, a country that had never been colonised, I was too naïve at the time to really understand the full extent of colonialism and my friends' resentments.

Only in my later years did I make sense of the iniquities of European domination over Africans and Asians, and how many problems colonialism had caused in the world. I no longer blamed my Arab and Indian friends who had placed their hopes

---

* Known as University of the Toilers of the East in the 1920s. For a full description, see p18 from my book *The Siamese Trail of Ho Chi Minh* (Post Publishing Bangkok 2015).

on the Soviets for the way they felt, rather than on the self-proclaimed 'liberal' West.

Many anti-British educated Asians and Africans though – among them Mahatama Gandhi and Jomo Kenyatta – returned to their countries and introduced the benefits of their British education to their peoples, such as parliamentary democracy, the civil service and the rule of law, and became successful militant independence leaders.

In this present age of 'Black Lives Matter', Britain's colonial past is now under serious scrutiny. In British universities today, there is an emergence of a new breed of historians who are confronting the injustices of the past, where the legacy of Empire has turned out to be the forceful occupation and the cruel enslavement of other races and peoples. It is hoped that future generations will be taught that imperialism and slavery were very much intertwined.

Britain in the 21st century is very different from the country where I was born, just before the outbreak of the Second World War. I was nearly always the only non-white person at the schools I attended (outside of my country) and although I was in the minority, I was never consciously made aware that I was different. I can only surmise that I was lucky to have lived in a privileged environment with multinational and multicultured contemporaries, sons and daughters of diplomats, international civil servants, lawyers, doctors, Christian missionaries, corporate executives, and even royalty.

True, I had an identity crisis, but it had more to do with my multicultural background than with my ethnicity. The questions I wanted answered were who I was, where I wanted to be, and about the meaning of life, rather than whether I would be accepted - or not - based on the colour of my skin. Racism was a word that I rarely heard and never used in my youth.

It wasn't until there was mass-immigration of peoples from

the West Indies, India and Pakistan in the fifties and sixties, who had come to Britain to work as bus and train drivers, and as manual labourers, that I realised that a racial divide would become a serious social and political problem in Britain during the last four decades of the 20th century, and a major global problem in this millennium. Hospital workers, domestic help and taxi drivers in Britain and Europe, right up to the late sixties, were all white during my time in the West. Only a few of the coloured students from overseas I met in the UK made me aware of my native origins.* They were passionate about global political issues and talked about *apartheid*, about colonialism and the wars of independence on the African and Asian continents; they told me that they would be going back home to fight for change. Equality became the battle hymn of the century.

In 2007, the Equality and Human Rights Commission was set up in Britain to tackle not just racial inequality, but all forms of discrimination, to protect victims of police brutality, transgender prejudice, sexual abuse, bias against women in the workplace, and many other social injustices, especially those that excluded people from society simply for being different.

★ ★ ★ ★

By the autumn term 1957, as a third year six-former, there was no longer any place for me in Eltham's dormitory. I was too old to be a boarder and happy to get 'kicked out' of school, and found full board accommodation at 208 Court Road, next to Mottingham station. I lived there for a year to prepare for my economic history exam. I then happily moved to London to study law.

At last, I now had the opportunity to discover what I really

---

* Usage of the word 'native' today has an old fashioned feel and may cause offence. How times have changed!

wanted. I started to work at trying to find out who I was. The search for my identity was on.

The journey was to be long and arduous. It involved working not just to get through my law exams, but to gain experiences in the real world, as well as to earn a bit of extra pocket money. I decided that I would try different jobs, before deciding what I was going to do for the rest of my life. To the despair of my father, it took a long time for me to graduate. I was too busy doing all sorts of work not related in any way to getting the professional qualification that my father had sent me to England for.

What my father would call this period of my life as my 'wasted years', I called these years working at the 'University of Life'. I learned more of life than I did from learning at school. Not at all debauched and certainly not criminal like the *Rake's Progress*, my own progress turned out to be as far off as it could possibly have been from the protected life I had been leading up to then, but just as adventurous, eclectic and variegated. (Unlike Tom Rakewell, though, I never ended up in prison!)

P.S. After twelve schools in five countries, my schooling had finally come to an end. Eltham was my last stop. I had suffered and I had survived. I was not an exemplary Elthamian: I was not a rugby player and I performed miserably at the bottom half of my class in maths, the sciences, and even history and English literature, my two favourite subjects. Yet I surprised my fellows by coming first in French and close to the top in Latin.

At Eltham, I was never actually *unhappy*. To be sure, I was always uncomfortable, at times even feeling unattended, and I was certainly untrained for the real world, yet I looked forward to leaving school and facing an unknown future.

One happy school event still conjures up all sorts of magical memories for me. It was at the end of the summer term 1956. As part of the Ordinary Level Geography exam – which I passed – we were assigned to carry out a geographical survey of an agricultural area of Kent on bicycles, in the parishes of St Paul's Cray and St Mary Cray, between Bromley and Swanley. Before the area succumbed to light industry in the late 1950s, and morphed into commuter developments later on in the century, the agricultural lands were used for growing fruit and hops. The country lanes I cycled through, still pastoral, bordered with hedgerows of hawthorne, beech and poplars, and the public paths carefully marked in the Ordinance Survey map that I tramped through, were once known as the Garden of England.

I would come upon roadside stalls, displaying baskets filled with freshly picked fruit. I bumped into French farmers coming in the opposite direction on their bikes from Normandy, to sell their onions. I remember Derry Downs, Pratt's Bottom and Broom Hill, quaint names of tiny villages, their church spires visible for miles around, happy echoes of the past, that give me a frisson still.

The changeable English weather, mild, misty, with bright intervals of sunshine, formed an essential part of those magical moments. When I wasn't working on my geographical project, I would lean my bike against a fence and tarry for a while, breathe in the clean air and listen to birdsong, taking in the sweetness and harmony of the English landscape. I was transported back to my idyllic childhood in Virginia Water and the surrounding countryside of Bath in the early forties, when, as a displaced Londoner, I first encountered country life during the Second World War.

Most of all, I was savouring the pleasures of wandering through the beautiful countryside of England, a sense of freedom rarely experienced by us boarders at Eltham.

★ ★ ★ ★

The Garrick Club, London, 10 October 2007, 7 pm.

'Where's the old Elthamian's reunion?'

'Well sir, you go down the 'allway, up the stairs, then turn right and keep walking 'til you reach the ballroom. Can't go wrong sir!'

I carefully followed the commissionaire's directions. The ballroom's double doors at the end of the hallway opened up to a large group of rather old men standing around with drinks in their hands. Some were hugely overweight and bald. Others were walking around with walking sticks.

I must be at the wrong do, I thought. I made a hasty exit and went downstairs to the front desk to ask again where the Eltham College class of '57 old boys reunion was held.

'You just came from there sir!'

I thanked him and sheepishly sneaked back to the ballroom. Father time plays nasty tricks with the old memory. I remember them as they were 50 years ago: tousled hair, clean-cut, healthy, mostly sporty, eager to get on in life. Others, like myself, pale, skinny, unsure of the future. None had been fat, though many had suffered from acne, and every one of them had been virgins for sure.

After a while, faces began to take on a dimly familiar look. What I found totally difficult to explain, though, was how a few of my contemporaries could have become so out of shape, particularly those who had been champion athletes on track and field, while I, who had deliberately avoided any kind of sport whatsoever, had remained agile and thin.

All at once a roll call of names came rushing back to me. Purkiss, Stares, Brown (there were two of them), Bottoms, Norris, Edmonds, Williams (also two of them), Prothero, Wainer, Buckley, Beith, Gillham, Skelton, Smith, Moore, Bradnock,

Martin, Clark, Jones*... Apart from Robin Hay, a fellow barrister at Middle Temple with whom I had remained in contact over the years, I had a hard time matching the names with the faces. There were 37 of us that evening, and three of them had been conferred knighthoods by the Queen for services to their country. I was the only old boy there who was not British.

Sadly, some names I recalled were no longer with us.

Once I got over the initial shock of how much change the passage of time had done to us all, I realized how pleasurable it was to be reunited with my contemporary sexagenarians from Eltham. We had a lot of catching up to do.

---

* British public school customs dictate that we all addressed each other by our surnames, and used first names only after a close friendship was formed. In countries where I have either lived or worked, such as Japan, Hong Kong, Korea, Singapore and Vietnam, the surname is the given name. In America, I discovered that in both the business world and in academe, everybody addressed each other on a first-name basis, whether between professor and student, or corporate CEO and lowly employee. In Italy, France and Greece, the surname comes before the first name, particularly in documents and during introductions. In Thailand, everyone is known by their first, or given, name. Surnames are hardly ever used.

CHAPTER TWO
THE ROYAL MAIL

In the Britain of the fifties and sixties, the traditional place to look for a job during the winter holidays for school boys and girls above the age of 16 was at the Post Office, sorting out the Christmas mail. The work was simply putting letters in the correct pigeonhole according to their destination. The sorter sat in front of a banked wall of small compartments, and set to work, backaching after eight hours on the job every day. It was a Dickensian process, where incoming letters were first sorted by region, then by county, then by city, and finally by postal district, all by hand. It was the same process for letters and Christmas cards arriving from overseas, whilst mail destined for abroad had to be put into pigeonholes according to the address in different continents and countries. Curiously, people sending their letters to other countries in the days before jet plane travel used to add the *continent* on their addressed envelopes, like Lithuania, *Europe*, or Paraguay, *South America*.

There was something consoling about my job at the British post office. I felt a sentimental affinity with my maternal grandfather who had devoted his life to the Siamese postal service and had had, in 1930, the Royal title of *Phra Paisal Praisani*, Chancellor of the Royal Post Office, equivalent to the Postmaster

General today, conferred on him. Would he have been proud of me, I wondered? The Thai postal service was founded in 1883 during the reign of King Rama V, and is one of Asia's oldest nationwide postal systems. By 1886 there were already 76 post offices in the kingdom.

Considering the sanctity of the British mail – which legally becomes government property as soon as a letter is posted into the classic red pillarbox – and the confidentiality of the letter's contents, I felt it was a singular honour and privilege to work for the Royal Mail. Once a letter is put through the pillarbox, rather like a hasty tap on the 'send' command for your e-mail, there's no turning back. The letter was as good as delivered. It was a crime, we were informed, to tamper with the mail in any way. So here I was, together with fellow student workers, entrusted to look after the Royal Mail, in the service of Her Majesty's Government. I went to work at the Earl's Court Post Office Branch with earnest intent. It was Christmas holiday 1955. I was 17 years old. It was my first job.

★ ★ ★ ★

Devoted philatelists like me knew that the most expensive postage stamps in the world are the oldest. They are the Penny Black and the Two Pence Blue, created by Sir Rowland Hill in 1840 for the Royal Mail. The institution started in 1660 as the General Letter Office, and became known as the General Post Office. The postal system eventually came to be called the Royal Mail because it was created for the distribution of royal correspondence and official documents. There was a network of post office branches all over the country, from where letters were collected and sent to distribution points called sorting stations. There were no postage stamps at the time, and it was the recipient who paid for the delivery. If the recipient refused to accept the letter or was unable to pay, the Royal Mail would temporarily bear the cost and keep a separate account of each letter, eventually collecting from the sender. The cost of each delivery was calculated by the distance the letter had been carried, on foot for local deliveries, and by horse riders for longer journeys. It was a cumbersome process.

After the introduction of Rowland Hill's 'Penny Post', letters under half an ounce could be mailed to any part of the UK, replacing the previous rates and the unwieldy system of charges varying with size, weight and the shape of the letters. Mail deliveries became much more efficient. Prepaid stamps were self-adhesive and a uniform postal rate became universal. Letter writing became institutionalised. It was a matter of professional pride for the British GPO that a letter posted in the morning in one location would be sure to arrive the following day at another. A letter written in the early morning would be delivered that very evening, providing it was posted in the same borough, like Fulham, where I was born, or in a village like Mottingham, where I went to school. The British postal system was the most advanced in the world.

The American postal system wasn't far behind. In 1775, the US mail, or the United States Postal System, was established by the Second Continental Congress, with Benjamin Franklin as its first postmaster general. So important was the USPS that it is still one of the few government agencies explicitly authorised by the American Constitution. In the 1800s, delivering the mail to the western frontier was such a dangerous job that postmen on horseback were armed.

The most famous part of the US mail's history was during the era of the legendary Pony Express Riders, which carried mail bags from St Joseph, Missouri to Sacramento, California, a distance of 1,600 miles, starting in 1860. It lasted 21 years, until a telegraph service connected the east coast with the west. Riders, like horse jockeys, needed to be small and sinewy, weighing not more than 125lb. A copy I found of a contemporary ad for the job would not have attracted me even though, as a young man, I had the correct physical requirements: 'Young, skinny, wiry fellows, not over 18. Must be expert riders. Willing to risk death daily. Orphans preferred.' There were dangers all along the route: hostile Indians, cutthroat bandits, difficult terrain, violent tornadoes and grizzly bears, were the kind of hazards that a rider would encounter. It was the most dangerous job in America.

The route was divided into 75 to 100 mile lengths over which a lone rider would traverse, changing horses every 10 to 15 miles, before handing over the mailbag to the next rider. He would then stay in place for a few hours before taking over from a rider coming from the opposite direction, and ride back to the last exchange station. Pony Express Riders became part of American hero folklore. Buffalo Bill Cody made his name by outriding a posse of tomahawk wielding Red Indians who wanted his scalp. He ended his career as a showman in his Wild West travelling circus. He was only 15 when he enrolled as a rider. Wild Bill Hickok, another famous rider, saved a frontier woman, whose husband had just been murdered, by outgunning five desperados and killing or wounding every one of them, in true Hollywood fashion. Almost as skinny and wiry, Paul Newman was heroically cast as Buffalo Bill, while beefy Jeff Bridges played an ornery but likable Wild Bill.

Curiously, the first American mail during colonial times in the 1600s was only for correspondence between letter writers in Britain and the colony, when it took months for the mail to cross the Atlantic. There were no post offices in the colonies, and recipients had to collect their mail from designated inns and taverns. 'Just off to the tavern to collect the post, dear, won't be long!' must have been a good excuse for a thirsty husband to sneak off for a pint of ale.

From 1899 to 1910, reindeer were used to deliver the US Mail to more than a dozen post office locations in north-western Alaska, as well as several locations north of the Arctic Circle. Dog sleds, the traditional form of transportation across the frozen terrain of America's 49th state, could not carry as much weight as sleds pulled by reindeer, and took twice as much time. Today, 'Santa Claus' has been replaced by airplanes.

When I went to live in America in August, 1994, to start working at the School of Journalism in Missouri, the biggest front page news at the time was the 4 million pieces of undelivered mail left to pile up in trailers; Washington DC was reported as having the slowest delivery in the country, seriously affecting the smooth running of the administration, since a great deal of the mail was addressed to the federal government. David Brinkley, a witty television journalist, observed wryly that the American mail was so slow that 'your bills become overdue even before you get them.'

The US Postal System today is America's largest civilian employer, with almost half a million career workers. At the time of writing, the USPS is in serious financial difficulties. President Trump had refused to provide Federal funds to improve the postal services, and hoping, unsuccessfully as it turned out, to prevent Americans from voting by mail.

The first postal system on the continent of Europe was established on a very small scale in Paris by one Jean-Jacques Renouard de Villayer in 1653. He set up mail boxes from where the letters were posted, collected and delivered on the same day. Way ahead of his time, he came up with the concept of pre-paid postage envelopes, the precursor of the twentieth century air letter, and known internationally as an aerogram. It was a thin lightweight paper in which letter and stamped envelope were on one single sheet. It was folded into four, three parts for the letter and the fourth part for the envelope, where the name, address and country of the recipient was written. It was the cheapest way to send an airmail letter, and in my time in the 1950s and 1960s it cost only sixpence. Needless to say, all my letters home were written on these light blue aerograms. Enclosures were forbidden, so when I wanted to send photographs with my letter, the envelope was weighed and the postage was four times more expensive. Air letters were withdrawn from service by the Royal Mail in 2012, and were still in use in Australia, New Zealand, Singapore and the UN until they were recently phased out.

As far as we know, one of the earliest postal systems in history was in ancient Egypt, 4,400 years ago. The invention of papyrus paper made it possible. The postal service was originally developed for the ruling Pharaohs only, and their royal letters were placed in a box escorted by guards, sent up and down the Nile. It was not until 305 BC that the system was speeded up and express messages were delivered by riders on horseback for shorter distances, supplementing the river services. Lesser mortals were now able to use the postal services, but the new 'regular service' was much slower. The postmen could only deliver the papyrus missives on donkeys and mules.

Ending 500 years of state control, the British Royal Mail was privatised in 2014. The intention was to make the British postal system more efficient in this new electronic era of diminished letter writing, and to make it more competitive with courier services, and meet the growth of global on-line shopping and e-commerce.

The Post Office that I went to work for nearly seventy years ago has retained part of its historic name, but is now under the control of its shareholders, investors in The Royal Mail Group Limited.

★ ★ ★ ★

In the beginning the new job was fun. I learned a lot about different geographic locations, certainly more fun than 'O Level' geography at school, and discovered parts of Britain that were unknown to me. Some village names were charming. Upton Snodsbury, near North Piddle, Worcestershire; Great Snoring, Norfolk; Bishops' Itchington, Warwickshire and Havering-atte-Bower, Essex, come to mind. Some were just naughty, like Pratts Bottom, Kent and Balls Cross, West Sussex. My favourite was Shittington, Bedfordshire.

I was once lucky enough to be assigned to the overseas section, and with my transnational background I was thrilled to see postage stamps from countries that I never knew existed, particularly exotic outposts from the far flung British Empire. Triangular stamps were of particular interest, often from lesser known countries that sought world recognition like Mauritania, or where their stamps were a source of revenue. When I lived on the Continent, it was always fun to post letters from the Republic of San Marino, the Principality of Monaco or the Vatican City. In my early teens I was an avid philatelist, so it was nice to see that my love for postage stamps had not diminished, even though I no longer had the time to add new stamps to my collection.

Another enjoyable aspect of the post office job had to do with my fascination for picture postcards, especially those from foreign places that in those days we suspected we might never get to see: the Sphinx, Mont Blanc, the Taj Mahal, the Great Wall of China, the Empire State building. They opened up vistas of modern cities, unexplored panoramas and lost empires. On the back was the usually hastily written 'wish you were here', to make the recipient green with envy. Then there were commemorative, historic, artistic and naughty postcards (what-the-butler-saw bawdy cartoon pictures of scantily clad women, girls with big boobs, leering men and henpecked husbands, with *double entendre* messages), these latter a curious British custom of sending 'saucy' postcards *only* from seaside resorts.

The very first postcards were not illustrated. Called Postal Cards, they had the postage pre-printed on them and were issued by the postal authorities around the world, introduced in Austro-Hungary in 1869. The first 'souvenir' card was sent from Vienna in 1871, and later in the same decade cards carrying simple advertising messages appeared in the UK and the USA. In 1889, a postcard with a photograph of the Eiffel Tower to commemorate the Paris World Fair, took advantage of the new era of photography and mass production with cheap global postal rates, and ushered in a new trend in postcard greetings from faraway places and commemorative events, reaching its height in the first two decades of the last century. When public telephones – called payphones – were first installed in America, postcards were touted as the 'poor man's telephone', the postage costing less than a phone call.

During the course of sorting out the mail, I noticed, disappointingly, much fewer picture postcards being sent during the festive season, apart from the rare and much cheaper Christmas greeting postcard, which, curiously, never caught on after a brief period of popularity in the early part of the century.

The world's first Christmas card produced by Sir Henry Cole – the civil servant who helped introduce the Penny Post in 1843 – was not meant to be a Christmas card at all. It had always been a British tradition amongst the wealthy to write lengthy Yuletide letters to friends and relatives, to wish them season's greetings and keep them *au courant*. Sir Henry printed out 1000 cards with a merry Christmas message which he sent out to all his friends, thus solving the problem of maintaining correspondence with all his acquaintances throughout the year. Sir Henry's card showed a picture of his family, including his children, celebrating Christmas over a glass of wine. Temperance societies of the time accused him of encouraging underage drinking. Thanks to the Penny Post, enterprising printers started producing cards en masse, and featured pictures of angels, winter robins, holly and evergreens. By the 1880s, the

Halfpenny Post was introduced to facilitate what had become a popular tradition of sending Yuletide cards, provided that the envelope was unsealed.

In 1875, Louis Prang, a German lithogram printer in Boston, launched the first card in America, and mailing Christmas greetings became so popular that by the 1880s, he was producing 5 million cards a year. The advent of cheap Christmas postcards put an end to his business, and it wasn't until 1920 when regular Christmas cards came back again, that the festive season's greeting card spread to the rest of the world. By 2010, 679 million cards were sent in Britain and *1.5 billion* were sent in America.

As Christmas got closer, the mail piled up, even though there were posters all over the country encouraging the public to 'Post early for Christmas', a variation of the perennial campaign 'Shop early for Christmas'. But people were still posting letters and cards on Christmas Eve. In Post Office branches all over London, stacks and stacks of Christmas mail bags were piling up on the floor, several feet high. We had to work overtime to clear the backlog before more bags of mail arrived the following day. I no longer had the time to study individual addresses and admire the stamps. Just a quick look at the postal code and off it went into the correct pigeonhole. It was tiring work. Sorting out the Christmas rush at the Post Office gave me regular festive season employment for many years.

★ ★ ★ ★

Working at the Post office while still at school was not just a welcome change from the daily grind of studying for my exams, and being with my fellow alumni day in, day out, but it also gave me the opportunity to discover more about the country where I was born and where I had lived during the war. I wanted to meet the people. The Post Office was my introduction to the 'real world'. Here young people from different social backgrounds were thrown together. I was able to make friends with strangers of all ages and classes. I was ready to talk to anyone on almost anything.

The first impression I had when I met both my fellow workers and my post office supervisors was their spoken language, quite different from the English that was taught to me at Eltham. I was used to standard English, what was once called an 'Oxford Accent',* spoken by stiff-upper-lip actors like Anthony Hopkins and Judi Dench, and more recently by Benedict Cumberbatch and Keira Knightley, and of course by the BBC. Eltham College was in Kent, and the local accent was Estuary English, spoken by many of my school chums, which I was used to. But it was a far cry from the 'vernacular' that D.H. Lawrence's gamekeeper Mellors used when speaking to Connie, his upper class mistress, the lady in *Lady Chatterley's Lover*. His Derbyshire dialect was impossible to understand.

'Accent', I was to discover, was *the way people speak* English, to be distinguished from 'dialect', based on a combination of *the words people use* with their local accent. There are 37 separate dialects in Britain, according to a study conducted in 2020.

Many of the people I worked with at the post office were early school leavers from different parts of Britain who had moved to London to seek better prospects. A lot of them were from working class backgrounds and educated at state schools. They came from different parts of England, Wales, Scotland and Ireland, and I learned that they were, without exception, proud of their roots, and where they came from was more important than being British.

---

* Variously referred to as accepted, aristocratic, posh, public-school, upper-class, refined and conservative accents, BBC English and Queen's English, as well as received pronunciation, aka educated speech. See post for my attempts to explain the development of this complicated British cultural and linguistic peculiarity, and how it derived from their vexed class system.

They all spoke in the vernacular, local accents and dialects that I had never heard before. The most difficult to understand, even among the Scots themselves, was Glaswegian, the dialect of Glasgow. Equally difficult was the language spoken by the Geordies, in and around Newcastle. Until the advent of the Beatles, Scouse, the local language spoken by Liverpudlians, with its nasal twang and unique vocabulary, was little known in the rest of the country. Welsh, of course, was a totally different language entirely and impossible to understand.

The most pleasant was the Yorkshire accent. Spoken well, it is slow, relaxed, and easily understood. Harold Wilson, Labour prime minister from 1964 to 1970, was a history and economics don from Oxford University before entering politics, yet he never lost his Yorkshire accent. His was the voice of calm during Britain's economic crisis and forced devaluation of the pound in 1967. My dear friend Vivian Robinson QC, one of my legal classmates, became a successful criminal law barrister, and used his delightful Yorkshire dialect to win over the jury when he was called upon to prosecute or defend the accused in the dock. The most famous Yorkshireman to speak with his regional accent professionally was the entertainer Wilfred Pickles, whose distinctive voice was used during the Second World War to read the news to distinguish BBC broadcasts from German propaganda. I like to think that Wilfred's Yorkshire drawl was used to confuse the Germans as well!

While dialect is identified by its geography, the so-called Oxford accent (nothing to do with the language spoken by the locals in Oxford but all to do with the university dons) was once associated with the extremely privileged, the wealthy and the public school educated, wherever they came from in the country. The immediate post-war years was still an era where class and education highlighted the gap that had long existed in British society. In the army, commissions were granted almost exclusively to those with a public school education, and a heavy regional accent would prevent even the most qualified from becoming an officer. Once referred to as a 'posh' accent, and sometimes as a 'refined' accent, the Oxford accent is now officially called the 'Received Pronunciation'. It's also known as Queen's English, actually spoken by HM the Queen. Her father George VI, of course, spoke King's English.

Today, as we enter the third decade of the 21st century, Estuary English has gained popularity and has become more widely accepted as the nation's classless and regionless accent. Although originally spoken in southern England, it is now the normal language for BBC news announcers, Members of Parliament on both sides of the aisle, and higher institutions of learning. In their attempt to popularise the monarchy and to reach out to the people, both the hapless Prince Harry and the future king of England, Prince William the Duke of Cambridge, speak with an Estuary accent in public, rather than with the Queen's English of their grandmother.

Long gone are the days when Received Pronunciation was a mark of wealth and privilege, supported by the old boy network and the right connections. Professor Higgins, the haughty English language expert who could tell a person's class and origin from his, and in this case from her accent, in the musical *My Fair Lady,* based on George Bernard Shaw's play *Pygmalion,* is very much a product of the past. The most conservative of British prime ministers and the smooth actor who portrayed British upper class characters, came from modest backgrounds and took elocution lessons to get ahead in the middle of the last century. Margaret Thatcher, née Roberts, was born in Grantham, Lincolnshire, a grocer's daughter. When she aspired to higher office in politics, she put behind her provincial dialect, and became a staunch member of the ruling class. Roger Moore, the son of a London policeman, took English diction classes at the Royal Academy of Dramatic Art before taking on roles of the British élite. Both were products of their time. In the 21st century, accents 'to the manner born' are slowly becoming irrelevant and relegated to historic roles on the stage and film, to Shakespearean plays, and to traditional British stiff upper lip stereotypes in Hollywood movies. Prime Minister Boris Johnson is an exception, of course, but his élite place in the sun is starting to set. He may be the last of his species. By the next generation, he could very well be mimicked by stand-up comedians in music hall theatres as a foppish clown.

Today, in the so-called British 'classless society', it has become less desirable for actors to change their normal speaking voice to Received Pronunciation, unless the role they take on calls for it. The late Diana Rigg discarded the Yorkshire accent of her childhood to make her career in Shakespearean dramas. Albert Finney, with his midlands accent, started off in the early sixties in what were called 'kitchen sink' dramas, depicting working class characters, before taking on the role of Winston Churchill and other aristocratic roles in his later career, with a distinct plummy accent. Two actors of the last century who had successful careers and spoke with the accents of their birth were Sean Connery from Edinburgh and cockney Michael Caine. Paradoxically, in order to get on in today's modern Britain, those brought up with a 'refined' accent are now having to adapt to the more egalitarian voice of the masses, either Estuary English or a return to their roots, to take up the voice of their geographic origins. Could Connery and Caine have been the first successful exponents of this new world of English speakers?

There were people who spoke with a 'posh' accent who were *not even* English, and some may never have lived in England. They were educated abroad and didn't belong to any region of the UK. I have met Argentinians, Africans, Australians, Canadians and Indians, who went to English schools in their own countries (like Freddie Mercury the rock singer who went to schools in Kenya and India), or European nobility who had learned English from their tutors and governesses (like Prince Rainier of Monaco and Gianni Agnelli, the Italian owner of FIAT), where the English language they learned used the phonetic transcriptions from the Oxford English Dictionary for the correct pronunciation. They all spoke 'posh'. This is yet another curiosity of the English language.

How do I come to these conclusions, some admittedly outlandish, without any research to back me up? On what basis do I even *dare* to make such bald statements, particularly since I freely admit that I am quite unqualified to make judgments on the British language and culture? Allow me to submit my evidence. I've been listening to the BBC all my life and I've been a devoted viewer of BBC World, the Beeb's global TV news transmission, for the last 40 years. Dear readers of my generation will remember John Snagge's polished delivery of the BBC news in the Queen's English during and immediately after the war. More BBC broadcasters with the same refined accent were Richard Baker and Richard Dimbleby in the fifties and sixties, Angela Rippon and Robin Day in the seventies and eighties, and more recently Andrew Marr and Jeremy Paxman. As Britain progresses into the third decade of this century, there will be less and less broadcasters of that school.

The new generation of BBC newsreaders such as Carrie Gracie, Shaun Ley and Ros Atkins, all have a distinct Estuary accent, classless, less snobbish and more egalitarian. Their professional delivery is based on meritocracy rather than on where they went to school.

All of this must be a source of great confusion for foreign visitors who come to live and work in Britain, especially for students who are learning to speak English. But for me, the learning curve of the British class system and their peculiar accents was going up by the day, starting with my new employment at the Royal Mail.

It was furthermore my first paid job.

CHAPTER THREE
LITTLE SCARLET

'Have you ever worked on a farm before?' asked the secretarial assistant at the National Union of Students office in Villiers Street next to Charing Cross station, when I showed interest in a fruit picking job on a farm in Essex that was posted on their bulletin board.

It was coming up to midsummer 1958. I had just passed my Economic History exam. If I was going to move to London, my monthly allowance of 38 pounds wasn't going to get me very far. All Thai students had the same problem. In the fifties, the government imposed strict currency controls on Thai students studying in England, who were under the supervision of the Civil Service Commission – the '*Kor Por*'. The allowance had to cover rent, food, clothing, transport and other sundries. Fortunately, school fees were paid from a separate account. Not very promising for a young man who liked to dress up, enjoyed the theatre, loved eating out, and was a hi-fi enthusiast who wanted the latest jazz and Sinatra recordings. I was especially concerned, because I was just starting to date girls, a new kind of expense that I had to manage. Going to the cinema to steal a kiss or two and enjoy a mysterious fondle in the dark without interference from the usherette's shining torch, was a very frustrating way of discovering the beauty of the opposite sex, and even more so since I often enjoyed the film I was seeing at the same time. Clearly, I needed a place of my own for a bit of privacy. I had to find a job and earn some extra money to pay for what I hoped would be my new 'sophisticated' lifestyle in London.

The first place for students seeking holiday work was to check out available jobs at the NUS (National Union of Students) office, headquartered in London, where I was informed that a farm in Essex was looking for student workers. In the beginning it didn't seem that this farm job was the kind of work I was looking for. It wasn't that well paid, it involved working in the fields and it was far from civilisation (as I knew it).

I was given a leaflet to read. On closer inspection it didn't turn out to be as bad as I had been led to believe. It was located in a village called Tiptree in the county of Essex, about 80 km from London, and called the 'International Farm Camp', or simply the NUS Farm Camp. The job was described as a 'working holiday' and Wilkin & Sons, the renowned jam makers, invited students from around the world over the age of 18 to 'help' with the farm's harvest. Essentially, the work was to pick fruit. On the leaflet's first page, there was what looked like a Bolshevik propaganda photograph of a tractor trailer full of cheerful boys and girls being driven to work in the fields, except that they genuinely looked like they were having a lot of fun. Further enquiries revealed that *half the students were girls* from Scandinavia, Germany and other countries who came to the camp to learn English. Most enticing of all was the description of the evening entertainment. After supper the camp arranged games, film shows and dancing. Accommodation in tents (two per tent) and meals were free. That should save me a bit on food and rent for a while, I thought, as I signed on immediately for one month.

★ ★ ★ ★

Essex is farmland country. Rural, pastoral, and pretty. Canopied by the majestic trees of Epping Forest on its western borders, the flat agricultural areas of east Essex are not as picturesque. I would have preferred an idyllic farm near the Sussex Downs or on the warm coast of the West Country, but this was meant to be a place of work and not a holiday resort. I needed the money and a change of scenery wouldn't be bad. I packed my bag and took the train from Liverpool Street Station to Witham, from where I boarded a local bus to the tiny village of Tiptree. It has not grown very much since then, and today it is known as 'Britain's largest village', with a population of less than ten thousand people.

Up until the Industrial Revolution, Essex was one of the most prosperous counties in England. It had always been a cereal growing area, and for many years wheat was its cash crop. Despite the Corn Laws which had kept grain prices at a high level to protect farmers from cheap imports, a period of depression set in after the 1840s; there was widespread poverty due to the high prices of basic foods, especially bread. Ireland was suffering from famine, and there was severe hunger in the new industrial towns of England too. The decade would come to be known as the 'Hungry Forties'. The protective tariffs had made Essex landowners become too comfortable and overcomplacent. They had not bothered to develop any new entrepreneurial skills and had failed to invest in new agricultural products – in particular market gardening and fruit cultivation – to meet the growing demands of the wealthy middle class of London. New railway services meant that fresh fruit and vegetables could at last be delivered directly to Convent Garden, the capital's biggest fresh food market, where the money was and where the rich were willing to pay for natural produce direct from the farm.

Fruit growing at that time was a relative newcomer, and only added needed variety to Essex farming. The locals were still committed to the production of cereals, which was becoming increasingly unprofitable. Arthur Charles Wilkin, an enterprising young farmer in his twenties, inherited a small family estate, going back to the 1700s. He switched from arable farming to growing fruit in 1864, after he had decided to become a supplier of quality fruit to jam makers in London. However, his produce, mostly strawberries, often ended up decaying in their crates by the time they arrived in London. He could no longer rely on the vagaries of the English summer or on the erratic railway timetables to ensure his product remain fresh and whole. He decided to start his own jam preserve business, and used his wife Mary Ann's recipe, and her kitchen, to make the first batch. *He never liked the products from London anyway.* His wife's jams were natural; one could actually taste the fruit. In the beginning, Arthur Charles had problems recruiting locals to work on his farm. The labourers were used to ploughing and reaping and did not think fruit picking was a man's job, disparagingly calling it 'fruiting work'.

It was not until 1885, when he was absolutely sure he could deliver a quality product, that he confidently launched The Britannia Fruit Preserving Company. One Australian importer who could taste the difference from 'London jams' decided to buy his entire stock every year. Wilkin's products were glucose free, free from preservatives and added colouring, faithful to Mary Ann's original recipe. By 1901 the company had 8000 direct customers and the farm had grown to over 600 acres of land, with new fruits added to its product line, including gooseberries, cherries, damsons, plums and crab apples. In 1905, the company was renamed Wilkin & Sons Limited, to avoid confusion with 25 other companies trading under the Britannia name. Imagine a cup of tea with leaves processed from a Britannia rolling and drying machine, poured from a Britannia silver teapot, served with a Britannia strawberry jam sandwich, with a Britannia biscuit on the side, on the menu of the Grand Britannia Hotel in Venice at teatime. A branding nightmare! By 1920, Wilkin & Sons sales had exceeded 100,000 pounds sterling with 200,000 customers around the world.

When I started working at Tiptree farm in mid-June 1958, Wilkin & Sons was starting to become a global brand. Exports had grown by sixty-two percent and in 1954 a Royal Appointment was issued by Her Majesty Queen Elizabeth for the company to supply jam and marmalade to Buckingham Palace. At about the same time, the Tiptree International Farm Camp was opened to provide accommodation for 100 students from around the world, to help the locals pick the fruit.

One of Britain's finest traditions come in a Wilkin & Sons 'Tiptree' 12 ounce jam jar. It is hard to imagine breakfast without their tawny thick cut marmalade on toast, or scones and clotted cream without their fruity strawberry jam at tea time.

★ ★ ★ ★

8.30 am. My first morning at work. I squeezed on to a flatbed trailer with 20 eager European boys and girls towed by a tractor driven by Jim, a pleasant old farmer with a deep, gravelly voice. When we arrived at the strawberry fields, Jim handed us each a pail, got on his hands and knees and started to explain how to pick the fruit.

'Lemme showyer 'ow to 'arvess stawbwies. Follow me 'ands closely, loike. See 'ere.' He started to pull a strawberry plant from the ground. *'Old da stem between yer finga' and tumbnoil abaaht one inch abuv' da berry, and twist at da syme tyme. Let da stawbwie roll on yer 'an, gently-loike, den pull da next one 'aaht. Den put 'em gently-loike inter yer pile. Ollis be gen'l wid dem stawbwies. They's loike gawld fer us. Innit?'*

His demonstration was met with embarrassing silence. He was obviously expecting all of us to say 'yes' in unison.

'Innit?' he repeated.

John Carpenter, my English tent-mate, whom I had just met the day before, and I were the only ones who understood Jim's Essex dialect. We nodded enthusiastically. There were some French and Italian members of our group who looked as if they had just landed on the moon. Some Swedish and Norwegian girls were arguing fiercely about the meaning of the words. Two German boys pretended to understand everything. In the end it was all sorted out. John repeated Jim's excellent instructions in standard English and I did my best to explain what it all meant in French and Italian.

In the distant horizon, a majestic sycamore, the occasional sturdy English oak, sweet chestnuts and bushes of wild cherries fringed rows and rows of long strawberry fields, each row stretching up to 100 metres. On that mid-June day, the sun was out. Heat was building up and bright red strawberries, beautiful and inviting – and ready to be picked – were glistening through the narrow furrows of earth. We were spaced two or three metres apart and sank to our knees, and eagerly set to work. Jim, affable, helpful, was there to encourage us. It took well over a quarter of an hour to fill a pail. A light breeze every now and then was a welcome relief.

Most Essex days in June are blue, only a few are cloudy. Weather plays a big part in determining yield and flavour. Ideally plenty of light rain and a fair amount of warm sunshine will ripen the strawberry fruit to perfection. Extreme heat can ruin the crop. On this breezy June morning, the light flurries of a southwesterly had infused the fields with the sweet smell of strawberries. Simply gorgeous. But strawberry picking is back-breaking work. Our pay was calculated on piecework, so the more we picked the more we earned. Payday was at the end of the week. We were out in the fields from 8.30 am to 4.30 pm Monday to Friday, but now, during the peak season, we were expected to work overtime on Saturday and Sunday. On my first week I was put to work on picking the standard Tiptree strawberry that ends up in a 12 ounce jar of the popular 'Strawberry Conserve', which costs 5.59 UK pounds today. Wilkin & Sons produce two basic types of jams: 'Conserve' and 'Preserve'.

Conserve: comes from the Latin *con* (with) and *servare* (to keep safe and intact). It now means a type of jam in which the ripe fruit that cannot be eaten at harvest time and would otherwise spoil, is boiled to a pulp - with sugar whole or in large pieces - and immediately bottled. Other Wilkin & Sons conserves include blackcurrant, blueberry, rhubarb and damson, as well as strawberry, *all* grown in Tiptree.

Preserve: from the Latin *pre* (before, in advance) and *servare*. A preserve jam refers to a fruit pulp cooked with sugar to a thick consistency from fruit that has not necessarily been harvested recently, nor locally, and is processed to extend its useful life. To qualify as a preserve, the fruit must not be mashed, crushed or be in small pieces. Not an easy operation. Apricot, black cherry and gooseberry are typical preserves.

Marmalade is also a fruit preserve made from the juice and peel of citrus fruits boiled with sugar and water. Wilkin & Sons famous orange marmalade is made from Seville oranges. Other marmalades are made from lemon, lime or mandarin oranges. Unlike most Tiptree fruits, all citrus fruit are imported from warmer climes.

★ ★ ★ ★

A week later I fell in love with Little Scarlet. She had a beautiful, sensuous colour and the sweetest bouquet. She was rare and expensive, and used to be quite wild.

I was now assigned to a new group of pickers. Like me, they already had experience in picking regular strawberries. When Dave, our much younger tractor driver and foreman, explained this new assignment to us, he spoke with much gravitas and reverence. We were chosen to pick Wilkin's famous Little Scarlet strawberries. The berry picking was a delicate operation, and our hands and fingers had to be 'more nimble, more respectful and much, much softer.' Yet we had to work fast, and if necessary overtime, during the weekend.

Little Scarlet strawberry, *Fragaria virginiana*, is a variety native to the Eastern United States. This wild strawberry was brought back to England by Arthur Charles Wilkin on a visit to America in the 1890s. Little Scarlet is tiny, intensely flavoured, and one fifth the size of a regular strawberry. Its colour is dark crimson. Each 12 ounce jar of *Tiptree Little Scarlet Strawberry Preserve* contains 60 berries. Wilkin is the only commercial grower in the world. There is a narrow window of opportunity of three weeks to pick Little Scarlet across late June and early July. From pick to jar takes a few hours. Miss those deadlines and Little Scarlet is gone. No wonder we were briefed in great detail and had to be strictly supervised.

As we started picking – we learned the hard way – we were not supposed to throw the small berry into the pail. Dave was making sure that Little Scarlet didn't get bruised or damaged. 'Don't rush to fill the pail', he said. It was harder work than picking regular strawberries, but the pay was the same. Little Scarlet took about five times longer to fill a pail. Fortunately, the pail was much smaller. By the end of the day, our fingertips were stained crimson red and a great deal of dirt was embedded under our nails. Our backs were breaking, but we were happy in the knowledge that we were chosen to pick Tiptree's treasured fruit, the beautiful Little Scarlet.

★ ★ ★ ★

Scarlet is also a famous name in American Civil War fiction. This is not the place to write a sequel to *Gone With the Wind*. Neither time nor talent permit. And anyway, Alexandra Ripley, an American novelist, has already written a pretty exciting story about Scarlet O'Hara's subsequent reunion with Rhett Butler and her adventures in Ireland. Her book *Scarlet* became a best seller in 1991. But please indulge me, as I summarise *my version* of GWTW II in one short paragraph.

The beautiful Scarlet O'Hara does indeed survive for another day. For four more years, in fact. After the end of the American Civil War, she is destitute. After realising that she will not be able to rebuild her life in Atlanta, she goes up north to seek her fortune. She vowed, if you recall, never to be hungry again. She learns that New York is where the money is. It is also where the northerners are much more forgiving. She marries a good man, an upstanding member of the New York Bar, and gives birth to a beautiful girl, who is named Little Scarlet. GWTW II is this girl's story. In her late teens she returns to learn more about her mother's roots in the south. At a Ball in Charleston, she meets Rhett Butler Junior and falls in love with him…

I leave it to the dear reader to continue with the rest of the story.

Tiptree's Little Scarlet Strawberry Jam has played a small and sensual iconic role in modern literature. For two American novelists, Little Scarlet Jam has become a symbol of New York's rich life style. In Philip Roth's *Sabbath Theatre,* the novel's unstable protagonist Micky Sabbath, finds a jar of Little Scarlet jam in the kitchen of his rich friend's posh West Central Park apartment. He spreads it on a seeded pumpernickel, while contemplating sex and suicide. In *Aysymmetry* by Lisa Halliday, Ezra Blazer, a successful writer, calls up Alice, an aspiring writer and his much younger lover, and gives her detailed instructions on how to buy a jar of Little Scarlet that he describes as an expensive jam, and specifically spells out the brand: 'T-I-P-T-R-E-E', that they will later enjoy eating together in bed. Another Alexandra, Alexandra Schwartz, a book critic for the *New*

Yorker magazine, calls Little Scarlet 'the Rolls Royce of conserves'. In an early chapter of *From Russia with Love,* James Bond enjoys a hearty breakfast and includes a spread or two of Little Scarlet on his toast, and is, by inference, Ian Fleming's preferred jam.

When Queen Elizabeth hosts a tea party in the gardens of Buckingham Palace, Tiptree Little Scarlet Conserve is served with the royal scones and clotted cream. Her family's royal appointment is proudly, yet discretely displayed on every Wilkin & Sons white oval jar label, contributing to the brand's mystique.

★ ★ ★ ★

The evening's entertainment in the farm camp after a long day in the fields was just right. We all met in a central canteen hall for supper, and in the beginning the conversation was mostly about exchanging experiences of the day's work. Long oak tables, hard benches, reminiscent of English boarding school. Self-introductions for those who were not so shy. 'Good evening. I'm Walter Jodl from West Germany.' This was still a time long before East and West Germany were reunited. There were no German students from the communist East at the camp. 'Hello, I'm Katarina from Yugoslavia.' She introduced her two stunning friends, Ljuba and Natasha. We talked more and discovered they are of Serbian stock. All this, of course, before Tito's rule ended in 1980 resulting in the breakup of Yugoslavia ten years later. For the first time, I met Slavs. They were very good looking. There were a couple of Malaysian Chinese boys from Ipoh, and like many Asians, less extroverted, and more hesitant to introduce themselves. The most gregarious were the Italians. I easily joined their group. It was a pleasure to brush up my Italian that I had not used for four years. Like many Italians at that time, their English was appalling, and we were only too happy to exchange vocabularies.

The Tiptree International Farm Camp was a mini Tower of

Babel for high school students and university undergrads. The atmosphere was relaxed, and despite the diversity of cultures and languages, the communality of academic and student interests eased the flow of conversation. Around me were boys and girls in their late teens and early twenties, serious and earnest; they were all happy and full of enthusiasm, imbued with the joys of youth. English was the lingua franca. With my chronic habit of eavesdropping on peoples' conversations, I had a field day.

'... better strawberries in France but not so ...'

'... of course, there is a long tradition of academic study and intellectual curiosity, in common with institutions of learning everywhere ...'

'... the nearest Catholic church is in a town not far from here ...'

It was at the NUS farm camp that I was able to hone my eavesdropping skills to a fine art. Watching and listening without being noticed, became part of my eavesdropping technique, an essential exercise, together with observing minute details, for actors and writers.

The best way, then, is to work from a totally detached position, because if you get involved then the effect is lost. It is the difference between an overheard and not minding your own business. I call it the 'fly on the wall method'. *When* to wisely retire out of earshot is critical.

I had developed a code of conduct in my eavesdropping pursuits. I only listened to conversations between total strangers, people I didn't know. Overhearing snippets on politics, business and sex in hotel lobbies, buses and airplanes are the most intriguing, and even more so when you are on holiday in another country. Once in a while, in the foyer of a theatre, I would overhear to the great annoyance of everyone within earshot, the opinion of a person who had decided to become a critique of the play we were about to see: *'Act 1 disappoints ... not until the last Act does it redeem. ...'* Worst of all is when you overhear how the play ends.

My golden rule: never eavesdrop on private telephone conversations between people you know without their permission. You may overhear snippets that could be very personal or highly compromising, dangerous if you don't know the full story. MYOB.

I was even able to tell from the way people dressed what country he or she hailed from. It was an era when there was still a certain pride in one's national habits. Although young Frenchmen no longer wore berets and the Germans their lederhosen, there were certain *styles* that were unmistakably characteristic to each nation. For example, in summer, French males wore open-toe leather sandals *without* their socks, while Germans wore them *with* short socks. The English wore closed leather sandals – the type originally designed by Clarks – presumedly to keep their feet warm and dry, with *long knee-length* socks. Sandals were never worn with long trousers. Americans in those days did not wear sandals and shorts, and went around in jeans and gym shoes.* Today, the male universe, young and old, has ungainly converted to the ubiquitous shorts and light textile sports shoes on their days off, even in the coldest weather. So much on how fashions have changed in my lifetime.

Every Western European country was well represented at the camp. It was in the fifties, at a time when many African and Asian countries were either too busy fighting the West for their independence or had just gained it, so I did not meet any Africans or Indians at the camp. The largest group of foreign students in Britain at the time came from oil rich nations like Iraq, Persia and Saudi Arabia, yet there were no Middle Easterners working in the fields either. There were a few Israelis who must have felt at home in this kibbutz-like environment. It was too far (and at

---

* Also called plimsolls and trainers (both Brit.), sneakers (US), running shoes, tennis shoes, high-tops and basketball shoes, irrespective of the sport the wearer played (or didn't).

that time too expensive) for young Americans and Canadians to cross the pond just to work for a few weeks, and under Franco's totalitarian rule there weren't many Spanish students. The odd Australian and New Zealander occasionally cropped up. And of course, there were no Russians, or any East Europeans. I was the only Thai. *Oh you mean Siam, why didn't you say so!*

Dances to old scratchy gramophone records were arranged twice a week. *Theme from Moulin Rouge. The poor people of Paris. Wonderful Copenhagen. Magic moments.* No jazz, no rock 'n' roll. A lot of dirge pop. Not great swinging music, but at least it was a chance to *talk* to my dancing partner, once I got over my shyness. All I had to worry about were my two left feet. No romantic numbers either, but it didn't seem to deter a few brazen French and Italian boys from getting close to their partners. As soon as the music had a bit of rhythm – Glenn Miller's *In the Mood* comes to mind – the boys from Yugoslavia, looking very much like American beeboppers, took to the floor and showed off their jiving skills. I looked at them in awe. Can they do this under Marshal Tito's rule, I wondered? I later learned that the more repressive the regime in eastern communist Europe, the more its youthful denizens wanted to ape their Western brethren. On a short visit to Moscow in 1972, I remember that the local teens were eyeing my Levi's with envy, and were prepared to pay a fortune for them.

At nineteen I would break into a cold sweat when I was called upon to meet members of the opposite sex. I had never made the first step to get to know a pretty girl that I rather fancied. My voice trembled when I spoke to them. I discovered at Tiptree that the best time for me to have a chance to talk to some of the most beautiful girls I had ever seen in my short life, was when I was seated next to them at the supper table. Eltham College had not prepared me to talk to members of the opposite sex. It was even more difficult if we hadn't been introduced.

But in the free-spirited ambiance of the farm camp it was easier for me to communicate with girls. I boldly gave my name to one and all. I told them where I came from. Most of them had never heard of Thailand so that was an excuse to talk about myself. I was pleasantly surprised to find out that most girls I talked to were receptive, though some more than others. I learned to tell when a girl was interested. *I looked into her eyes.* I was particularly attracted to a beautiful blonde girl from Oslo. Her blue eyes just oozed with approval. She nodded and smiled when I talked to her. Her name was Anne, pronounced *Aahneh* in Norwegian. Anne Schjelle. We spent a lot of romantic moments together. I was in love.

★ ★ ★ ★

Essex, I was to discover, was an amazing county. Few stretches of England have been the setting for so much history.

I was probably put off by a previous visit to this county when I was younger. I had spent an unremarkable day with one of my Eltham school chums at Southend-on-Sea, an Essex seaside town. It's famous for its long pier. Apart from its fresh oysters, there was very little else that would have lured me back. There was a cheesy promenade on the seafront, and noisy arcades, fish and chips stalls, and cheap souvenir shops all over town, bustling with hyperactive day trippers from the capital. New York City has Coney Island. For Londoners it's Southend.

At the end of four weeks of hard labour in the strawberry fields, I decided to visit other parts of Essex. I opened my eyes and discovered Colchester, half an hour's bus ride from Tiptree. I remembered my history. The Romans invaded Britain in 43 BC and built a fort in Colchester the following year, and Camulodunum, its Latin name, became the most imperial city in Roman Britain. A stone temple dedicated to Emperor Claudius was built there ten years later.

I also remembered Boadicea, the brave Celtic queen, who was flogged and her two daughters publicly raped by the Romans, when she was no longer protected following the death of her husband, Prasutagas, King of the Icani tribe and a reluctant Roman ally. By all accounts, a tall, striking redhead with fierce eyes and a harsh voice, Boadicea was a trained warrior. With an army of 100,000 Celts, she attacked the Roman fortifications at Colchester, laying the city to waste. Roman cemeteries were desecrated and the statues mutilated. A bronze statue of Claudius was decapitated and his temple totally destroyed. She went on to successfully attack and raze two other important Roman cities: St Albans and London, where legend has it that she rode out in her chariot along the Strand to do battle with the Romans. An equestrian statue of her stands by Westminster Bridge, close to the Houses of Parliament, a triumphant hyperbole in the city that she destroyed. According to Tacitus, the Roman historian, she massacred 70,000 Romans. The Romans reacted with a vengeance and in her final battle near Nuneaton, 80,000 Britons were slaughtered. Her rebel army was no match for the battle-trained Roman centurions, who surrounded her and won the war with two massive salvos of javelins.

She was the stuff of legend for all English schoolboys. Before her first battle, like King Henry V's rousing speech before the Battle of Agincourt 1355 years later, she rallied her troops with these stirring words: 'Nothing is safe from Roman pride and arrogance. They will deface the sacred and deflower our virgins. Win the battle or perish, that is what I, a woman, will do.' To avoid capture, in true Shakespearean tradition, she poisoned herself and her two daughters. It is curious that the Bard never wrote a play about her.

Colchester has a checkered history. After the fall of the Roman Empire in AD 405, the city successively passed through the invading hands of Anglo-Saxons, Vikings and Normans. King William, the Norman conqueror, recognised the strategic importance of Colchester, and built his castle on the vaults of the Temple of Claudius in the 1070s. In 1642 the town became the headquarters of the Royalists during the Second English Civil War. In the wet summer of 1648, the parliamentarian Roundhead army laid siege to Colchester for ten weeks and their heavy cannon barrage severely damaged the inner city. It was one of the key battlegrounds of the Civil War. The Royalists only surrendered after they received news of their army's defeat at the decisive battle of Preston.

There is a sympathetic folk story to come out of the siege, which eventually became an amusing nursery rhyme that children have been reciting for centuries:

Humpty Dumpty sat on a wall
Humpty Dumpty had a great fall
All the king's horses and all the king's men
Couldn't put Humpty Dumpty together again

Legend has it that Humpty Dumpty was the nickname of a huge royal cannon that sat on one of Colchester's defensive walls. During the Roundheads' bombardment in 1648, the cannon was knocked off the wall and came tumbling down to earth. With the help of 'all the king's horses and all the king's men', the Royalists were unable to move the massive cannon to another part of the wall. As history is often written by the victors, Humpty Dumpty has become a fanciful nursery rhyme, neither pro- nor anti-royalist. Had the victors been the Parliamentarians, and England become a republic, who knows what Humpty Dumpty would have become?

Two gifted sisters, Ann and Jane Taylor, lived in West Stockwell Street, Colchester, between 1796 and 1810, where they composed the best-known and much-loved nursery rhyme in the English language:

Twinkle, twinkle, little star
how I wonder what you are!
Up above the world so high,
like a diamond in the sky.

This charming lullaby continues its dreamy tone for another four verses, and expresses the tenderness in the relationship 'twixt mother and baby, as they look at the night sky together.' It was published in *'Rhymes for the Nursery'* in 1806, a compendium of children's poems, and later sung to an old French melody. Today, there is a plaque in front of the house where they lived, and a life size statue of the two sisters, dedicated to the children of the world, has been put up in the high street, with Jane pointing up to a star.

My meanderings in Colchester ended up in the old castle, built on the site of Claudius' Roman temple. It had the longest castle keep in Europe. I was curious to inspect Colchester Castle's famous keep, a large fortified enclosure where the Royalist defenders retreated to safety as a last resort during the siege. It was the securest part of the castle, a dominant feature of Norman castle construction. I spent hours inside, pretending to be one of the royal Cavalier defenders. I continued to explore and discover all the sites of this historic town.

I end this section with a number of interesting snippets that have emerged from the history and geography of Essex. Four American presidents' forbears hailed from Essex: John Adams, John Quincy Adams, George H.W. Bush and his son George W. Bush. In 1799, Charles Henry Harrod, the founder of the world renowned luxury department store Harrods, was born in Colchester, son of a local tax collector. At 350 miles (905km), Essex has the second longest coastline after Cornwall, and with 35 islands off its coast, more than any other county. Colchester is the earliest recorded town in English history, with annals going back to AD 77. After the Romans departed, it became one of the earliest towns in England to convert to Christianity. To mark 70 years of Queen Elizabeth's reign in 2022, Colchester was granted the prestigious Platinum Jubilee city status, highlighting the city's royal associations and cultural heritage.

★ ★ ★ ★

This side trip to Colchester paradoxically became an event that brought me closer to my Thai roots. I was having lunch at a restaurant on the high street. While I was waiting for my order of the usual meat-and-two-veg, I was jolted by the sound of the Thai language gently wafting from somewhere in the restaurant. Thai is a soft language. I looked around and saw a group that I assumed to be three young Thai men sitting at a table across the room. It has always been a cultural shock for me to hear my language outside of Thailand. I had not spoken Thai for quite some time. Their table was too far away to enable me to eavesdrop. I got up and pretended to go to the toilet. I wanted to make quite sure that I was hearing correctly.

I recalled being in a queue in Paris once, at the *Restaurant Universitaire,* a self-service dining room for students, waiting with my tray to select lunch. I suddenly heard the musical sound of an Asian tonal language. It was coming from a group of young Southeast Asians in the queue ahead of me. *Thai!* As I edged closer, I discovered that they were Vietnamese.

This time I didn't want to get it wrong. I left the bathroom of the Colchester coffee shop and bravely went to their table. They were in the middle of an animated conversation. It must have sounded idiotic when I asked them *in Thai* whether they were Thai or not. *Of course they were Thai, who else in Colchester would be speaking Thai?* All three of them looked up at me, more amused than surprised. We became friends immediately, exchanged names and addresses, with plans to meet in London where they would be living, once their English course in Colchester was over. I continued my close friendship with all of them back in Thailand. It was yet another of those seminal moments in my life when I was grappling with my identity. I realized that I was consciously seeking the company of my own people. I desperately wanted to be Thai. I needed to improve my Thai language skills. I was now determined to seek the company of other Thai students in England whenever I could. After all, it had always been my intention to return to Thailand after attaining my law degree.

★ ★ ★ ★

I was sad to leave Essex, but a new exciting life was about to begin in London.

CHAPTER FOUR
ARRIVALS AND DEPARTURES

London, November 1958.

I was getting short of cash again. I checked at the NUS office to catch up on the latest job openings. I could have easily gone to the post office to sort the Christmas mail, but I wanted to explore some new horizons.

Thomas Cook caught my eye. They were looking for assistants in their airline ticketing department.

Thomas Cook, pioneers of global travel! In the back of my mind, I remembered their slogan, 'Don't just book it, Thomas Cook it!'

I eagerly went for an interview at their London head office building in Berkeley Street, Mayfair, hoping to get a job at a travel desk where I could help customers plan their holidays. With my international travel experience, I fancied myself as an expert overseas vacation consultant. But there was never an interview. I didn't get beyond the ground floor where a gruff clerk with serious dandruff handed me a form to fill. After approving my carefully crafted application with a brief nod, he gave me a voucher with instructions to proceed to an address off the Tottenham Court Road.

It turned out to be a huge warehouse space, where I was herded with five other people to a narrow table about fifty centimetres wide and eight metres long, with a small writing surface and pigeonholes on the partitioned wall, not unlike the sorting desks at the post office, but less work friendly and with many more workers. We were seated on grey metal office chairs, wobbling on four castor wheels that squeaked at the slightest movement, and given instructions on how to write airline passenger tickets. There must have been dozens of people working with me on rows upon rows of long work tables, not unlike a factory assembly line. So much for Thomas Cook's airline ticketing department.

Thomas Cook would have approved of the simplicity of our working space. A simple man himself, he started work at age ten, often for a penny a day, to help support his family. Born in Derbyshire in 1808, he was self-educated, and as a Baptist preacher, he would walk thousands of miles to save money. So meagre was his income when he started out that he would work in the dark to conserve candles and oil.

Had he been alive in 1920, he may not have been too happy with Thomas Cook's expensive luxury tours for the super rich, although his Protestant work ethic would probably have allowed his conscience to reconcile the pursuit of wealth with his religious piety. But he certainly would *not* have approved of the offer of free drinks on board the company's premium class flights, just before the world's oldest travel agency went bust in 2019.

A prominent leader of a temperance movement in Leicester, Thomas started off organising a round trip excursion on a Midland Railway Company train for 485 teetotaling devotees, to an anti-liquor meeting in Loughborough in July 1841. It was the world's first tour group to quite possibly the world's first convention. His organised excursions to temperance meetings in nearby towns became so well known that he soon realised the commercial opportunities of group travel. In 1845, he organised a one day leisure tour to Liverpool for 1200 train passengers.

The Liverpool excursion was so popular that he was asked to repeat the tour two weeks later for 800 customers. This was a time when the majority of people in Victorian Britain had never travelled beyond their home town. After a successful tour of Scotland, Thomas introduced the Scottish Highlands to the English public in 1846 for the first time.

In 1851, he was responsible for sending 150,000 visitors from the provinces to attend the Great Exhibition in London, the first time a great many Britons saw their capital. It was the largest movement of people ever for leisure. Within ten years, Thomas expanded his travel services to destinations in Europe. The modern tourist was born.

When I wrote airline tickets for Thomas Cook in 1958, there were around 50 million tourist arrivals around the world. In 2018, there were a staggering *1.46 billion* international tourist arrivals. That's 1,460,000,000 people.* Travel had become the planet's largest service industry, providing employment for every tenth person in the world.

According to IATA,** 4.54 billion airline tickets were sold in 2019. In 2020, only 1.8 billion were issued, and air traffic fell as much as 70 percent when compared with the previous year, because of the Covid-19 pandemic.

Who knows what the future of global airline travel will be for the rest of the decade, with the Covid-19 and its Omicron variants present in many countries around the world? As more governments gradually remove travel barriers for fully vaccinated passengers with a World Health Organisation approved vaccine, and provided airlines are able to solve their staffing shortages, pilot attrition levels and high fuel costs, IATA has optimistically expected overall travel numbers to reach 4 billion in 2024.

---

* The largest number of tourists came from China, 170 million in 2019.
** International Air Transport Association, the airline industry's trade body.

After opening up the continent of Europe to British travellers in the 1850s, Thomas Cook continued to make trailblazing travel innovations around the world.

The first all-inclusive tour that combined travel, accommodation and food into one reasonably priced package was launched in 1855. The trip started at the port of Harwich, and took travellers to Brussels, Cologne, Heidelberg, Strasbourg, and ended in Paris for the International Exhibition, enabling working class travellers to visit the Continent for the first time.

Long before Thomas Cook's group tours, there had already existed a more sophisticated travel market in the 1800s; wealthy British independent voyagers with a higher purpose of travel – education, health and pilgrimage – regularly visited their favourite Continental destinations. They would frequently bump into Thomas Cook's popular tours in the Rhine River Valley, the Swiss Alps and the French Riviera. They wrote indignant letters to the *London Times*, complaining about the uncouth and uneducated common traveller, calling them 'Cook's Hordes' and 'Cook's Circus', or simply 'Cookites'.

Thomas Cook was a marketing genius. He realised that there was a lot more money to be made from the wealthier traveller, so he segmented his clientele into separate target groups, and began to develop exclusive tours that appealed to the more educated class. His Biblical tours to the Holy Land were inaugurated in 1860, the first time a group of higher-class travellers could discover the Middle East.

In 1865, Thomas Cook opened shop in Fleet Street, London. Wealthier Victorian travellers could now visit countries across their global empire where 'the sun never sets'. The shop also sold travel accessories, maps, guide books, telescopes, luggage and footwear. *Cook's Tourist's Handbook to Palestine and Syria* published in 1886 became a best seller.

In 1869, the first River Nile cruises were launched on board two steamships. Tours to the Pyramids became one of Cook's most popular upmarket destinations. The company was known by the locals as 'Cook Pasha'.

When John Mason, Thomas' son, joined the firm in 1871, the company traded under the new name of Thomas Cook & Son. Over the next few years, father and son launched the first escorted tours to the USA, and put their more adventurous clients on stage coaches. For those who wanted to continue their journey on to Japan across the Pacific, paddle steamers were made available. From there, the itinerary continued overland across China and India. The company now served the British aristocracy and called Thomas Cook the 'travel agent of the British Empire.'

Now that the company had become an important part of the empire's establishment, John Mason was approached by the government in 1884 to help transport General Garnet Wolseley's army of nine thousand men and 40,000 tons of stores and munitions 1500 miles up the Nile – a massive logistics operation – as part of an expedition to rescue General Charles Gordon, who had been ordered by Prime Minister William Gladstone* to evacuate Sudan, but who had foolishly decided to stay on and defend Khartoum. Surrounded by the enemy, he and his entire garrison of six thousand men were massacred by the army of Mahdi Mohammed Ahmed, a self-styled prophet and liberator of Sudan.

Sadly, Wolseley arrived too late.

---

* Gladstone, the great Liberal PM, was unusual in an age of imperialistic expansion, and way ahead of his time, because he possessed humanitarian principles and sympathies with minorities abroad. His policy was not to get involved with new colonial adventures and fight wars with nationalist independent movements. Under his watch, he saw the end of the Anglo-Afghan war in 1880 and Britain's withdrawal from Afghanistan, following the massacre of the British Residency staff in Kabul by Afghan freedom fighters. Interestingly, President Biden evacuated US forces from Afghanistan in 2021, ending America's longest war.

Again, in 1886, John Mason was asked by the government, this time that of Colonial India, to help transport the subcontinent's Muslim population to Mecca, as part of the hajj pilgrimage.

British travellers in Queen Victoria's time were often at the mercy of local thieves and highwaymen. With their well-tailored clothes and upper class bearing, they were the world's richest sightseers, and were frequently robbed of their money and left penniless in an alien country where there would be no one to help them. Thomas Cook Circular Notes, the first traveller's cheques, were introduced in 1874, so that currency could always be made available to travellers on demand, whenever and to whomever the signed circular was presented. Intrepid travellers could now journey safely without fear of losing their money.

In 1872 they launched the first round-the-world tour. The journey took 222 days and covered nearly 30,000 miles. In 1875 Cook's exclusive 'Midnight Sun' tours to the Norwegian fjords were introduced.

Thomas Cook developed the concept of 'enclave tourism' whereby the traveller would be confined to luxury hotels and to a prescribed itinerary, providing a safe corridor of protection from hostile locals at all times. Visitors touring the Pyramids were isolated in a bubble, far away from beggars and thieves. The Shepheard Hotel in Cairo was the first of its kind to cater for élite excursionists, with all the services they would ever need available in-house, protecting them from perceived outside dangers.

Modern enclaves have now become entire destinations where tourist activities are planned and confined to one small geographic area, and the traveller is cordoned off from the rest of the country's general population. In Sharm el Sheikh, a beach resort in Egypt, visitors from Europe are able to roam around scantily dressed to their bodies' content without the risk of ever offending their Muslim hosts. The chances of either party coming face to face were nil. Giant cruise ships are another prime example of enclave tourism. There was no need for passengers to leave the safety of their floating enclave, and when they did, they were well-protected. Unfortunately, the rapid spread of the Covid-19 virus has today put cruise ships at the top of the danger list for mass tourists, overtaking the threats of terrorism to air travellers.

My own experience with enclave tourism disturbs me still. On a luxury cruise down the Irrawaddy, I was on deck of *The Road to Mandalay* at sundown, nibbling on caviar sandwiches with a chilled glass of Moët & Chandon, before sitting down to a sumptuous dinner. Poor Burmese villagers on the banks waved to us. They had no electricity, no running water and hardly any clothes. Not one of them benefitted from the sixteen well heeled passengers on board who had each paid around $2000 for the two day cruise. We were using their river free of charge. The contrast between us, the privileged traveller, and the underfed peasants, will forever disturb me.

★ ★ ★ ★

At age 63, Thomas decided to see for himself some of the overseas destinations he had made famous. In 1872, he departed from Leicester on a tour of the world, travelling from Egypt to China through the newly opened Suez Canal, and then on to North America, crossing the States by railway from San Francisco to New York. He was away for 8 months.

Thomas Cook & Son was appointed the Official Passenger Agent for travellers wishing to attend the first modern Olympic Games in Athens in 1896.

Thomas Cook's business was not only confined to outbound British travellers. The company also arranged travel to Britain for visitors from overseas. In 1870 Thomas Cook facilitated a visit to Britain for the Maharaja of Kolhapur, who ended his memorable tour in Scotland. It was quite a formidable logistics exercise. He travelled with seven 'native' servants, and '22 packages of bags, boxes, hampers, including his own spices and cooking utensils.'

In 1887 and 1897, Thomas Cook was assigned by the British government to organise and manage the travel arrangements for foreign dignitaries coming to London to attend Queen Victoria's Golden and Diamond Jubilees.

By the turn of the new century, there were several Thomas Cook branches in the United States, Australia and New Zealand. In 1919 Thomas Cook was the first travel agent to market pleasure flights. An ad was placed in the *London Times* announcing this new concept in travel. A Handley Page bomber left over from the First World War was converted into a passenger plane. Air travel for pleasure was launched. In 1927, Thomas Cook's American office organised the first passenger flight from New York to Chicago, purely for the experience of air travel, rather than for touring the sights of Chicago.

Interestingly, the Prohibition law in the United States between 1920 and 1933 enabled alcohol seeking Americans to select tours on foreign cruise ships that served as much booze to intemperate passengers as they wanted, which inherently crippled the US passenger trade. Tours to popular destinations in Mexico and the Carribbean, especially Nassau and Jamaica, were on carriers booked through Thomas Cook, an ironic turn of events considering the Baptist founder's original business for teetotaling travellers in the previous century.

In 1926, Thomas Cook moved offices from Ludgate Circus to Mayfair, the chicest area of London, and became the world's most exclusive travel agent. They were a stone's throw away from the Connaught, the Dorchester and Claridges, London's most expensive hotels, where their clients lived. The first safari tours, part of a five-month tour of Africa from Cairo to the Cape, were developed during this period.

For $5,000 (in today's currency around 50,000 pounds) an American traveller in 1928 could experience the world's first luxury cruise in a marketing tie-in with Cunard Lines. Starting in New York, the liner would sail to Buenos Aires via the Caribbean, across the South Atlantic to Cape Town, and from there along the east coast of Africa, up through the Suez Canal to Cairo, Naples and Monte Carlo. After three months, the happy but by now exhausted traveller would return home to New York, stopping at Madeira along the way.

In the 1900s, Thomas Cook had prestigious offices located at the best addresses in Europe. Among them were Place de l'Opéra in Paris, Piazza San Marco in Venice and the Spanish steps on Piazza di Spagna in Rome. During the nineteenth century the area around the piazza was inhabited by dozens of English poets and writers: Byron, Keats, Shelly, Edward Lear, George Eliot and the Brownings. The doyen of them all, the Romantic poet John Keats, lived and died at No 26, overlooking the steps. Nearby was the grand office of Thos. Cook & Son, the focal point for English tourists who congregated here during the Roman leg of their grand tours. In the fifties and sixties when I lived in Rome, I often took visitors there to cash their traveller's cheques and exchange their money into lira.

The company's advertising slogan at the turn of the twentieth century was short and sweet: 'From heir to the throne to the humblest greengrocer, travel with Thomas Cook.'

★ ★ ★ ★

By the time I worked as an airline ticket writer in 1958, the company had already changed hands many times and its new owner was now the recently nationalised British Railways. The new emerging middle class wanted to leave the drabness of post-war Britain behind and Thomas Cook catered to their needs with its 'inclusive tours' at prices they could afford. The first modern packaged holidays were introduced, launching unusual destinations and modes of transportation once the preserve of the rich. In 1959 about 2.5 million Brits had travelled abroad on holiday and by 1967 the figure had doubled. Such was the desire of British families to spend two weeks in the sun that the number of holiday makers travelling overseas increased by 230 per cent over the decade of the sixties, whilst the number of people holidaying in the UK increased by only 20 per cent.

The cheapest destination was Spain. There was even a tour company called 'See Spain Ltd'.

An airline ticket basically consisted of 9 parts: the passenger's name, the issuing airline, the ticket number, the destinations the ticket was valid for, the flight number, the class of travel, baggage allowance, the fare and the dates of the ticket's validity. The ticket itself was a flimsy booklet measuring approximately 3.5 by 7 inches. The travel details were hand-written with a thick biro pen on the first page, and the following two pages were carbon copies. It did not require great skills to write a ticket, but the job was tiring. To make sure that the details of the passenger's air journey appeared clearly on the carbon copies, one had to press the pen hard on the top copy. Eight hours and two hundred tickets later my right hand was ready to fall off. It was more demanding than writing answers for the Advanced Level Economic History exam I had taken earlier in the year.

Most of Thomas Cook's packaged tours in 1958 were for cheap holidays in Spain. Typically, a couple would take their annual two weeks in the sun to popular seaside destinations on the Costa Brava, so BCN (Barcelona) was their nearest airport. More adventurous passengers went further afield to PMI (Palma de Mallorca) and AGP (Malaga). The issuing airline was BEA (British European Airways).

Each ticket that I wrote was like writing a cheque. Before computers, paper tickets were the only proof that passengers had paid for their flight before they would be permitted to board. After nearly 80 years of handwritten paper tickets, IATA, the International Airlines Travel Association, announced on 1 June 2008, that air travellers would henceforth be issued with e-tickets to enable them to board the aircraft. Simply explained to old school air travellers such as myself, who had written hundreds of paper tickets and flown on dozens of flights to all four corners of the globe, an e-ticket is located in the airline's computer database, instead of in my briefcase. Lose my paper ticket and I lose my flight. The termination of paper tickets was said to have saved as much as $3 billion worldwide and cut the cost of issuing a hand-written ticket from $10 each to one dollar. According to IATA, the elimination of paper tickets had saved 50,000 trees a year. It must have also eliminated thousands of ticket writing jobs all over the world.

After two weeks and several hundred tickets later I'd had enough working in Thomas Cook's slave galley. I left in early December with a little extra cash to see me through the Christmas holidays.

I was never a customer of Thomas Cook. I have always been what the trade calls an 'F.I.T', a Free Independent Traveller, avoiding group tours like the plague. Consequently, the only time poor students like me could go on a plane in those days was when the seats were paid for by our parents. Immigrants and guest workers didn't travel by plane until the seventies. Otherwise, my friends and I would hit the road with our backpacks, and hitchhike our way across the Continent. In those carefree days of the late fifties, it was a safe way to travel.* We were blessed. It was an age of innocence, before drug abuse, terrorism, illegal immigration and political correctness.

★ ★ ★ ★

---

* I have safely hitchhiked in Britain, France, Germany, Switzerland, Italy, Spain, Malta, and even Morocco, between 1958 and 1962.

On Monday morning 23 September 2019, the world woke up to the sad news that Thomas Cook had gone under after 178 years of business. It had run up colossal losses of up to 1.5 billion pounds and failed to convince banks to back a rescue plan. The British government had also refused to grant the bankrupt company a 250 million pound bailout. Over half a million customers were stranded around the world.

It was the decline in packaged tours, the high cost of operating an airline, 550 unprofitable high street retail shops, intense competition from low-cost airlines and internet companies, and the new market of younger consumers who plan their trips online, that led to its demise. It was the first major Brexit casualty.

It is hoped that Thomas Cook's new owners, Fosun Tourism, develop original creative ideas to meet the needs of the modern generation of experiential travellers, based on eco-friendly destinations, wellness tourism, cultural enrichment and personal development, enabling travellers to connect with nature, with communities and with themselves. Only when management understands that the travel market has become niche will they be able to restore the company to its former glory. Since the Covid-19 pandemic, it has now switched its operations online.

Item: By early 2022, at least 40 airlines have collapsed since the beginning of the corona virus pandemic. Two serious casualties: Avianca, the world's second oldest airline, and Alitalia, an 'old friend' since 1947, that ended its run with its last flight from Rome to Cagliari on 15 October 2021. Although Thai has gone into bankruptcy, the government has so far been determined to keep the airline going.

Item: On 8 October 2020, British Airways retired their entire fleet of 31 fuel hungry Boeing 747 Jumbo jets, in service since 1989. They either finished up in a giant parking lot in the Californian desert or broken up and sold for scrap metal. Alas, another 'old friend' that has bitten the dust. Just one Jumbo survived, ending up in Dunsted Aerodrome in Surrey, to be used as a film set.

Item: The Airbus A380, the largest, and arguably the smoothest and most comfortable passenger jet that has ever flown, has slowly been retired from the skies by many airlines. The defection started with Air France in 2020. Dozens of A380s are parked in the deserts of California and Australia, waiting for better times, when some may be resurrected. Otherwise, they too, will be consigned to the scrapyard.

A sad turn of events for the airline and aviation industries.

II

'Suoi mani sono troppo piccole per questo tipo di lavoro.'

This is what an Italian co-worker at Frankfurt Airport told me. My hands were too small for this kind of work.

It all started in early 1959. I had fallen in love with Regina Berthold, a German girl I met at the Metro Club in Old Compton Street where young au pair girls went dancing on their nights off. After her English course came to an end she returned to Germany and found a job in Frankfurt. By July, when I went over to Frankfurt to be with her, we sadly discovered that we were not meant for each other, but I decided to stay on in Germany to learn more about the people that had started two world wars in the last half century, and had lost both of them.

I rented a comfortable room in Westend Platz that cost a bit, so I needed to find work. I made my way to the Goethe University of Frankfurt where the NUS in London had informed me that I could look for vacant jobs for students, once I presented my membership card. A reasonably well paid job was available at the *Flughaven Frankfurt am Main*, the local airport. They were looking for baggage handlers, 'no previous skills necessary.' The university arranged all the formalities and the next day I presented myself at the new east terminal, the *Empfangsaulage* (the arrival facility east), completed in 1958, to handle the growing international traffic. In March 1960, Lufthansa had launched the first non-stop flight from Frankfurt to New York, on the newly designed Boeing 707 long distance jetliner. Frankfurt Airport was starting to become an international airline hub.

I was put to work right away. Diametrically opposite to the sedentary job I had writing airline tickets for hours on end at the travel agency, little did I realize that I would be required to be on my feet all day long on the airport tarmac, at the other end of the air travel industry spectrum. 'Baggage-handling' was a gentle way of describing the physical lifting and moving of heavy luggage and trunks from the airplane's hold.

This was an era before passengers were able to leave the aircraft through the exit door straight on to a boarding bridge that directly connects to the terminal. In the fifties and sixties a passenger would deplane (to use an Americanism) onto a mobile boarding staircase that was wheeled up to the exit door of the aircraft, and then proceed to the terminal by coach. A crew of four baggage handlers on a tractor trailer – I was one of them – would accompany the mobile staircase to the rear bulkhead of the plane to unload the luggage from the hold. When it was my turn, I was assigned to crawl inside the luggage compartment, and drag out items that were deep inside the hold. It was an uncomfortable job, and on Aeroflot's Tupolov 104 aircraft, clearly dangerous. There were bits of sharp metal edges and rusty surfaces throughout the narrow space. Safety and quality control were not the Russian engineers' strongest points.

We emptied the luggage holds on turboprops like the Vickers Viscount, four-propeller piston-engines like the Lockheed

Super Constellation and the Douglas DC6, as well as on the much larger jet propelled Boeing 707, which had its maiden commercial flight on PanAm in 1958, from New York to Paris, and launched the modern Jet Age. Frank Sinatra was on the return flight back to New York and was inspired to launch his best-selling album *Come Fly With Me* later on that year.

★ ★ ★ ★

I often reminisce about my first flight experience in 1951. It was a KLM flight from Bangkok to Rome on board a Lockheed Constellation – the 'Conny', as it was nicknamed – stopping at Rangoon, Calcutta, Karachi, Basra, Beirut and Athens, before arriving in Rome nearly 48 hours later. I wore my best suit and joined 56 other well-dressed passengers in the first class cabin – there was only one class in those days – with seat configuration for families based on the deluxe wagon-lits dining car train compartment of the 1930s. My kid brother and I sat *opposite* our parents, with a low dining table in between. We were looked after by uniformed 'stewardesses' with little hats on their heads. Young passengers were supplied with toys and colouring books, apparently to keep them quiet on this rather long and certainly very tedious journey. For passengers who were travelling on their own, the configuration was not much different from that of a modern aircraft, but with much more legroom and larger seats.

Before 1954 flights from Europe to Britain landed at Northolt Airport on the edge of Ruislip, while flights from the rest of the world landed at London Airport in Feltham. In 1954 London Airport was relocated to Heathrow, originally at the turn of the century an area covering several tracts of wasteland, with an undergrowth of gorse, row upon row of heathland. The locals called the nearby hamlet 'Heath Row'.

★ ★ ★ ★

By 1959, when I started working as a baggage handler, two cabin classes had been introduced, first and economy, and the deluxe seating plan that I experienced on my first flight on KLM no longer existed. Business class didn't come in until well into the seventies. Occasionally, baggage handlers were called upon to search the airplane's cabin for small suitcases and other bits and pieces that passengers had inadvertently left behind. At other times, we were assigned to move luggage inside the terminal, putting them on to special carts and loading them on to different airline coaches.

It is interesting to note that students and casual workers were required to *unload* the aircraft only. There were specialist crews that *only loaded* luggage and freight on to the aircraft. I was told that this was a specialised job requiring handlers to work inside the hold, working on their knees, and stack the bags and freight as neatly and efficiently as possible. Anyway, whether it was loading or unloading, both were rough jobs, and left workers exhausted. We were supplied with thick gloves and heavy overalls to protect ourselves, but they didn't make our job any easier. I only lasted a month.

At that time in Frankfurt, there were many casual workers, displaced refugees of all ages, who had fled from the harsh dictatorship of the German Democratic Republic, an absurdly oxymoronic name for totalitarian communist East Germany, and some of them worked side by side with us. To stem the flood of escaping refugees, many of them East German technical school and university graduates seeking a better life in West Germany, the Berlin Wall was put up at great speed two years later, in August 1961.

The students working at the airport were mostly German, and the biggest foreign group were Italians. I was happy to put my Italian language skills to work again. In the short time that I worked there, I easily made friends with many German high school leavers – *Sekundarschulabganger* – and undergrads – *Grundstandiges.*

One of them, Wido Praun, was extremely affable and warm, and was to become a lifelong friend. He spoke good English and patiently helped me learn his difficult language. He taught me *Hochdeutsch* – High German – 'the language of Goethe', he told me, and spoken by the cultured class. He told me not to learn from the common East German workers with whom we mingled at work who spoke a 'rough' form of German. But like many other post-war Europeans of their class (including the UK) who were now learning how to speak their national language correctly, many retained their provincial speech for use with their families and in their home towns. For a moment, I was reminded of the English class system. He himself spoke English with an American accent. He was an avid listener to the *Voice of America*, the most popular English language radio program in Germany in the fifties.

I was privileged to meet Wido's family. His father worked at Höchst, a chemical company with headquarters in Frankfurt. His mother was a small lady, blonde, kind, and motherly, with a beautiful smile. They welcomed me to their home like a long lost son. Wido was not a typical German name. His forbears, the Prauns, came from Schleswig-Holstein, on the northern Danish border. Their dialect, *Plattdeutsch*, or Low German, is less guttural, and their language sounds almost Danish. I learned from Wido that English spies who were posing as Germans during the war were less likely to get caught if they spoke *Plattdeutsch,* an easy accent for them to learn.

Wido's father, Herr Praun (that is how I addressed him, as the Germans were very formal in those days so I never got to know his first name) was thin, underweight, and had a permanent cough. His hands were arthritic, and his fingers crooked and misshapen. His face was craggy and deeply lined. He couldn't stop shaking. He was only 55, yet he looked eighty. He was one of the very few Wehrmacht war survivors from the Eastern front, where 4 million German soldiers were either slaughtered in battle fighting the Russian army, or died of exposure and frostbite from the freezing Russian winter. The war between the Nazis and the Soviets on the Eastern front was the largest military confrontation in history and the bloodiest theatre of World War ll. When it was clear that the Germans were losing, he could either have surrendered to the Russians or run for his life. He chose the latter. Wido told me that his father had rather braved the bitter winter steppes through Russia and Poland, and suffer severe frostbite, than be taken prisoner by the Russians, known for their cruel brutality. He walked the entire 1000 miles. In the end, he said he was fortunate to have been captured by the *humane Amerikaner* and was later released in 1946.

★ ★ ★ ★

Germany in the late fifties was a country trying to forget its past. Everyone I met, everyone I talked to, and everyone I made friends with, seemed desperate to atone for the sins of the Nazis. Led by Chancellor Konrad Adenauer, a former mayor of Cologne imprisoned by the Nazis in 1934 and again in 1944 for plotting to kill Hitler, he was single mindedly determined to lead post-war Germany back to international respectability. It was the period of West Germany's 'economic miracle' when its currency was strong and its trade and productivity performance became the first in Europe. In 1956, Germany overtook the UK as the world's leading car exporter. By the sixties, the Volkswagen Beetle was the world's best-selling car. In this atmosphere of rebuilding their country from the rubble of defeat and destruction, every German I talked to and met had a positive attitude. All the talk was about their future plans – *Zukunftsplane*. The word *Krieg* – the war – was hardly ever mentioned.

A serious topic of conversation in Britain at that time was still about the proud and brave country that stood alone against Hitler, when Russia and Germany were still allies, and before the Americans came on board in 1942. In fact, Britain was the *only* combatant nation that fought continuously in the Second World War from the very first day to the last. The island race that stood alone against all adversity was a metaphor for all British people of my generation. Depending on the person's age, it was either '*during the war*' in which case it was about the heroics of the British people, or '*before the war*' when the nation's global territorial empire and the good times were harked back to. '*After the war*' was invariably about the current deprivations of a country that was suffering from post-war economic hardships, rationing, reconstruction and decolonisation. During the fifties, and even up to the early sixties, 'the war' was often referred to in daily conversation in Britain. In Germany nobody hardly ever talked about the war.

German is the only language I know that has at least *sixteen* different words to describe 'efficiency'. Whether it is for a person, a machine, a service, an organization, a method of production, an art, even music, each has a task with its own rules of efficiency. Learning how to unload luggage from a plane had its unique system that I had to familiarise myself with. Instruction books often contained phrases like *Arbeit wird so logisch und rationell wie moglich organisiert* – work is organised in the most logical and efficient way – a somewhat dogmatic way of describing the German mind. Working for as short a while as I did at the airport, I was made to believe that nothing could go wrong if I followed the rules.

German is also a language where the sheer number of syllables in one word make it very difficult to learn. Try reading *Geschwindigkeitsbeschrankung.* That's 28 letters and 7 syllables for the words 'speed limit'. Now try pronouncing it. Of course, the word was hardly ever used, and that's just as well. There used to be no speed limit on the *Autobahn*, the German motorway. Now, only a few unlimited speed sections remain. It must have been quite a mouthful for a diligent speed cop to utter, not to mention the effort of having to write it out in full, each time he wanted to issue a traffic summons, during the days before they were processed electronically.

The Germans I met and made friends with were honest, hard-working and sincere, with a deep craving to make friends with the world. This was a time when Thais, and indeed everyone else from almost every country, did not require a visa to enter, nor a residence permit to live in Germany.

Unlike the French, the Germans were very sympathetic when I attempted to speak their guttural language, and they accepted my mistakes, not with a Gallic shrug, but with sincere empathy, notwithstanding their sometimes tiresome attempt to correct and teach me the right way to speak and pronounce some of their impossibly inflected words. Whenever there was a misunderstanding of any sort, be it a set of instructions that I didn't follow, a particular grammatical rule that I didn't get when I was learning German, or a story that I didn't quite grasp, the corrected version was repeatedly and dogmatically made at great pains, to ensure that all was understood. I found myself saying *ich verstehe* – I understand – all day. I was often required to repeat what I had just learned several times. *Wiederholen das nochmal?* The Germans take everything, big or small, very seriously. It is in their DNA.

There were a number of unique characteristics about the Germans that I would like to share with my readers. Unlike the British or Italians, Germans were not quite as masterly at humour. Upstanding citizens by nature, heaven help the person who innocently infringed even the simplest regulation, like going through the left door only meant for pedestrians walking on the right. And of course, they were proud of their technology and efficiency. The trains ran on time. Even as far back as the fifties, most young Germans born after the war were hopeful that their country would one day be reunited. My university friends were often annoyed when letters to Germany were addressed 'West Germany', as if to tacitly approve the existence of (Soviet occupied) East Germany. The biggest no-no: any mention of the war.

I stayed on in Germany for the next 6 months. Wido had kindly put me up at his home through Christmas and the new year. The warm welcome that the Praun family extended to me will forever remain in my heart.

★ ★ ★ ★

Several decades later, in 1992, I returned to Frankfurt for a few days on a business trip. Frankfurt had become the financial centre of Germany, and the second biggest in Europe, vastly different from the provincial town where I had once lived. I boarded the metro train from the airport with my carry-on shoulder bag to get to my hotel near the Hauptwache, a 17th century building and a city centre landmark. I asked a passenger or two to let me know when the train arrived at the Hauptwache station. The airport train service was new to me. After thirty-five minutes, at least ten people yelled *'Hauptwache!'* and enthusiastically pointed out the station's name on the platform for me. They were all concerned lest I miss my stop. This was German efficiency and hospitality at their best. They were the same people that I came to know in the sixties: honest, friendly and super competent. They hadn't changed at all.

CHAPTER FIVE
ABBOTTS LODGE

It was March 1961 and I was short of money again. The local news vendor's general notice board on Earl's Court Road posted an advertisement for a temporary job vacancy at the Abbotts Lodge Hotel in Cromwell Road. I often checked at the shop's Jobs Vacant notices for local employment opportunities. There were the usual notices like 'French lessons available'*; 'Brown cocker spaniel answering to the name of Joey lost in Philbeach Gardens. If found please call KEN 5639. Reward'; 'Morris Minor, 56 model, 200 pounds o.n.o'** and 'Single room for let, Collingham Place, 1 pound a week'. Hidden amongst all these notices was a job vacancy at the Abbotts Lodge Hotel.

There was no job description, just that the work was for the mornings only. And it was only temporary. Perfect. That would leave me free for the rest of the day, I thought. I was curious to know what kind of hotel it was though. I have always considered myself a seasoned traveller when compared with my fellow British contemporaries. By the time I was fifteen I must have stayed in dozens of hotels of all descriptions in England and Continental

---

* Call-girl service.
** An abbreviation for 'or near offer' used in classified ads and private notices boards.

Europe, and in as far flung places as Singapore and Thailand. So I knew a good hotel when I saw one. Was Abbotts Lodge one of them, I wondered?

The golden age of hotel accommodation for me was during my travel across provincial France, Italy, Spain, Portugal, Switzerland, Austria and Germany with my parents by car. It was in the late 40s and early 50s, after years of hardship during the war, marking the end of an era of grand hotels that had been part of *la belle époque* of the previous century, yet still a few years away before the advent of international hotel chains.*

It was also an era when motor travel for most holiday makers was rare. Many urban families chose one destination – the sea or the mountains – for their annual summer break in August, and they normally went by train. Not my family though. The longest road trip we ever took was from our home in Rome to Lisbon, through France and Spain, and back home again. That was when we lived in Italy in the fifties. My father loved his car and he was a good driver. Only once did we come close to an accident, and that was on a German *autobahn*. It was raining, and the Chevrolet Bel Air went into a 180-degree spin. Fortunately, he wasn't going very fast and my father cleverly avoided a collision. Unlike Germany, the highways in France and Italy in the early fifties were narrow, and the potholed roads of Spain were forever in a state of repair. *Obras* (work) signs were everywhere. The network of motorways, *autoroutes* and *autostrade* had not yet been constructed. There was very little traffic on the country roads and long-distance drivers were generally French businessmen travelling in their fast Citroens and Bugattis from Paris to Nice on the *Route Napoléon*, or wealthy Italians in their Alfas and Lancias from Genoa to Rome on the old *Via Cassia*.

---

* Today, according to the BBC, there are nearly 800,000 hotels and resorts around the world.

No one would ever think of going to an out-of-town hotel by car. Local motor traffic mostly consisted of families going about their business within a small radius of their home province in their tiny Fiats and VW Beetles.

Gone are the days when my father could park the family (Morris/Austin/Chevrolet/Oldsmobile) right in front of the grandest hotel in town where it would safely remain for the rest of our stay. Before checking in, my mother would be allowed to view two or three rooms, and select one that met her particular list of needs: cleanliness – especially under the carpets – comfort, peace and quiet. This was post-war Europe when bathroom taps were often out of order. She rejected rooms with peeling paint and wallpaper, unpleasant smells, and curtains that were difficult to draw. A good view was never a criteria. Front rooms were noisy, she would say, not unless they were on the top floors. Space was never an issue either, because hotel rooms in those days were, by modern standards, enormous. Hotel occupancy in the early fifties, particularly in provincial towns, were at most half full. My mother would always get the room she wanted and within budget.

Not all hotels we stayed at were necessarily fashionable or famous. We were on holiday and certainly couldn't afford the rates of the George V in Paris or the Bauer au Lac in Zurich, where we would stay if my father was on a diplomatic mission. Once, at our hotel in La Coruña, General Franco, the Spanish dictator, happened to be staying there too. He was in town for the *corrida*. The hotel was crawling with fascist uniformed *Guardia Civil* officers brandishing firearms. At another time, in San Remo, we were annoyingly woken up at 1 am every morning. We didn't know that it was the month of the Italian pop music festival and the singers were returning noisily to the hotel after their performances. On one trip to Savona in autumn 1948, we had the entire hotel to ourselves, when no one was travelling.

ABBOTTS LODGE

My parents were opera fans, so in the lovely country towns of Italy – Parma, Piacenza, Verona and Vicenza – they would always select a hotel near the opera house. Not necessarily the best or biggest hotel in town (they were generally near the station) but certainly the cosiest; it was the kind of hotel with not more than 30 rooms that would today be pretentiously called 'boutique'.

★ ★ ★ ★

All these fond memories came rushing back to me when I started to work at Abbotts Lodge, a small, traditional establishment in Cromwell Road, now long gone. It was the 'boutique' of its time. I worked there for 6 weeks over Easter 1961. It had 30 biggish rooms, a vast dining room, and I got to know many of the guests. It was an era when many occupants were permanent residents. Rather than checking in to an old people's home, many well off British retirees, widows and war veterans preferred to spend the rest of their days in a warm, comfortable and well serviced hotel. Abbotts Lodge was one of them. The other section of the hotel welcomed visitors from overseas.

The hotel was ideally located next to the West London Air Terminal on Cromwell Road, a check-in and arrival facility for British European Airways passengers flying to or from the Continent. Before it closed down in 1974, I had always used the terminal to check-in for my flight to Rome when I visited my parents in the sixties. A BEA coach would transport passengers to Heathrow and deliver them straight to the customs and immigration desks, since baggage check-in had already been completed in town. European visitors arriving at the terminal, mostly from France, Germany and Italy, picked up their luggage here in town and simply walked a few metres to Abbotts Lodge, the closest hotel to the terminal. Travellers from Asia and the Americas did not enjoy this convenience. This was a time when the most sophisticated world travellers were American.

Much to my chagrin, I was employed to perform one of the most laborious jobs in the hotel. Every morning at 6 am, whatever the weather (normally wet and cold, this was England after all), I had to make my way to the hotel – luckily only a 10 minute walk – to stoke the boiler. Mr Grove, the man who normally added coal to the boiler to keep the hotel's heating system working, showed me how to do it before going away for two weeks. The work was simple but dirty. It was one of those jobs that looked easy when someone showed you how to do it, but became a total disaster when called upon to do it on one's own. I listened carefully to Mr Grove's lecture on how to open the dampers to regulate the draft, when to make it draw, how to light the flame and get the fire going before actually stoking the boiler. There was a pile of coal on one side of the cellar, and a furnace on the other. After that, all I had to do was shovel coal into the firebox, rather like the stoker on a steam locomotive train, until the gauge on the boiler reached a certain temperature, and then 'Bobs your uncle!' which in cockney means that the job was satisfactorily done.

The next morning, I arrived at my new place of work one hour early. I did as instructed and lit a little fire in the furnace with a bit of wood and paper, adding some coal as it started to blaze up. But to no avail. The furnace never seemed to get going. Mr Grove arrived an hour later. He saw me covered with soot and there were cold ashes all over the floor.

'Wot's wrong wiv the boyler?' he asked me, incredulously. I told him of my predicament. Apparently, I had kept the wrong door open (there were two of them) and all I had to do was put only two knobs of coal on top of the burning paper and wood, and once it started to glow, simply add more coal as it started crackling. 'Easy like,' he said. Mr Grove looked at me as if I were half-witted, which I admitted to him that I was.

Thank God this job was only for a short while, I thought to myself. Do it all wrong and the hotel guests would be up in arms, he told me. 'Why isn't there any hot water this morning?' 'What the hell happened to the heating?' they would ask angrily. Mr Grove had the most important job in the hotel.

After a few days, the manager asked me if I could stay on for an extra two hours after stoking the boiler, and take on an additional duty. A small increase in pay was offered. The hotel needed someone to prepare the hot breakfasts, until the manager was able to find a suitable person to do the job. The last one had recently retired. It was too much work for Mr Martin, the hotel's resident chef, to do in the morning and whose hands were already full preparing dinner every evening. I accepted with alacrity. It would be fun to do something totally new and the pay wasn't bad either. Mr Martin showed me the ropes.

The kitchen of Abbotts Lodge was a vast, dark tiled room in the basement, with a majestic iron range and more cooking utensils than I had ever seen anywhere. Huge drying racks for the hotel's sheets and towels hung from the high ceiling like ships' sails. This giant Victorian clothesline could be hoisted up and down on pulleys. I called it 'the schooner'. Never mind that the sheets and towels carried the greasy odours from the previous evening's roast dinner.

Every morning, after the boiler was well stoked, I went to the kitchen to make breakfast. I had to prepare 40 hot meals, quite an undertaking if the guests wanted their cooked breakfasts all at the same time. Fortunately, such occasions were rare, I was told by Mr Cochran, the resident waiter, whose job was to take breakfasts up to the rooms or to guests in the dining room, and to serve dinner in the evenings. Normally, overseas guests had their breakfast between 7 and 8 am, whilst the local residents had a good lie-in and didn't eat breakfast until 9 am. It was much the same fare every day: fried egg with bacon, sausages and beans, prepared on a giant griddle, accompanied by toast. I was given 42 eggs, 40 for the guests plus two spare ones, which were mine to take home if I didn't break any. Trying not to break any eggs became an art form. Tea, coffee, bread rolls and cold cereals were served on a buffet table in the dining room. After 11 am Mr Cochran left the hotel to his lunchtime job at a restaurant in the West End. At 1 pm a scullery maid would arrive to wash all the dirty breakfast and dinner dishes and launder the sheets and towels. Abbotts Lodge seemed to be a well-run hotel. It did not serve lunch, although it was open for tea at 4 pm.

In time, I took on a few additional duties. It happened entirely by chance. A French couple were not able to express their requirements adequately in English so I was able to help out by translating their needs. When it became known that I was available to be of service to guests, I found myself performing small chores for individual visitors before I quit work at midday. There was no in-house switchboard for overseas calls, so it was my job to direct them to the West London Air Terminal next door from where they were able to call home. For an American guest, I would buy and deliver a copy of the *International Herald Tribune* to him every morning. Occasionally, I would help guests – there was no porter – take luggage up to the room. There was a dear old lady in Room 14 who just wanted to talk. She was bed-bound and would occasionally ask me up just to have a chat. I could see that it made her happy to see me, and she would often give me a pound. Her name was Miss Veal. She was interested in my life and she would then talk about her own childhood in India. She wasn't lonely but simply enjoyed young company. In time, I became acquainted with many of the guests. There were other guests who totally ignored me, not out of rudeness of any sort, but simply because they had no need for my services, such as they were.

If the reader is under the impression that all was well at Abbotts Lodge, it would be partly true, as I did quite like the work I was doing, apart from stoking the boiler. However, I was soon to learn from experience that in every organisation there was always a type of person who was generally unhappy with the job they were doing and was always complaining. Up to now, my co-workers at the Royal Mail, the farm camp and in the travel business, were mostly recruited as casual labour, and were mainly students who had not quite decided what to do with the rest of their lives. On the whole they were a happy lot, provided they got paid at the end of the week.

I had only been at Abbotts Lodge for about a week to discover that the staff who were meant to be working together as a team were each trying to assert themselves as individuals. The manager, Mrs Dempster, kept very much to herself, and never joined the staff at teatime, insisting on having her meals taken up on a tray to her room by Mr Cochran. Fortyish, thin and ever so prim, looking beyond her years in her severe pinafore dress, she personified authority and could have easily been mistaken for a school headmistress. Her infrequent visits to the kitchen were only conducted to inspect the larders and store cupboards, and to make sure that the staff were not pilfering any of the provisions. I only met her when she initially interviewed me for the job, or on her inspection tours and on paydays.

The rest of the staff – the chambermaid, the pantry maid, the cook, the waiter – were all conscious of their positions, and I was never quite sure of each one's status in Abbots Lodge's hierarchy. I wasn't even sure where *I* stood. The only thing they had in common was that they were all complainers. They all addressed each as either 'Mr' or 'Mrs' – I was 'Mr Palestine' or 'Mr Palestra' – except for the plump, spotty faced chambermaid whom everyone called 'Doris'. Poor thing, she was obviously at the bottom of the pile.

The waiter, Mr Cochran, was the unhappiest person of all. He was always complaining about his co-workers, and in a whispered aside to me – he treated as me if I was a co-conspirator in a plot to overthrow the hotel – he told me that he didn't really belong here at all.

'I'm more used to a classier establishment,' he would tell me. He kept on muttering about the Savoy Grill, but I was never quite sure whether he had ever worked there at all. I rather suspected that he would very much like to have had a position in London's 'classiest' hotel, but could never quite make the grade. Either that, or he didn't have the right connections.

After the manager, Mr Martin was next in line. He would get upset if anyone called him 'the cook'. I was advised by one and all to always refer to him as 'the chef', especially in front of guests. He was treated with revered deference. The entire staff were very careful never to upset him, including Mrs Dempster herself. Losing the chef would be like losing the pilot of a ship. It wouldn't sink, but it wouldn't get very far either.

Once in a while I was caught up in French or Italian guests' conversations on the stairs going up to their rooms, in the drawing room, or in the entrance hallway, whenever I was called upstairs to help out. It was always amusing to hear snatches of conversations from entire strangers, as I continued with my work, pretending to be oblivious to their presence. I was up to my old tricks again, eavesdropping and not minding my own business.

'*Les Anglais. Ils ne mangent pas bien du tout,*' I heard an elegant Frenchman say to his wife. '*Le diner ici etait affreux. Ce soir, on va manger dehors –* '.

'*Mais le petit dejeuner anglais n'etait pas mal, quand meme,*' was Madame's reply.

He was complaining about the hotel's evening dinner – he used the word '*affreux*', disgusting, to describe it – and told his wife that they would definitely eat out that evening. His wife tried to calm him down and told him that the English breakfast wasn't at all bad. I was happy that my morning work was appreciated, but Chef Martin would have been livid.

On other occasions I picked up little snippets of comments from German and Italian guests; on the whole they seemed to be happy with the hotel, particularly the large sized rooms. A common complaint was the lack of bidets in the bathrooms. Separate hot and cold water taps also posed a problem. Overseas guests either scalded their hands or froze their fingertips. They could never understand why the British preferred to wash their hands in cold water. Another was the struggle they all had with different English accents, especially the inimitable cockney accent they encountered in London.

Apart from the quirks of different local accents across the British Isles, I was often called upon to explain the *pronunciation* of common place names to our foreign hotel guests. Their local tube station was *'Gloster Road'* and not *'Gluesester Road'* or *'Gluekester Road'*. To get to theatre-land in the West End, they had to get off at *'Lester Square'* station, and not *'Leisester Square'*. For Americans from Alabama, it's *'Birmingum'* not *'Birmingham'*. Likewise *'Fullum'*, *'Clappum'*, *'Ballum'* and *'Tottenum'*.

In the dining room, foreign guests would need to ask Mr Cochran for *'Wooster Sauce'* and not *'Worcestershire Sauce'* if they wanted to add more zing to Chef Martin's rather insipid Irish stew. For Thais and Cantonese who enjoyed a few drops of their favourite English sauce on their fried egg and had great difficulty *reading,* let alone *pronouncing* the brand's name, they called it *'Rabbit Brand'* sauce. On the bottom right-hand corner of the orange coloured Lea and Perrins Worcestershire Sauce label, there was a small picture of a rabbit that used to sit there since 1837.

Another source of great perplexity for non-English speakers was the required etiquette when two people are introduced to each other. It became apparent one morning as I happened to be at the hotel's entrance helping to collect the mail. A man in a charcoal grey double-breasted worsted suit, black bowler hat, leather gloves and rolled umbrella, formally dressed in the style of a City stockbroker, stepped out of a taxi and into the hotel's rather narrow foyer (Abbotts Lodge, and indeed most hotels in Cromwell Road in those days, did not have a lobby). He was one of those gentlemen who would be instantly recognisable as English wherever he went in the world.

He looked around. He had an appointment with Mr Brandini whom he had never met. After seating him in the hotel's small drawing room, I went up to inform Mr Brandini, an Italian guest in Room 8, that Mr Grenville-Smith was waiting for him downstairs. One of our jobs was to make sure that guests were not left waiting in limbo if Mrs Dempster wasn't there to greet them. I hung around for a while when the two strangers met. As usual, I eavesdropped.

'How do you do?' said Mr Grenville-Smith. He extended his right hand and introduced himself. They shook hands. Mr Brandini looked perplexed. 'I am doing very well, thank you,' he replied. He was not used to total strangers asking him about the state of his health, after they had just met.

The most common form of salutation in Italy after being introduced was *'piacere'* – 'pleased' to meet you. More or less the same words are used all over Europe, as well as in many cultures around the world, upon being introduced. The French are 'delighted' to meet you – *'enchanté'*, and the Germans find the experience 'enjoyable' – *'angenehm'*.

Although somewhat archaic among young people in Britain and America today, the how-do-you-do is still a formal greeting of introduction in polite society, and the reply should be the equivalent 'how-do-you-do'. Had our Italian guest known the correct Anglo-Saxon form, he would have replied 'I am Giuseppe Brandini. How do you do.'

Modern Americans take a more casual and neighbourly approach to introductions, and dispense with the how-do-you-do custom entirely. If an American approaches you at a party with a

'Hi! I'm Orville Applebaum Junior,' the answer would be to tell Orville who you are immediately, and the introductions would be in order. Shaking hands is an option. A grin or eye contact would help to complete the friendly encounter.

'*Howdy*' is an American rural version of 'how do you do', mostly in Southwestern states, especially in Texas. It is used as a friendly greeting but never in introductions. Curiously, '*howdy*' first appeared in Southeast England in the sixteenth century, also as a greeting, a shortened version of '*how do ye?*', but soon fell into desuetude.

Curiously, there is one small country in Asia of seven million people that greets people with a how-do-you-do. '*Sabai dee*' in Laos means 'How are you?' which is used upon introduction, for which the correct answer would also be '*Sabai dee*', in this case meaning 'I am well.' '*Sabai dee*' is also used as a general salutation.

The most complicated aspect of Britain for overseas visitors in those days was the vexatious pound sterling monetary system. There were 12 pence to a shilling and 20 shillings or 240 pence to a pound. Furthermore, the penny itself was subdivided into 4 farthings (until 1960), and there were halfpennies or 'ha'pennies' still in circulation right up to 1969. To further befuddle metric-minded visitors, one guinea was equivalent to 21 shillings, traditionally used to settle barrister's fees – the additional shilling was used to pay the barrister's clerk – as well as to pay for horse racing and greyhound racing winnings. The specie itself was confusing. The two shilling coin was known as 1 florin and the two shilling and sixpence coin was half-a-crown. The crown was five shillings, but curiously there was no coin for this regal sounding denomination. The smallest sized coin in the realm was the sixpence, smaller than a farthing, equivalent to half a shilling, and was curiously converted to 2.5 new pence when the British currency was decimalised. There was also a threepenny coin, commonly known as a 'thruppeny bit', a twelve-sided nickel-brass coin in use until 1971, equivalent to 1.25 new pence. 'Threepenny' can also mean of little worth.*

Even more confusing for overseas visitors was the slang and the spelling used to describe each denomination. One pound was called a 'quid', one shilling was a 'bob', half a shilling or sixpence was called a 'tanner', five pounds was a 'fiver', and a 'pony' was ten pounds, a 'monkey' 500 pounds, and 1,000 pounds was a 'grand'. 'Tuppence' and 'tuppenny' were variations in spelling and pronunciation of two pence and two penny. 'Twopenny' and 'halfpenny' are also used as *adjectives* to describe something that is unimportant or worthless. A 'pennyworth' in America means a small quantity or a bargain.

A penny-farthing is something else altogether. It is the name of the very first bicycle, with a very large front wheel (the penny) and small back wheel (the farthing), on the roads of Britain and France in the 1880s. It was a front-wheel pedal-powered bicycle.

I was not about to explain the vast cultural gap that existed between the British Isles and the Continent (and exists still) to all the guests, although I made a point of warning families with children from America and Europe about the perils of crossing Cromwell Road, advising them to look *right* first, and then left, not left to right, even on the zebra crossing.**

American guests I encountered were polite and showed an earnestness not found in British and Europeans. They were the wealthiest travellers in the world at the time, and I was well tipped for even the smallest chore. I once hailed a taxi for an American family and directed the cabby to take them to the Tate

---

* '*The Threepenny Opera*', an anti-capitalist political satire composed in 1928, was based on '*The Beggar's Opera*' of 1728, so named because it would be so cheap that even the very poorest could afford to see it.

** In America, called 'Crosswalk' in speech, 'Pedestrian Crossing' when written, and 'PED XING' on signposts. In Italian it's *strisce pedonali* (pedestrian stripes), in French *passage pietons* (pedestrian way) and in German, a seventeen letter word: *Fussgangeruberweg* (foot corridor level crossing).

Gallery. I thanked them for a tip of 2 shillings and told them I could not possibly accept it, and that it was my pleasure to help them. They asked me whether 'I was working my way through college' and when I told them that I was indeed a student, they kindly informed me that in America it was 'customary' for students to accept tips however small the 'assignment'. I accepted gracefully. When I eventually lived in America, I realised that tipping was not only customary, but compulsory.

The English staff, and even more so the Irish and Scots, much preferred their American guests to other nationalities, including their own. The Americans were easy to get on with, they were respectful, they tipped well, and they spoke English like Hollywood movie stars. Like so many of their compatriots, the British people have long felt a strong cultural, religious and political affinity with their *American cousins*, who came from across 'the pond', an affectionate reference to the Atlantic Ocean, approximately 3,500 miles away. Europeans who came across the narrow 21 mile Channel were *foreigners*. It is interesting to note that in 2008, Sir Michael Palliser, former head of the Diplomatic Service, told history professor Peter Hennessy, that 'we British never compare ourselves with Europe; only with America.'

★ ★ ★ ★

To work at Abbotts Lodge was to work in the heart of cosmopolitan London, where people from different cultures could come together in a hotel where they were able to meet the locals, and who, like me, could learn about the wider world beyond their borders from overseas visitors. Both Thomas Cook and Abbotts Lodge linked Britain to the world, and together, in their own different ways, they helped make it smaller. Even the neighbourhood post office, with addresses to foreign countries and the exotic stamps on incoming Christmas mail, connected the local people with the geography of the world. The international Tiptree farm camp encouraged students from all over the world to work together in harmony. As a young survivor of the Second World War, I honestly believed, as I still do, that peace could be achieved once the peoples of the world solved their differences through friendly dialogue and the free exchange of cultures and ideas.

The first attempt to bring the world together in peace and unity was the founding of the League of Nations on 10 January 1920, at the end of the First World War. Its objective was 'to develop cooperation among nations and to guarantee them peace and security.' Thailand, or Siam at the time, was one of its charter members. Although the League initially had some success, it started to fall apart after the invasion of Manchuria by Japan in 1931, the annexation of Ethiopia by Italy in 1936, and that of Austria by Hitler in 1938. In 1940, the League convened for the last time in Geneva, just when a world conflict was about to start. My father was a member of the Thai delegation and witnessed this final attempt to bring peace to the world. After the war, the League reconvened on 18 April 1946 and handed over its responsibilities to the newly created United Nations.

At last, the start of friendly dialogue and the free exchange of ideas through the forum of the United Nations could finally bring us closer to world peace and unity. The end of the Second World War produced a vast array of specialist UN bodies to deal with common global issues: the World Health Organisation, the Food and Agriculture Organisation, the United Nations Educational, Scientific and Cultural Organisation, the UN Refugee Agency, to name but a few.

In 1951, Germany and Italy, both wartime allies, got together with their former enemies Belgium, France, Luxembourg and the Netherlands, to sign the Treaty of Rome, and form the European Coal and Steel Community, which eventually became the much enlarged European Union. The Treaty declared that its purpose was to 'lay the foundation of an ever closer union among the peoples of Europe.' Its underlying philosophy was to ensure that the nations of Europe would never go to war with each other again.

As I write this, the unity of the world is now being seriously challenged. The structures of international organisations seem to be falling apart. In just the first three decades of this century, the British left the European Union, President Trump withdrew the US from several international organisations, and President Putin invaded Ukraine. Were they attempting to return to the perceived glory days of the past: the heyday of the British Empire, the post-war dominance over the world in the 20th century by America, and the vast Union of Soviet Socialist Republics?*

The world of the 2020s appears to be a world in disarray, resulting from the emergence of a new populist breed of isolationist and nationalist leaders, many of whom have little concern with human rights and the declining quality of the world's environment. If we are to survive, we will need to get used to what seems to be a New World Order that will be totally different from the post-war days of my innocent youth. Nevertheless, I will continue to remain optimistic that the peoples of the world will use the incredible advances in information technology to come together for a better future and lasting peace.

★ ★ ★ ★

Now that I have had my say on the divided world that I fear we have now entered, let us go back to 1961, and return to Abbotts Lodge.

It was coming to the end of my fourth week stoking the hotel's boiler on Mr Grove's days off and preparing the daily breakfasts.

---

* Aptly called 'nostalgic nationalism' by the *Financial Times*, 2 April 2022.

I was getting good at my job and hardly breaking any eggs. The new assistant cook, I was told, would be arriving the next day. Her name was Miss O'Leary. She would be living on the premises and would be responsible for making the breakfasts, as well as helping out Mr Martin with the evening dinners. The timing was just right. I needed to devote more time to pursue my studies in Roman Law and Constitutional Law.

Miss O'Leary turned out to be a frail whisp of a woman, thin as a rake, from County Clare, Ireland. Her weak appearance stood out in total contrast to Mr Martin, a large, beefy man – as one would expect a professional cook to be – with perfect Central Casting looks: a jolly round face with a jovial personality to match, especially when he donned his chef's white hat. I wondered what he would make of his new assistant.

Fortyish and sad, Miss O'Leary spoke with a strong western Irish brogue and didn't seem to be at all comfortable in Abbotts Lodge's vast kitchen. It was her first day on the job, and together with Mr Cochran, we explained how things worked. We showed her where all the pots and pans were stored and taught her how to operate the food lift. I placed a breakfast tray on the lift's shelf and showed her how to pull the rope, pointed out the pulleys above, and hoisted the lift up the shaft to the dining room level, where Mr Cochran would be waiting to collect the bacon and eggs and serve them to the guests. Mr Cochran called it the 'dumb waiter', an Americanism, which, coming from a waiter, I found mildly amusing. Miss O'Leary's weak hands had difficulty getting a firm grip on the lift's knotted rope. Already I was beginning to feel sorry for her. She seemed to be dwarfed by her surroundings.

'How does 'dis t'ing work?'

It was clear that Miss O'Leary had never worked in a big kitchen before. Mr Cochran had already gone off to his lunch job, and I was preparing to go home. She was examining the huge industrial cast iron cooking range with curiosity and wonderment. She was fiddling around with the different switches and knobs, and opening and closing the wide doors of the oven. She looked like a little boy trying to work out the mechanism of a new toy car.

'How does 'dis t'ing work?' she repeated, more to herself than to me. No sooner had she said that when I heard a mighty explosion. She had stuck her head inside the giant oven and lit a match. Her hair was on fire. She started to scream.

'Help me! Help me!'

I had never attended the fire emergency drill at Abbotts Lodge. I didn't even know where the fire extinguisher or the fire alarm were located. I vaguely remembered a fire hose in a framed box on the wall of the ground floor. Even if I could reach it on time, I wouldn't even know how to operate it. Filling up saucepans with water to pour over her head wouldn't have been much good either. I had to think fast.

I frantically lowered the laundry hoist and quickly grabbed several towels and sheets that were hanging out to dry, and threw them on her burning hair. Under the pile of wet laundry her wretched screams were gradually reduced to a faint whimper. She was saved by *the schooner*. I removed the swathe of wet cloths wrapped around her head and sat her on a chair, as far away as I could from the oven that was still blazing away at full blast. I kept on asking her how she was feeling. She eventually looked at me in a daze, tears running down her cheeks; I will remember that frightened look on her face for as long as I live. She looked like a bald chicken.

Doris, the housemaid from upstairs, came running down to see what the commotion was all about and took her up to her room. 'Dat yong man soived me loif,' she kept on muttering as she was being gently led away.

I was about to leave for home when Doris came back to let

me know that Miss O'Leary was well and had asked to see me. I entered her tiny attic room. She was sitting on the edge of her bed; a small battered suitcase was by her side. She had covered her head with a loosely knotted woolen scarf. 'T'ank you for soivin' me loif,' she said weakly, and handed me a glass of sherry, my 'reward', as she called it. She told me that she was leaving, never to return, adding, 'De English are troying to kill me.' Before I left her she said that the English were plotting to kill all the Irish people. 'Me advoice to you is to leave England before dey kill you too!'

Miss O'Leary departed for Ireland that very afternoon. Mr Martin never met his new kitchen assistant. Two weeks later I left the employ of Abbotts Lodge to swot for my exams.

★ ★ ★ ★

Postscript. Abbotts Lodge, alas, is long gone. Together with many similar Victorian mansions of the period situated between Marloes Road and Lexham Gardens, Abbotts Lodge came under the wrecking ball in the mid-1970s, to make way for a new modern block of buildings that is today the BUPA Cromwell Hospital. The adjacent British European Airways Terminal has been turned into a shopping centre. I still go there, not to reminisce about the good old days, but to have a splendid meal at a Thai restaurant on the premises.

CHAPTER SIX

'IS ANYONE IN?'

Middle Temple, June 1962, end of Trinity Term.

I needed a break and I needed money.

I had just sat my first law exams at the Council of Legal Education, the governing body of the Inns of Court that had been training English barristers since the 1400s. In the Middle Ages, the Inns of Court's residential premises – The Temple – were built close to Fleet Street and the royal courts, and have not moved since. An élitist institution since the late fourteenth century, its objective was to create 'gentlemen' for a particular class of society and train them not just in the law, but in the 'moral and social' aspects of life, including the fine arts, music and dance. In those days, there were only three academic institutions that provided such an education in England: Oxford and Cambridge Universities, and the Inns of Court, which became known as 'the third university of England'.

There were four Inns of Court, or colleges – Lincolns Inn, Grays Inn, and two within The Temple area on the River Thames, Inner Temple, and my own college, Middle Temple. They were the precursor of the modern law school, and Barristers were, and still are, trained through lectures and 'Moots', where legal issues are argued in mock courts before the Benchers – senior members of the Inns of Court – and the compulsory attendance of 'Dinners' at the Inn's dining hall. The purpose of these ritual dinners was to introduce the student to the traditions of the Bar and the corporate life of his or her Inn, and thus create a Pupil and Master relationship. There were eight Dining Terms and I was required to attend Dinners in Middle Temple Hall on three separate days of each term. It is also in Hall that graduating Barristers from my college were called by the Treasurer 'to the Degree of the Utter Bar', appropriately wigged and gowned, as I eventually was in 1968.

The Middle Temple Hall is one of those grand historic dining rooms that are a hallmark of British college campuses – a vast rectangular space of 4000 square feet, about twice the size of a tennis court, spanned by a double hammer-beam roof, dating back to 1572. A table, known as 'Drake's Cupboard', on which newly called barristers are required to sign their names on a roll of members, is made from the timbers of Sir Frances Drake's galleon *The Golden Hind,* the ship that circumnavigated the globe between 1577 and 1580. The oak panelled walls bear the coats of arms of members since 1597, and there are giant portraits of King Charles I and II, James II, William II and a young Queen Elizabeth I. The Hall is the only building surviving from Shakespeare's time where it is known that one of his plays – *Twelfth Night* – had its premiere, on 2nd February 1602, attended by the Bard himself. In 2002, to commemorate the play's 400th anniversary, it was performed again in Hall, with memorable interpretations by Eddie Redmayne and Mark Rylance.

Famous members of Middle Temple include Sir Walter Raleigh, Elizabethan explorer and responsible for introducing tobacco to Britain; John Rutledge, signatory of the American Constitution in 1787, who became the first US Chief Justice in 1795; Lee Kuan Yu, the first prime minister of Singapore; Tunku

Abdul Rahman, the first prime minister of Malaysia; Phraya Manopakorn Nititada, the first prime minister of Thailand, then known as Siam, in the early 1900s, and two other former prime ministers of Thailand, Pote Sarasin and Sanya Dharmasakdi. I was in good company. The present leader of the British Labour Party, Sir Keir Starmer, was called to Middle Temple in 1987. Honorary Middle Temple Benchers include Queen Elizabeth the Queen Mother, appointed in 1944; Princess Diana in 1988, and her son, in line for the throne of Britain, Prince William, Duke of Cambridge, in 2009.

In the mid-19th century The Temple was also hallowed ground for writers and poets. Charles Lamb, the Romantic essayist and playwright, loved The Temple, and was inspired to write this beautiful description of it:

'I was born and passed the first seven years of my life in The Temple. Its Church, its Halls, its gardens, its fountains, its river', he wrote. 'Indeed it is the most elegant spot in the metropolis.' These lines are from the *Essay of Elia* that he wrote in 1823, where he commented on the 'collegiate aspect' of 'that fine Elizabethan hall where the fountain plays.' He was, of course, referring to Middle Temple Hall.*

Lamb was to later spend his happiest and the most rhapsodic years of his productive life at Inner Temple Lane, where he entertained Coleridge, Keats and Wordsworth. Thackeray lived in rooms nearby.

It is interesting to note that Charles Dickens wanted to become a Barrister, but thankfully his literary talents and writing career took precedence. In 1839 he was admitted as a student at Middle Temple, attended all the necessary Dinners in Hall, and

---

* The Lamb of God is the symbol of Middle Temple, and is engraved above the entrance to Lamb Buildings, and has nothing to do with Charles Lamb's family and his past residence in The Temple. I am a 'Floor Tenant' (Honorary Barrister) at Lamb's Chambers in the same building.

was planning to get called in 1846, but this period of his life was some of his most prolific years as a writer. He wrote 12 titles in those seven years, including *Nicholas Nickleby* in 1839, *The Old Curiosity Shop* in 1840, *A Christmas Carol* in 1843, and *The Battle of Life* in 1846. He never graduated.

A great chronicler of London life, Dickens' affection for The Temple is poetically brought to life in *Barnaby Rudge*: 'There are still worse places than The Temple for basking in the sun, or resting idly in the shade. There is yet a drowsiness in its courts, and a dreamy dullness in its trees and gardens: for those who pace its lanes and squares may yet hear the echoes of their footsteps on the sounding stones and tread upon its gates in passing from the tumult of the Strand or Fleet Street, "Who enters here leaves noise behind". There is still the splash of falling water in Fair Fountain Court...' This charming vignette was written in 1841, and The Temple today remains very much as Dickens described it.

★ ★ ★ ★

Introducing Gerald Hart, my tutor. No chapter on my law studies would be complete without mentioning the inimitable Mr Hart, crusty, eccentric and authoritative. His chambers occupied the entire second floor of Farrar's Building, overlooking the Temple Church quadrangle, with space enough for twenty students. His reputation for getting results was an institution in the Temple, his teaching style strict and Victorian, and his wing collar, stiffed shirt, black jacket and striped trousers draped around his gaunt, thin figure, distinctly Dickensian.

The empty coat sleeve of his left arm was permanently tucked into the pocket of his jacket. He had lost his arm fighting in the brutal trenches of the Battle of the Somme in 1916, the bloodiest in the First World War. Mr Hart, who was in his late sixties, never talked about the war, but the trauma had never fully left him.

On my first day, while he was perusing my application form, he asked me: 'How is Somboon doing?' I was totally nonplussed. How on earth did he know my father's name, I wondered?

'He's now Thai ambassador to Italy,' I replied.

'Well, I expect you to be as clever as your father,' he said, totally without emotion, although I did detect a slight look of satisfaction on his deadpan face. I later found out that Mr Hart was indeed my father's law tutor in the thirties.

Mr Hart ran his tutorial classes with military discipline. His right arm and large hand were strong and forceful; he liked to project a no-nonsense image. For a teacher, he was curiously a man of few words, and the atmosphere in his sombre chambers was distinctly non-collegiate. He was known to be tough, yet I felt that underneath it all, he was good-hearted. He was also a gifted single-handed pianist and organist. I once had the singular privilege of listening to him play Chopin's *Marche Funebre* with aggressive brio, when he invited me to his home in Hampstead one festive season. He was vigorously banging the keyboard, his arched back shaking from side to side over his dilapidated piano, as if in pain. I was a bit terrified, then moved to tears.

We were given essays to write on legal sized exercise books in the spartan rooms of his chambers, from nine to five, Monday to Friday, for the entire term, all the completed essays to be handed in for correction at the end of each week. There was never any homework. His method of getting us through the tough Bar exams (in those days with only a 30 percent pass rate) was to grind away at the essays all day long, five days a week, at his chambers. When he returned our work to us, there were rubber stamped corrections on every page, like 'Wrong', 'Untrue', 'False', 'Unproven', 'Incorrect', and the most frequent: 'Rewrite'. Rarely used was the rubber stamp 'Balls', which meant that we were totally off-track. If there were 'Balls' stamps on every page, it clearly meant that one would seriously need to reconsider a career at the Bar. He neither made written corrections nor verbal comments. It was assumed that one did well if there were no stamp marks on the essay pages whatsoever (rare). It became a matter of honour for us to have *at least one* 'Balls' stamp on our exercise books each term. On Mondays and Tuesdays, we would hear vigorous and continuous banging sounds on a desk, emanating from Mr Hart's room. He was correcting our papers.

Banging sounds aside, the working rooms where we wrote our essays were eerily quiet, apart from the scratching sound of writing, of noisy flipping of text and exercise book pages, and the legs of chairs grating on the bare wooden floor. Any chatting and Mr Hart would come out of his room and give us hell. We were all a little afraid of him.

One would assume that in this monastic atmosphere of silence, there would be no shenanigans. Wrong. It was in this very kind of environment that the restricted schoolboy thrived the best and was at his most creative. Public-school humour can be very puerile. Drawing naughty pictures and handing them around, making funny faces and rude gestures to get us laughing, even using sign language to tell jokes, or any other attempt to get us to break our vows of silence, were tame, compared with some of the more inventive pranks that Mr Hart's schoolboys (average age 23) got up to. One chap by the name of Rex Bragg removed the red phosphorus heads from matchsticks and patiently stuffed the powdery substance into the cylindrical end of his mortise house key, slid a matchstick into the cylinder hole, lit and pointed it as one would a gun. The matchstick shot out of the cylinder like a fiery projectile, almost setting alight a bookshelf of rather important Law Reports at the other end of the room. It also made quite a bang. Mr Hart was not amused.

College friendships are often the most enduring. After fifty years, reminiscing with fellow internee Anders Grundberg, the first Swede to be called to the English bar, we remember

Gerald Hart with much affection, and recall the rowdiness in his monastic chambers with unforgettable regalement.

★ ★ ★ ★

Right across from Mr Hart's chambers is one of England's oldest churches dating back to the twelfth century, the Temple Church, built by the Knights Templar, the order of crusading monks founded to protect pilgrims on their way to the Holy Land. It was consecrated in 1185 by Heraclius, the Patriarch of Jerusalem, who came all the way from the Holy Land for the occasion, as well as to persuade King Henry II to participate in the Crusades, a Holy War to fight the 'enemies of Christ'. The Temple Church is one of only four Norman round churches in England. Its circular nave was named after the Temple of Solomon and modelled on the Church of the Holy Sepulchre in Jerusalem, the site where it is believed Jesus Christ was crucified, and subsequently where he was buried before his resurrection. In the 13th century, King John of England used the circular nave as his London headquarters, and it was here where he was forced to formally sign the Magna Carta, after he had capitulated to his barons at Runnymede in 1215 and granted them history's first bill of rights.

If I may be allowed a brief digression – for non-British readers – on the ill-starred King John, the only monarch with that name in English history. He was the youngest son of Henry II, who never intended to bequeath any land to him and gave him the unfortunate nickname of 'John Lackland'. John was never expected to rule. He was small, unattractive and had little presence when compared with his handsome brother King Richard – the chivalrous Richard the Lionheart – who was always away on the crusades, and won many battles against Saladin, the leader of the Muslims who were occupying Jerusalem. Saladin's relationship with Richard had been one of chivalrous mutual respect, as well as military rivalry. After the last battle of the Third Crusade in 1192 at Jaffa, both kings wisely negotiated a long -lasting truce.

Richard spent only a few months in England in his ten years as King, and left his only brother John to defend the realm. Yet King Richard was much revered in history, and English schoolboys have always looked up to him as one of the kingdom's bravest monarchs. As for King John, known in story books and swashbuckling Hollywood films as the 'Bad' King John, for ordering the Sheriff of Nottingham to arrest the legendary Robin Hood for robbing the rich, many historians have doubted whether King John even knew of Robin Hood. If he did, Robin Hood was just another outlaw who robbed the barons and the clergy of their wealth, consequently leaving less tax monies available for the king's deep royal coffers.

Unlike his legendary brother, John was not a born soldier, and he lost Normandy, the foundation of his family's continental possessions. His image as a failed warrior was further exacerbated by his failure to work with his barons, who raised an army and forced him to capitulate at Runnymede. The war with his barons continued after he had signed the Magna Carta, and with the support of Louis, the crown prince of France, and Alexander II of Scotland, the rebel barons tried to wrest the crown from him. In the last year of his life, John turned into a capable military leader, and prevented the capture of London. Before John could reverse his image as a failed soldier he succumbed to dysentery on the battlefield and died in 1216. Exceptionally, the reviled John of history was the first king to speak English, the language of the people. All the other kings of England up to this time, including heroic Richard, only spoke French.

By the fourteenth century The Temple area was leased out to the legal profession, and in 1608 the Temple Church came under the joint ownership and management of the Honourable

Societies of the Inner and the Middle Temple. The church is not a parish church and carries the status of a *Royal Peculiar*, which means it falls under the direct jurisdiction of the British monarch, and not subject to the bishopric of the area.

Today, the Master of the Temple, the Reverend Robin Griffith-Jones, elegant and articulate, with a shock of brilliant white hair, conducts regular church services, including Holy Communion and Matins on Sunday mornings. He used to deliver weekly lectures to American tourists who visited his church on the Da Vinci trail, when the Hollywood film *The Da Vinci Code* first came out, pointing out some of the historical inaccuracies of author Dan Brown's story, explaining how little is true and how much more is pure fiction. He also performs weddings for members of the Inner and Middle Temple. My wife Patricia and I were honoured to have our marriage blessing in the chancel of the Temple Church on 6 June 2019, presided over by Master Robin.

★ ★ ★ ★

By the end of the term, I had had enough of the law for a while. I desperately sought relief from the monotony of writing essays day in, day out, in Gerald Hart's gloomy chambers, and escape from the cloistered surroundings of Middle Temple. I also needed more money to sustain my expensive lifestyle as an aspiring bon viveur.

Once again the National Union of Students came to my rescue. This time there was a job opening at the London County Council, universally referred to as the LCC, the principal local government body for the County of London until 1965. The LCC was the first municipal authority to be directly elected, and its offices were located in a grand, iconic building known as County Hall. In those days LCC was one of the most famous abbreviations in England.

Young people in London today have no idea about the immense power and influence the LCC had had over Londoners' lives in the last century. London's famous abbreviation is almost forgotten, and today means so many other different things, among them: London Cricket Club, established way back in 1722; London Capital Communications, a remote-working business Consultant; London Cycling Campaign, founded in 1978 to encourage Londoners to take to their bikes for a healthier and cleaner capital city; *Leukoencephalopathy Calcification* and *Cysts*, commonly known as Labrune, a terrible brain disease, with progressive deterioration in cognitive function and mobility. Enough said.

Visitors to London were frequently introduced to County Hall, hailed as the headquarters of the greatest municipality in the world, more of a parliament and government than a city municipality. Londoners at the time would proudly boast about the twin bastions of democracy in their city: the Houses of Parliament *and* County Hall, conveniently located opposite each other on the River Thames. It has often been said that if Parliament closed down for twelve months, the country would continue to function regardless. But close down County Hall for a few days, and London would come to a grinding halt. The LCC operated on a budget larger than those of some nations.

County Hall is an imposing English Renaissance style building covering about six and a half acres on the south bank of the river next to Westminster Bridge. Construction started in 1911 and the building was opened with much fanfare by King George V in 1922.

As I passed through County Hall's massive portals and reverently walked along its gleaming marble floor and its impressive oak lined space, it was like moving through the corridors of power. I was in awe. The only other time I felt like this was on my first visit to St Peter's Basilica in Rome. I half fancied bumping into the Lord Mayor, but I wouldn't have recognised him nor did I know his name anyway. This was long before the modern era of social media celebrities, when London mayors like Boris Johnson and Sadiq Khan have become household names. I followed the directions given to me by the porter's office and immediately lost my way. It was not surprising really; the building contained about nine hundred rooms. I eventually found myself in a dark meeting room on the south side of the building. There were several dozen applicants, mostly students like myself, who had responded to the ad. The LCC was looking for 'Canvassers'.

The job of an LCC canvasser was to knock on doors and find out the names and numbers of occupants there were in each household. The objective was simply to keep the County of London's Electoral Register up to date. We were given an official identification card (*without* our name) to be kept in our pockets, not pinned on to our lapels or hung around our necks, and a hefty Voting Registry Record book that we carried around in a satchel. It was similar in size and weight, and certainly in aspect, to an accounts ledger that Scrooge would have had in his counting house. Keeping the voting registry up to date was a massive task, requiring hundreds of canvassers.

We were assigned different wards. Each London borough was, and still is, divided into a number of wards for local elections. Each ward is a primary unit of English electoral geography, and the composition of its residents needed frequent updating. I was charged with canvassing households in Westbourne Park Road, in Colville Ward, in the district of Notting Hill.

When I related to my friends that I would soon be in the service of the LCC, I was greeted with both the 'oohs' and 'aahs' that came with respect and envy. Why, they teased me, I could even become the Lord Mayor of London one day! Little did they know that my work with the LCC would be a far cry from the warmth of a comfortable office in the palatial County Hall, but disappointingly involved pounding the pavements of Notting Hill, a down at heel area of slums, squats, boarded-up houses, cheap lodgings and decaying streets.

Here a great number of immigrants from the West Indies, and a lesser number of Indians and Pakistanis, had settled alongside the white working class, an uncomfortable coexistence that was one day bound to flare up into racial conflagration again, as it did during those dark days of August 1958 in Notting Hill, and again during the St Pancras rent riots in September 1960.

A bit of historical background is in order here. During the height of the West Indian immigration into Notting Hill, and indeed to many poor areas of North Kensington in the mid- and late-fifties, there were unscrupulous property speculators who would buy decaying mansion blocks, where the rent and tenure of flats and rooms were inhabited by poor British working-class families paying pre-war rents, through statutory rent-controls. Known as 'controlled tenants' – who paradoxically had *no control* at all – their new landlords forced them to leave through nefarious means, by making their lives intolerable. Their electricity and water would be cut off, for example, or their lavatories would be removed, and more West Indians would be crammed into the properties that were increasingly subdivided into more flats to increase the number of tenants not subject to rent controls.

The immigrants had already found difficulty finding accommodation elsewhere, so they were also charged higher rents. The West Indian immigrants were not protected from eviction like the controlled tenants; it didn't take long before entire properties in Notting Hill were emptied of their original pre-war tenants, who were to find life there increasingly untenable. The racketeers could now sell their empty properties at huge profits. Violent racial feelings were stirred among the few controlled tenants who remained, a perfect storm for future conflicts.

The most notorious property racketeer was Peter Rachman*, a penniless immigrant from Poland who arrived in the UK during the war. Each time he sold a building that was emptied of controlled tenants, the return on his meagre investment would be five times its cost price. In 1959, after investigation by the police, he was denied British citizenship. A self-made millionaire, he died in his lavish Hampstead home of a heart attack. He was 43. His infamous legacy was the word 'Rachmanism', which entered the Oxford English Dictionary, meaning the exploitation and intimidation of tenants.

It was just as well that I had temporarily forgotten the race riots of August and September of 1958 that had taken place in Notting Hill before I started my new job.

★ ★ ★ ★

I hit the road on my first day with great enthusiasm and fancied myself as an official inspector, with authority from the LCC to knock on doors and ask questions. I donned my dark suit, stiff white collar and old school tie to lend authenticity to my new role. Westbourne Park Road was a street of stucco-fronted pillar-porched houses, the homes of the upper middle class intelligentsia in the twenties, but on this rather overcast day in June 1962, it was a slum.

To bolster my spirits, I started with the best looking house on the street. It had a window box with drooping petunias desperately trying to reach out to the sun, and an olive green front door. Just as I was about to ring the doorbell, a man in a beret and bicycle clips suddenly opened the door. He almost bumped into me.

---

* Although he charged the West Indians exorbitant rents, he claimed that he was actually doing the West Indians a favour by not barring them from renting his properties!

'Can I help you?' He asked abruptly when he saw me. 'I'm a canvasser from…'

'I suppose you think I'm going to vote Tory?' he said, before I could complete my introduction.

'Actually, I'm a canvasser from the LCC and my job is to…' I was struggling to fish out my identification card from my trouser pocket.

'As you can see, I'm in a bit of a hurry. Come back tomorrow.' He rushed down to fetch his bicycle from the basement and disappeared down the street before I could thank him.

So much for my first interview. I was about to ask him for his name, whether he was either the head of the household or a lodger, as well as the names of other members of his family or other people who 'abode' in the same house. I made a note to come back the following day.

The next house was less prepossessing. The front door's grey paint was peeling and there were torn lace curtains on the dirty window of the front room. I thought I spotted a rat scampering across the front basement floor. I pressed the doorbell. It didn't seem to work so I reluctantly stretched across the rusty iron balustrade and started tapping on the window. I tapped a bit harder and after a few minutes the lower sash of a first floor window from the house next door was raised noisily. A tousled red haired man in a pyjama top stuck his head out.

'*Can you not plainly see* that the house is empty and has been so for weeks? *Did you not know* it's condemned?' he shouted. I detected the unmistakable cadence of a lyrical-talking Irishman.

I immediately decided to talk to him. His house looked just as bad though. The same dilapidated front door entrance and the same dirty windows. It was probably rat-infested as well. The pillar's stucco was almost stripped to its bare brick. It was number 21, but the 2 was missing from the column. At least the doorbell worked. And *there was somebody* at home. It took him quite a long time to come to the door. He looked as if he had just got out of bed. I apologised for waking him up and presented my credentials. He was friendly enough, but kept on yawning. When he opened his mouth to talk, his teeth and mouth were black, and his breath reeked of stale alcohol. His name was Mike O'Conner and he told me that he was a poet and 'a simple lodger trying to make an honest living in this country.' He was unable to give me any details of the other occupants as he didn't know them, and he informed me that 'the world would be a better place if we could all mind our own business.'

'Besides,' he added, 'there's nobody in.' After a short rhetorical discussion on the Irish contribution to England's very existence ('they can't do without us') I found out he had a night job as a guard at a building site in the West End.

I thanked him and pondered for a while on the steps. Here I was, on my first day, already two hours into the job, and getting nowhere. A morning wasted and nothing to show for it. I decided to have an early lunch at The Duke of Wellington, a pub on Portobello Road around the corner, to get over my disappointment. First a hearty steak and kidney pudding and chips, and *then* I'll put my important canvassing mission back on reset.

Suitably victualed, I went straight to the first house on my voting register. No more picking and choosing. Just start at the first house and go on to the next house, and then on to the next, and the next, and so on, until the job is done. This time I had more luck.

It was the same rundown house like all the other houses on the street, but with its own unique shabbiness: paint that was peeling so much from the top window down to the front door that it was difficult to know its original colour, a basement full of filthy dustbins, and a dull brass door knocker hanging precariously on its last screw. I was afraid that it might come off in my hand so I avoided using it. Naturally, the doorbell didn't work. I could hear loud voices and people moving about, so I knew there was life inside. This time I knocked on the door.

'Is anyone in?' I shouted, and knocked again, this time a bit harder.

'Comin' mon, comin.' I couldn't quite make out whether the man – it was a strong, gravelly male voice – was saying that he was coming or whether he was asking me to come in. The door opened and there in front of me stood a tall, gangling black man of about 60 with the biggest mouth and friendliest smile I had ever seen. He wore a cream double-breasted sharkskin jacket with shoulder pads so wide that it looked like it was draped on a giant coat hanger. His palm tree patterned tie was as colourful as a Caribbean post-card.

'What you want, mon?' he asked me.

I produced my LCC identification card, and before I could introduce myself, he snatched it from my hand and started reading it. He then looked me up and down, and when I brought out my voting registry book, he made a grab for that too. I managed to save the book from his grasp and asked him to please give back my identification card. I was relieved when he returned it. I decided that I would need to soft pedal my act and do my best not to sound officious. Assuming that he was the head of the household, I got out my ballpoint pen.

'I work for the LCC and all I want to know is your name and the names of all the occupants in your house, and I will write them down in this book.'

'Why you want our names?' he asked suspiciously.

I explained to him that it was his legal right to have his name recorded in the local government's voting register, and that he and all the adult members of his family were entitled to the benefits of a British citizen to vote. He nodded with approval and started shouting down the hallway.

'*Alvita! Nevis! Jade! Winton! Tasha! Chalky! Delane!
Henry! Zachary!* Come down here *now!*'

He shouted at the top of his voice and called out to every member of his household. His booming vociferation reverberated through the house. Within a few minutes, a huge group gathered at the front door. The narrow hallway was filled with at least 30 West Indians of all ages, including six babes in arms.

'Dis mon want all your names because we British citizens now an' we have de right to vote,' he told them proudly.

'M'name's Aloysius. Aloysius Mundle. Dis lady here's Alvita, my wife. Dat man dere my son Zachary: Zachary Mundle. My daughter Delane,' he pointed to a buxom woman in a bright pink and purple dress, who was at least eight months pregnant and held a baby in her arms. 'She married dat man Winton: Winton Chewitt. Dis here's Winton's elder sister Laurette, married Delane: Delane Devon. Dey got three children. Dey's all at work...'

It took me well over an hour to get all their names. I wanted to make sure that all the spellings were right.

They waved me goodbye. I left them in good spirits and I felt invigorated, wondering what awaited me as I eagerly made my way to the next house.

It was one of the most depressing houses on the street. It looked as if all the grime of London had got into every nook and cranny of the building. The window frames and doors were a sooty grey colour. There was only a hole where the doorbell ought to have been. I could just about discern a dangling light bulb through the broken window pane. There was movement inside. As I approached the door I inadvertently kicked over four empty milk bottles that rolled down the front steps onto the pavement, and made enough noise to announce my presence to the whole neighbourhood. I needn't have knocked. But I did anyway.

'Is anyone in?' I shouted.

As I waited for someone to come to the door, a horrid, rancid smell reached my nostrils. Could it be the decomposing body of a dead animal, I wondered? The door was slowly opening so I banished these nasty thoughts from my mind. The ceiling of the hallway was strung with cobwebs, and the air was musty and thick with dust.

A small stout woman of about fifty, wearing a drooped apron, her grey hair tied up in a scarf, stood menacingly in front of me. She held a broom in her right hand, upright like a spear.

'Yeah?' She asked me in the angry tone of: *who are you, what do you want and whatever it is make it quick*. When she spoke, she shouted: 'I don't need any more of what's yer got to sell me!'

I showed her my LCC card and politely explained that I was not a salesman, but a canvasser whose job was to keep the voting register up to date.

'We already 'ad somebody from yer people last week!' She slammed the door in my face. I didn't even get her name but I was happy to get away.

We were instructed not to pursue uncooperative and belligerent cases: 'just leave the space blank and a senior inspector would follow up at a later date.'

I returned home that night totally exhausted.

To give a clearer idea of my work in this tumbledown neighbourhood, I will go through some events that still stand out in my memory, selecting a few more households and describing the residents who lived there, and the sorry state of their homes. This was a good three decades before properties in Colville ward were redeveloped into multi-million pound residences. The slums of Notting Hill of my canvassing days were a far cry from the chic location of the soppy 1999 film of the same name. Today, a tiny 60 square-metre *leasehold* second-floor two-bedroomed flat in Westbourne Park Road would fetch well over half a million pounds.

The next day started well. The sun was out. In the bright light, the houses looked grimier than usual, and I noticed the gutters were full of litter. There were a few cars parked on the road, a lot of them abandoned wrecks. Yet, on this warm morning, the decaying tenements of Westbourne Park Road seemed to take on a happier air.

I approached my next house with less trepidation.

I was getting used to dilapidated front doors. This one was streaked with peeling black paint over what was once a cream coloured door. Makeshift curtains made from newspapers covered the windows. It had a battered brass lion head knocker and the ring was missing. There were four electric button doorbells, labelled with typed names which had faded so much that they were barely legible. I could just about make out three of them: Murphy, O'Brien, Quinn. I rang all three bells.

I was preparing to be charmed by a wee bit of blarney and a lengthy polemic discussion with the Irish occupants. To my surprise, a black man answered the door. Not so elegant and not as imposing as Aloysius Mundle, he had the same sing-song voice, but he looked unhappy. He was wearing a colourful short-sleeved Hawaiian shirt. He could have been anywhere between thirty and fifty. A look of fear overcame him when I produced my identification card. He kept on looking back into the hallway, as if he had something to hide.

'Ain't done nuttin' wrong so what's you want?'

When I explained to him what I was doing and asked for his name and the names of the other occupants of the house, he asked me why. I started to explain my position all over again, this time with more emphasis on his rights as a British citizen and their corresponding benefits.

'You ain't the fuzz then?'

I assured him that I was quite definitely not the police. He started to relax. Taylor Lenworth, for that was his elegant name, introduced me to all the occupants of the house – all men, ranging in age between fifteen and forty – and in a little less than an hour, I had completed all 44 names. I never found out whether they were hiding anything or not, nor was it my job to do so. Like many colonial immigrants, they had difficulty in communicating with the British authorities. What I did learn though, was the terrible overcrowding that existed in these poor dilapidated homes, which meant that they would often be four people to a bed, with day and night shifts to sleep in the available space.

The relatively well-maintained house next door was opened by a handsome man from Barbados of about 50. He wore a white shirt with his pin-striped trousers, and his black shoes were beautifully polished. I learned that he had come over to London in 1948, one of the very first to take advantage of the British Nationality Act of the same year, which allowed all Commonwealth citizens the full right to settle in the UK as British citizens. He was part of the 'Windrush generation', named after the *Empire Windrush,* the ship that brought the first groups of West Indian immigrants to Britain.

Once he was satisfied with my credentials, he immediately co-operated with me and proudly told me his name, *Mister* Antoine Fennel. He ran a lodging house of one-room flatlets, and he gave me the names and ages of each of his tenants. When he found out that I had just interviewed the rather overcrowded house next door, he got visibly upset.

'Problem is that there are too many of dem spades movin' in to the Gate and they all give us a bad name in this good neighbourhood!'

He spoke slightly better English than the other West Indians who had immigrated to the UK more recently.

I complemented him that indeed his house was one of the better ones on the street, clean and welcoming. I asked him how much his rents were, just in case some friends (Thai government scholarship students on a very tight budget) would be interested in renting a room. His rents were reasonably priced and much cheaper than South Kensington where I was staying. He asked me where my 'friends' came from and when I told him 'Thailand' he asked me whether it was in India. I assured him Thailand was a totally different country and I asked why he wanted to know.

What he said took me by surprise. He told me that he never took in boarders from India, though he didn't say why. Neither did I ask him. Was Mister Fennel a racist or just a snob? He didn't seem to like more West Indians coming to live in the 'Gate' – slang for Notting Hill Gate – either. I never recommended any Thai students to him.

On another sunny day I approached a ramshackle house that looked empty. Paint was flaking off the entrance door. There were no curtains in any of the windows, by far the dirtiest in the street, and there were no milk bottles on the top steps, normally a sure telltale sign of abandonment. But I did see a glimmer from a naked light bulb coming from the front room.

A weary looking woman answered the door after several knocks followed by a couple of 'is-anyone-ins?' She held a duster in her hand and her hair was covered with pink rollers and what looked like a cloth shower cap. Through the open door I could see piles of magazines and newspapers, bits of clothing in a basket, several packed cardboard boxes and a few battered suitcases.

I produced my LCC identification card and went through the usual voting register routine.

'Yer wasting your time, ducks,' she told me. 'Me 'usband an' me, we're movin' next week to a council flat, in a much 'igher class area.' Despite her tired looks, she gave me a happy grin. She considered herself as one of the lucky ones.

I wished her all the very best and moved on to the next house on my register list.

One of the most memorable households I interviewed on my Notting Hill journey was that of an Indian family. In 1961 the number of Indians and Pakistanis who arrived in Britain represented about one third of the total immigrants from the Commonwealth. On Westbourne Park Road they were in a minority, judging by the number of families I came into contact with during my canvassing expedition.

As I approached a particularly dilapidated house, the window panes stained with years of thick grime, a strong smell of curry and ghee wafted on to the pavement, to my greatest delight.

Chandra Banerjee came from Bengal where he worked as a stoker on the North Eastern Railway of India. But times were hard back home in Calcutta. He learned that there were ample opportunities available in England for railway workers. Born under the British Raj, and educated in the English language, he imagined England as a land of palaces and the people the wealthiest in the world. But he and his wife and two teenage children were shocked by the poverty they encountered. They arrived at a time when the British people were war-weary, the country still scarred from the effects of the wartime bombing, and the government struggling to come to terms with the dismantling of Empire.

While he was waiting for a job-opening at British Railways, he worked as a porter at Waterloo station. He was better educated than his West Indian neighbours, mockingly calling himself, with a shake of his head, an 'East Indian'. I thought this was funny and we both laughed together. He was the first working class Indian from India I had ever met. I enjoyed talking with him. My old Indian school chums at Eltham were from rich Gujarati families, sons of shop owners and merchants in Kenya, and had never returned to India. They were very different from Mr Banerjee. They hated the British. But this Bengali immigrant actually *loved* Britain. The other inhabitants of this house were all from the

Caribbean, and they didn't seem to mind Mr Banerjee. I decided not to tell him about Antoine Fennel.

By the end of three weeks the novelty of the job was starting to wear off. I had covered sixty households and I was tired. It wasn't easy traipsing the streets, come driving rain or bright sunshine, heavy registry book in hand, talking non-stop to strangers on the front door steps of their dingy homes, not feeling particularly welcome, for days on end. I was happy at the end of my foray into the deserted and derelict houses of Westbourne Park Road to return to the 'Vatican' with my completed report.

Although I was adequately well reimbursed, I was uncertain how to accept the experience of witnessing the way the other half of the world lived. It was too close to the moment to conclude that it was anything but one of the saddest three weeks of my life. It wasn't easy to forget the abject poverty of the people I had interviewed.

★ ★ ★ ★

After County Hall lost its role as the seat of London's government in 1986, the building was subsequently sold to a Japanese investor, and now that the London Eye is located in front, it has sadly been turned into a tourist attraction. A small theme park, an amusement arcade, an aquarium and two hotels, are all housed in this grand historic building. Today, the best view of the Houses of Parliament at sunset can be seen from the Marriot Hotel's County Hall Restaurant.

County Hall's extensive river frontage and grand crescent-shaped facade has been used for several film locations, among them a Parisian night club, the palace of the Viceroy of India in Delhi, the KGB headquarters in Moscow, *and* the CIA headquarters in Langley, Virginia. What an undignified ending for one of the most important London landmarks of my youth.

CHAPTER SEVEN
MESSRS HARRODS AND SIMPSON

It was the Great Freeze of the winter of 1962-3.

I considered myself lucky to be working in the Men's Fragrance Department at Harrods where it was nice and warm. I found out that I could always rely on Harrods for a holiday job behind the counter during the Christmas rush and the January sales.

Harrods has not always been London's lifestyle destination store for Arab sheiks, Russian oligarchs and crazy rich Asians. When I worked there in the sixties, it was a larger version of Macy's in New York and Galeries Lafayette in Paris, one of many high quality department stores where Londoners could buy anything and everything. There were other London stores that had better quality fashions and carried a far superior cachet: Liberty in Regent Street, Burberrys in the Haymarket and Simpson of Piccadilly, were considered way ahead of Harrods in terms of style and exclusivity. The food products at Fortnum & Mason were unrivalled. And of course, there was always Aspreys on Bond Street, the kind of store where you couldn't afford to shop if you had to ask the price.

The owner of Harrods when I worked there in 1962

was the House of Fraser, a giant British retail group that also owned a number of other iconic London department stores of my childhood, where I used to go to with my mother in the late forties, like Barkers in Kensington and Dickins & Jones in Regent Street, alas both long gone.

It was a far cry from the humble beginnings of Charles Henry Harrod, the founder, born in 1799 in Colchester, Essex – yes, the very same county where I worked on a farm – whose parents died when he was only twelve, leaving him and his siblings as orphans to fend for themselves. A sympathetic neighbour took him on as a miller, and in his late teens he worked hard in the drapery and haberdashery trades in Colchester, educating himself with the ins and outs of the retail business, and discovering along the way that he had keen entrepreneurial skills.

He moved to London where there were more opportunities to make money. By the time he was 35, he opened shop as a wholesale grocer and tea merchant in the East End. Ten years later he moved to the new up-and-coming suburb of Knightsbridge and invested in a single-storey grocery shop in Brompton Road, with only three employees. Hard work and many setbacks – he was once narrowly missed being sent to the penal colony of Australia for receiving stolen goods from a crooked partner (one hundredweight of currants) for which instead he served a short prison sentence – had aged him before his time and he retired. He sold his business to his son Charles Digby, a much more dynamic trader than the father. Digby expanded the business and in 1884 built a five-storey emporium on Harrods' present day premises. Charles senior surprisingly lived to the ripe old age of 85 and died peacefully in his beautiful home in Chiswick. The Harrods name never looked back.

Since then, Harrods Stores Ltd has only changed hands four times. It went public in 1889 and after the end of World War I, trading under the name Harrods Ltd, the new company began an aggressive expansion program, acquiring high street department stores all over the country, including three major West End names: Dickins & Jones, Swan & Edgar and D.H. Evans. In 1959, all these brands, including Harrods, were gobbled up by the House of Fraser.

In 1983, a battle royal between two foreign investors of somewhat dubious reputation to control Britain's prestigious department store turned into a vitriolic slanging match in the boardrooms, the media and the courts, that lasted eight years. Ironically, both players were outsiders, both immigrants, and both had a long-standing feud with the British establishment.

One was German, born in India in 1917, and went to an English public school. He successfully passed himself off as an English gentleman, suitably dressed in bespoke suits from Savile Row and speaking with an upper-class accent. He was suspected of having Nazi sympathies during the war and changed his name from Fuhrhop to Rowland. Because he was a big boy as a child, his English nanny nicknamed him 'Tiny' and this name stuck. In the fifties and sixties, Tiny Rowland made his money through clandestine dealings with African leaders of less than unsullied reputation, helping to supply their armies with British-made weapons. He became chairman of Lonrho, the London-Rhodesian mining company, and turned it into a massive infrastructure and agribusiness conglomerate, acquiring hotels, motor car dealerships, shipping lines, oil, gas, textile and distribution companies along the way, including the prestigious British Sunday newspaper *The Observer,* in 1981. Well-known for being an aggressive corporate raider, Rowland was described by a rival newspaper, *The Guardian,* as 'greedy, ruthless and arrogant'. Tiny's fervent dream was to one day own all of Harrods.

The other protagonist was the equally flamboyant Egyptian businessman, Mohammed Fayed, who grew up in a poor neighbourhood of Alexandria. As a young man Mohammed worked in a variety of jobs, including selling Coca Cola in the streets to Egyptian teenagers and later on as a sewing machine sales representative. Like the impoverished Charles Harrod a century before him, he was ambitious, hard-working and a fast learner. His big break came in 1954, when he married the sister of Adnan Khashoggi, the Saudi arms dealer, who helped him set up successful shipping and construction businesses in Dubai.

In 1974 he moved to the UK, when he added '*al*' to his name and operated under the aristocratic title 'al-Fayed', claiming to descend from an old cotton growing dynasty on the Nile since the 1850s. He was rumoured to be a compulsive liar, and unlike his sophisticated rival Tiny Rowland, an inept social climber. He was described by the High Court as 'deeply dishonest, with an evil habit of vindictively pursuing those he regarded as his antagonists.' He too desperately wanted to own Harrods.

Like two fast gunslingers in the Wild West, they were bound to have a shoot-out one day in the boardrooms of London's financial jungle. They first met in 1975 when al-Fayed joined the board of Lonrho.

Rowland had already accumulated 29 percent of the House of Fraser's stock, and now expressed the desire to acquire the remaining stock. He was blocked by the British Monopolies & Mergers Commission from doing so, on the grounds that such an acquisition would be against the national interest. Lonrho had already been under government investigation for questionable business practices and the extensive use of tax havens.

Al-Fayed offered to buy Rowland's shares and 'look after' them until the political climate changed, with his assurance that he would sell them back to Rowland at a more appropriate time in the future. But events didn't quite work out that way.

In 1985, al-Fayed made a takeover bid to control the House of Fraser's remaining stock for 615 million pounds sterling right under Tiny's unsuspecting nose. There were no objections from the British government at the time, and al-Fayed became the outright owner of the holding company that controlled Harrods. Tiny Rowland was furious. He was humiliated and outwitted by al-Fayed. To his delight, his paper *The Observer,* called his Egyptian rival the 'The Phoney Pharoah'.

Accusations of dishonesty, theatrical insults and court actions ping-ponged back and forth between these two arch-foes. According to Rowland, the British government failed to fully investigate al-Fayed's credentials, while his company Lonrho had unfairly faced three government enquiries. He claimed that al-Fayed had lied about his background and the source of his wealth, and misrepresented his ability to finance the takeover. Al-Fayed was continually called upon to prove his solvency and wealth. A huge stuffed 10-foot shark on display in Harrods Food Hall had 'Tiny' written on its fin.

At a certain point, the warring parties must have realised that they would both be heavy losers if they continued to expose each other's dirty linen on the front pages of the British press. The shoot-out ended in 1993. All smiles for the cameras, Tiny Rowland and al-Fayed ended their feud with a public reconciliation in the Harrods Food Hall, although they would never speak to each other again.

In 1994, al-Fayed let go of the other House of Fraser businesses in a stock market flotation, and Harrods came under the private ownership of al-Fayed and his family.

The ownership of Harrods changed hands once again in 2010. In the final saga of the Harrods story, al-Fayed sold the profitable store to the Qatari royal family for 1.5 billion British pounds.

The ultimate British retail institution, once the exclusive domain of the United Kingdom's élite and the royal family, Harrods is now a shopping emporium for the world's nouveau riche and aspiring wannabes. Old-school English customers who accidently wander into Harrods today would find themselves uncomfortable in the opulent halls and vast rooms of flagrant luxury, getting unexpectedly caught up with hundreds of shuffling people, hordes of been-there-got-the-t-shirt tourists, wandering aimlessly, as if they were taking a stroll in the Piazza San Marco.

This is very different from the Harrods of 1962 where I worked for a while, when the majority of customers were British, and who actually had a shopping list.

★ ★ ★ ★

For that year's Christmas rush, I was assigned to the Men's Fragrance Department on the ground floor. In those days, men were generally hesitant to splash themselves with cologne for fear of appearing dandyish or effeminate. Against my wishes, my mother used to sprinkle a few drops of *4711 Kolnischwasser* on my handkerchief, or dab a bit on my pulse, before going out. I felt like a sissy, but at last I didn't smell like a goat.

After the war, a gentleman's first experience with any kind of fragrance would normally be at the barbershop. *Old Spice* or *Aqua Velva* aftershave lotion, or *Listerine Aftershave Antiseptic*, were applied to one's face largely for sanitary or medicinal purposes. The pleasant sting from the aftershave lotion was bracing and meant to close the facial pores to prevent bacteria and dirt from getting in, as well as to help heal shaving cuts and soothe razor burn. The perfume was an added bonus and found to be attractive to the opposite sex. Lady friends always knew when I had just visited the barbers. Men's colognes like *Guerlain Vetiver* and *Pour Homme de Caron* that appeared on the scene in the fifties generally attracted men who admired other men. However, in the ladies' perfume department, small men's fragrance counters were beginning to appear in the big stores; Harrods was the first to install a totally separate fragrance department for men.

There were dozens of men's cologne brands that were coming onto the market, so I had quite a job keeping up with their alluring names: *Chanel Pour Monsieur, Terre d'Hermes, Aqua di Parma Colonia, Pino Silvestre, Guerlain's Mouchoir de Monsieur, Givenchy Gentleman, Floris Special No 127*, not to mention their unique fragrance notes: *earthy but sweet, herbal and fruity, lavender with a touch of vanilla, spicy-floral, musky, warm and woody* ... At the end of my working day, I was heady with the assault of so many fragrances on my nostrils, that I couldn't tell the difference between one brand from another.

The only person who could was our good-looking and beautifully turned out department head, Mr Jack Lane, or 'Jacques', as he liked to be called. Fortyish, his combed-back shiny blond hair was thick with brilliantine and he had a thin pencil moustache. He wore a raffish Pierre Cardin suit and shoes so pointed that they curled up at the ends. Amusingly, this style of shoe was called 'winkle picker'. Jacques couldn't speak French, but pronounced all the brand names like a native.

'No dear, it's pronounced *Dyor owe de sovarge*, not *Dor ho de savidge*,' he would instruct an untutored sales assistant, pursing his lips like a French schoolteacher.

He charmed his customers, he was a good supervisor and he always rushed over to help me out to clinch the sale, whenever he realised I was faced with an undecided customer. I discovered that in the world of fragrances, there were quite a number of customers who were in the undecided category.

But some customers knew exactly what they wanted right away. The best seller for gay men was *Guerlain's Vetiver*. Girl friends and wives preferred *Chanel Pour Monsieur*, and the best seller for every other guy (disappointingly for Jacques) was that tried and true standby *Old Spice*. It was a safe choice and it was cheap. I made some calculations of my own. The receipts from the sale of four bottles of *Old Spice* were equivalent to the sale of one bottle of French cologne. It took ten seconds to sell a bottle of Old Spice, and at least three minutes for a customer to even *decide* whether to buy a French brand of cologne, two of those minutes being spent sniffing and re-sniffing the scent; and even then it wasn't always a done deal. The customer could walk away and often did, undecided. I sold hundreds of *Old Spice* during my short time at Harrods, including one bottle to myself at a staff discount. I rest my case.

For the first time in my life I was discovering *the thrill of the sale*. I had never sold anything before and I enjoyed taking in the receipts for Messrs Harrods, as I liked to call the store. Once in a while I was given the cash and came back with the change, but I normally directed the customer to pay at the cashier's counter. Making money was a heady exercise, and even though I was not making anything extra for myself – part-timers were not on commission – it was exciting to know the total takings at the end of each day from Jacques. It spurred us on. The star performer, a young fellow from Yorkshire, Mr Carver, resented making all this money for the store. One day, he told me, he was going to open his own shop, and make money for himself. Here was an entrepreneur in the making. He was full of northern charm, and I was sure that he would end up rich and successful.

I learned the two most important ingredients of successful salesmanship, by observing both Jacques and Mr Carver at work: respect for the product you were selling and oodles of charm.

I have often returned to Harrods, if only to drop in on the vast Food Hall and have a bite at the Oyster Bar. On many of my morning visits in the nineties, I would sometimes catch sight of al-Fayed making a tour of inspection of what I could clearly see was his pride and joy. He ran a tight ship. Looking like a caricature of a Mafia boss in his sharp Italian suit, he would walk briskly through the store, followed by a group of well-groomed English bodyguards, pointing out areas where there were clear infractions of Harrods' (*his*) regulations: a child messily eating ice-cream outside the Food Hall; a young man sporting a rucksack on his back when he should have been carrying it; a rack of clothes not quite in order; an employee not properly dressed in the prescribed manner; a rowdy group of customers. A member of his inspection team would break away from the group to gently inform the errant individual, customer or employee, of the store's specific regulation that was being infringed.

Al-Fayed was not popular with his employees. He was neither generous nor gentlemanly with his staff, and there were sexual complaints by young women who worked for him in his office; but he proudly ran his store with a high degree of professionalism and elegance. His dress code for customers was strict. He instructed his uniformed doormen to stop people in shorts, flip flops, sweatshirts, athletic singlets, revealing clothes and crash helmets, as well as in their bare feet, from entering the store. Today, alas, the dress code is not as strictly enforced, although the security staff still have the right to refuse entry to people in dirty or unkempt clothing.

I took on another holiday job at Harrods for the January 1963 Winter Sale. The sales were always mayhem on the ground floor, and that's where I was sent to help out. The cramped shoe department in those days carried all the top British brands – Lotus, Churches, Loake – as well as Harrods' own house brand, not so well made, heavily discounted for the sales, and I was selling them like hot cakes. Gucci and Ferragamo had not yet arrived on the local scene. I did not enjoy fitting shoes on customers, and their smelly socks made me long for those heady days in the fragrance department. I begged Jacques to take me back, but he told me that had no say in the matter. After a week I could stand it no longer so I quit.

Today I marvel at Harrods' shoe department on the top floor, the 'Shoe Heaven', 42,000 square feet of space, carrying over

100,000 pairs of shoes from over 55 designers. Each brand is showcased in its own private boutique and run by a professional sales person, a far cry from the hectic shoe department where I worked in 1963.

★ ★ ★ ★

One of the greatest things in my life in 1963 was the very fact that I was in Britain at that time. It felt as if the country was turning a corner. The post-war hardships that I encountered at school were well behind me, and the unpleasant memories of austerity and gloom of the fifties were beginning to fade.

A new, more exciting Britain seemed to be emerging. For the first time, the Establishment, personified by the Tory government of Prime Minister Harold Macmillan, was the subject of satire in a theatrical revue, *Beyond the Fringe,* written and performed by four young Oxbridge intellectuals: Peter Cook, Alan Bennett, Dudley Moore and Jonathan Miller. From a successful run at the Lyceum Theatre in the West End, it transferred to Broadway, introducing a new brand of British political satire, more acerbic and more savage, to a new post-war generation of young, critical and idealistic public in the English-speaking world.

In an interview with Joan Bakewell on BBC 2 in 2000, Jonathan Miller aptly summed up the current mood of the country: 'England was stuck in the Thirties until the Sixties.'

In November 1962, BBC Television took political satire to another level and to a broader audience of 12 million viewers, with *That Was the Week That Was,* a fifty minute Saturday night programme presented by David Frost from November 1962 to December 1963. It didn't just lampoon the politicians and the class system, but broke hallowed ground by attacking the monarchy and the British Empire. My girlfriend Margaret Bettesworth and I were glued to our TV sets every Saturday night after dinner.

The metaphor that summed up the new Britain of 1963 was the Beatles. Three songs, *'Love Me Do'*, *'Please Please Me'* and *'From Me To You'*, dominated the radio airwaves that year, and whether you liked their music or not, they conveyed the general feeling that Britain was on the move.

★ ★ ★ ★

I had just sat my Trinity term exams. As I lay awake at 3 am in my bedsit flat in Onslow Gardens, I reviewed my situation. I desperately wanted to spend some time in the Mediterranean. The English winter of 1962/1963 was long and bitter, and it wasn't until the middle of March that I saw the last of the frost. I desperately needed the warmth of the sun. I also needed the money. London in summer is a good time to find employment, and I thought the sales job I had in the fragrance department of Harrods was a pleasant way to earn a bit of extra pocket money. I was also fascinated by the retail business and wanted to learn more about it. I had always enjoyed visiting Simpson of Piccadilly,* arguably one of the chicest fashion stores at the time. Viewed from across the street, Simpson was sandwiched between two drab Victorian buildings, and stood out as the most modern structure in the West End. The store was designed as a Bauhaus steel edifice, its front emblazoned with a giant Simpson logo, and seemingly moored like an luxury ocean-going liner, with lengths of horizontal windows forming a glass wall that spanned the entire width of the building, as if ready to transport passengers to an exciting new world of the future. Its distinctive non-reflecting concave show windows at street level was the first of its kind in the country.

Step inside through the thick glass plate and steel door, and immediately one is blown away by a massive Travertine marble

---

* Not to be confused with Simpson's in the Strand, a classic restaurant that still retains its traditional Englishness, a vast Edwardian room, serving the best roasts and traditional puddings in the country.

staircase that dominated the ground floor, its chromed and glass rails spiralling majestically upwards to the top floor. One could almost see Fred Astaire and Ginger Rogers tap-dancing and jitterbugging up and down this grand Art Deco stairway, evocative of the glamorous Thirties.

Simpson was launched in April 1936. Its owner, Alexander Simpson, hired Joseph Emberton, Britain's leading modern movement architect, to design a steel and glass structure that has now become a Grade 1 Listed Building. On opening day, Sir Malcolm Campbell, the world's first racing driver to exceed 300 mph, or 482 kph, on the Bonneville Salt Flats in Utah, was invited to cut the tape. Three full-sized airplanes were exhibited on the fifth floor. It was London's most exciting event of the season.

Poor Alexander never saw his creation become the epitome of London elegance: the outfitters of choice by the Royals, MPs, dignitaries and country land owners. He died of leukaemia in 1937, one year after the launch of his store. He was only thirty-four years old.

Fortunately, his brother Samuel, a brilliant endocrinologist, took over the management of Simpsons, and was able to successfully run the store without giving up his medical practice and research, finally being appointed chief consultant to St Mary's Hospital in London.

Although Simpson began as a cutting-edge fashion store for men, by 1963 it had become a symbol of traditional, classic-cut clothes for a middle-aged customer base, exemplified by its famous DAKS self-suspending, beltless trouser range. It still had a strong appeal with older film actors like Richard Attenborough, Michael Rennie and Bryan Forbes, whom I was able to spot browsing through the store. Its snob appeal was also strong with a certain Anglophile generation overseas and a dying breed of British colonial expatriates.

On an overcast day in July 1963, I put on my best blue mohair suit and presented myself at Simpson's management offices on the sixth floor. The fact that I had worked at Harrods didn't seem to impress them in the slightest. They were more interested in my ability to speak French and Italian, and a smattering of German. Thai didn't seem to register with them at all. When they found out that I was capable of interpreting their foreign customers' tastes (*lapels, cuffs, stiff collars, soft collars, cutaway collars, wing collars, club ties, cravats, brogue shoes, patent leather shoes, tweeds, worsteds, two buttons vs three buttons, single-breasted vs double-breasted, dinner jackets, smoking jackets – not to be confused with 'le smoking', French for dinner jacket – raglan sleeves, turtlenecks, V-necks, lamb's wool, cashmere, fisherman's knit, trouser turn-ups,* etc.) to their English sales staff, I was signed on *immediately*.

In those elegant days, there were clothes for every occasion. It was always a pleasure to dress up for the opera or the Temple Ball. I would be invited to bashes that required wearing my DJ (dinner jacket in the UK, tuxedo in America) and black tie every month. I was taught by my father how to tie my bow tie in the dark (blackouts were frequent in those days), the test of a true diplomat. Today, I am aghast at the garb of theatregoers seated around me in London's West End. Pullovers are bad enough, but sweatshirts, cargo trousers and running shoes are beyond the pale. In Asia, tourists from the West, even of my generation, wear clothes in hotels and restaurants, *and even in museums and temples,* which display their worst bodily features: huge buttocks and stomachs bulging out of their t-shirts and shorts, and open sandals that show off their ungainly feet. Why do these relatively affluent tourists demean themselves in front of the locals who are poorer but neatly dressed in a more dignified way?

During my first week at Simpson, I was assigned to the cashmere section on the sixth floor, where most overseas visitors headed for first. I worked under the supervision of Mr Price, an old hand, who knew everything there was to know about cashmeres. He instructed the head sales person, Miss Derby, to show me the different styles – for both men and women – and where the stocks were kept in the back storeroom. She was thin, elegant, fiftyish, and I could always sense when she was around, because that cloying combination of perfume and cigarette smoke followed her wherever she went. She taught me how to fold, wrap, box and bag the precious pullovers, cardigans, and scarves. She had a slight American accent, an affectation she had developed, after serving so many customers from the other side of the pond seeking '*genoo-ine Scotch kashe-meeres*'.

She also showed me how to carefully fold and wrap delicate tissue paper around ladies' expensive twinsets – a classic cardigan worn over a round-necked short-sleeved pullover in the same knit and colour, adorned with a string of pearls and bought by women of a certain age who reminded me of my mother, Princess Margaret and Grace Kelly. It was Miss Derby who taught me that Americans called both jumpers and pullovers 'sweaters'. I told her that the French called them 'les pulls', an Anglophile word that surely must have upset Charles De Gaulle, the anti-British President at the time.

On one quiet day, when the store was not so busy, Mr Price and I got chatting, and he shared a trade secret with me that I have not forgotten to this day.

'Why is this pullover,' he pointed out the *Made in Scotland expressly for Simpson by Ballantyne* label sewn onto the back of the pullover's neck, 'more expensive than exactly the same garment in other stores in Regent Street?' he asked me rhetorically.

'Particularly since they all come from the same supplier,' he continued, when I looked to him for an answer with a quizzical look of ignorance.

He told me that there are only two or three cashmere

manufacturers in Scotland that knit the same products for *all* the brands.

'What makes the difference is the *cachet* of the Simpson label, supplemented by the unique service you and I give our customers.' I was taught my first lesson in branding. For the remaining two weeks in the cashmere department, I was to learn about customer service.

Most cashmere shoppers from abroad were American or from the Argentine. On the whole, Americans preferred Argyll designs with matching socks. They liked to try on the sweaters for colour and size, and if they were on their own, they would invariably ask me for my opinion. My answer would always be honest. If a certain colour or pattern did not suit them, I would say so and bring out other models for them to try on, to see if they didn't 'look better'. On one occasion, a mother and her teenage son disagreed about two different styles, one V-neck and the other round-neck, that the poor boy kept trying, on and off, hot and bothered, his hair becoming a right old mess, and I was reluctantly asked to help decide. I thought the young fellow looked great in both sweaters and I told them so. I convinced his mother to buy both. Mr Price approved.

The Argentinians were more concerned with the *total look*. The pullovers had to go with their traditional wardrobe of tweed jackets, old-school blazers and Prince of Wales check suits, which they had already bought from the other departments. They wanted to look totally British. By the time they tried on the complete ensemble, they looked more like a parody of a British gentleman. Secretly, I thought, they wanted to look like David Niven, and some did. Curiously, they preferred the Pringle brand cashmeres over Ballantyne. They were the richest shoppers in the store. And they knew what they wanted.

I was then transferred to the ground floor, near the grand staircase, a huge space where silk, cotton and poplin shirts were displayed and sold. Mr Barclay was 'head of shirts' and he introduced me to his team of six salesmen. The man I was working closest with was Mr Glossop, short and heavy, who worked slowly, and did not have the visage of friendliness to attract new customers. He did his very best to prevent me from selling any shirts at all. I could only guess that he was afraid that I would pinch his customers. He obviously didn't know that I wasn't on commission and I didn't bother to tell him.

What probably irked him the most could have been the fact that there were tiny French and Italian flags pinned to my lapel, with the word 'interpreter' printed underneath. It was the tourist season and I was called upon to help out sales staff who had trouble understanding their foreign customers. I did not have a privileged position, nor was I paid any more than my sales colleagues. If anything, I was paid much less. But to the casual outsider, I looked important. And if I was to be quite honest with myself, I *felt* important.

After a week of helping out on the ground floor, I was given an additional job. I was assigned as a guide to accompany big spending clients throughout the store, from cashmeres on the sixth floor, down through to coats, mackintoshes, bespoke tailoring, ready to wear DAKS suits and trousers, shoes, and the sports shop on the lower floors; and finally to the gift shop, the barber shop and a restaurant in the basement. There was a women's fashion department on the fifth floor. It could often be a full day's exercise.

As I guided my customer from one floor to the next, I was required to sign off a form provided by the department's sales assistant after each purchase, called the 'With Other Goods' or 'WOG form', a procedure whereby all the purchases would be tallied together and added up to a single bill at the end of the day. It was a convenient system for the customer to settle payment and collection for all his or her purchases in one go.

There was a free delivery service to hotels within central London. Some bills totalled a few thousand pounds, particularly if it was a family.

However, there was one flaw in the system that I pointed out to all the department managers. The 'WOG' denomination could also be misconstrued as a derogatory and racially offensive slang word referring to a non-white person, as it did in those far off days. At its best, 'WOG' meant 'Western Oriental Gentleman' or 'Wily Oriental Gentleman'. At worst, it was a racial slur, and very insulting. Either way, it was agreed with all the sales assistants, that we would avoid using this acronym in future, and gave the form its full official description: 'With Other Goods'.

What was supposed not to happen, happened.

I was assigned to accompany a big spender, an elegant and sophisticated Indian Maharajah, who was hurriedly going through the store, buying everything that caught his fancy.

In the shoe department, he was being helped into a pair of black Chelsea boots by Mr Guerney, a doddery old retainer who should have long been furloughed, and had obviously forgotten about our agreement not to use the 'WOG' word.

'I suppose we need to use the WOG form then,' he said, looking first at our distinguished customer and then at me. I was thinking of hitting old Guerney in the head. Instead I just blinked. When I regained my composure, I was faced with a very angry customer.

'How dare you! I have never been so insulted in my life!' cried the Maharajah, as he sprang to his feet.

Mr Guerney, realising his mistake, quickly put a hand to cover his mouth and tried to explain. But it was too late.

The Maharajah then looked at me, his dark eyes focussed on mine, 'wog to wog', as it were, as I spluttered out an apologetic 'with other goods' and other inane words that did little to rectify our terrible blunder.

He continued to look at me. 'How you – '. His voice trailed behind him as he quickly stalked out of the store. His tab had already run up to almost 1000 pounds and it seemed as if he was ready to fork out quite a bit more.

The next day I was invited by management to explain the incident to the executive board of directors. It was decided that the WOG form procedure would be revised. I never found out what took its place, as I had already left Simpson's employ by the time it was implemented.

★ ★ ★ ★

That unpleasant politically incorrect blunder aside, there were some memorable moments at Simpson that I cherish still.

I made many friends in the store. I was particularly fascinated to look at the display team at work. They called themselves 'visual merchandisers'. The curved windows facing *inwards* on both Piccadilly and Jermyn Street must have presented a challenge, but the final results were always works of art. I remember Malcolm, a very tall man of about thirty, one of the decorators, continually tweaking and repairing the displays. At night, he would be seen working with his creative team at the show windows. He was the only employee in the store who not only never wore a suit, but 'wouldn't be seen dead' in a 'baggy pair of DAKS trousers' either. He proudly stood out a mile in the store with his colourful sweaters and tight jeans. He confided in me that visual merchandising wasn't really his thing. He was waiting for a position in the Drury Lane theatre as a set designer.

For people who have never worked in a shop before, it is difficult to describe the thrill of welcoming your first customer of the day. It is a delightful experience.

Celebrities, particularly those in the film business, tended to shop very early in the morning. Being used to early morning calls at the studios could be a reason. Avoiding the crowds was probably the other. They always entered through the less public Jermyn Street entrance. Another thrill was to introduce new product lines that had been advertised and had just come into the store.

We all dreaded Saturdays, when the customers were 'less refined', as one saleslady described them, and the shop was much more crowded. In those days, all the stores in the West End were open only up to 1 pm on Saturdays, so the weekend crowd had only four hours to do all their shopping. It was mayhem. Simpson, and indeed all the other stores in Britain, were closed on Sunday.

Some of London's finest restaurants were in the Piccadilly area, including less expensive teashops and sandwich bars that catered to the West End retail workers. I was glad to get away from the store at lunchtime if only to get a breath of fresh air, rather than eat at the staff canteen on the top floor, where I would invariably be seated next to one of my co-workers. The conversation would always end up talking shop (pun intended). Like the workers at Abbotts Lodge, they were all complainers, and it wasn't always about the management either. It was the astonishing rudeness of customers who were more often the subject of their gripes.

I would invite my new friend Chris Hyde-Smith to join me for lunch. A simpatico South African from Capetown, Chris had to leave his country after being caught running night classes for black Africans, a criminal offense. It was the sad era of apartheid. During the day he sold ties and accessories. In the evening he worked on stage as an extra in the hit musical *My Fair Lady*. We would have long conversations together after work, solving the problems of the world.

We were both in love with Sue, a beautifully slim brunette with dimples, in accounts. She never joined us for lunch despite our many invitations. I met her again in Rome in the late sixties where she found a secretarial job. I tried to get closer to her, but she was won over by the charms of my Italian-Thai cousin Roberto. She eventually returned to England, got married, and lived in suburbia happily ever after.

Chris decided to make his career in retail and continued in the business as a buyer for the British Home Stores (an upscale Woolworths), ending up running the lighting department. Alas, BHS was one of the first of many British high street department store chains to go bust in the second decade of this millennium.

After two months, some aspects of my job at Simpson were turning out to be a bit of a grind, despite my initial enthusiasm when I first started. The daily routine was beginning to pall. Half an hour before closing time, all the sales assistants would start to tidy up, putting away the shirts and sweaters, hanging up the suits, clearing the fitting rooms and putting the merchandise back into their boxes. By five-thirty, all the dust covers were carefully put on the shelves and glass top counters. The last customers were being gently herded out of the store, before the commissionaires closed the doors of both entrances. All the staff were checked before leaving and if we had bought any items in the store, we had to show the receipts. I did my fair share of apologies in French, Italian and German to customers who lingered on in the store. All the staff seemed in a hurry to get home, although I couldn't understand why. It was not much fun cramming into the Piccadilly tube station at rush hour and getting crushed in the train all the way back to South Kensington.

The dress code in Britain in the sixties for sales employees in Harrods and Simpson was always a suit and tie, which would sometimes cause a bit of confusion. It was often difficult in those days to distinguish the customer from the salesman. 'Excuse me, do you work here?' was often asked of me, when I was not standing behind the counter, by male customers wearing a suit just like me.

Today, the confusion persists, but in the opposite direction. *Everyone,* shoppers and sales alike, are dressed as if they were going jogging or off to the beach. What is accepted as 'smart casual' (whatever that means) is a visual challenge. I now have great difficulty when I am shopping in the UK and the US trying to find a sales assistant to serve me. Not only are they far and few on the ground, but also because they are all casually dressed just like their customers. Except, of course, in Harrods, where the sales assistants are super-suited in black, as if they were attending a funeral. In Italy, Switzerland, Austria and Sweden, suits are still worn by the locals on both sides of the counter, although in more relaxed styles.

Once, way back in the eighties, on a business visit to a city in the Midwest United States, I went into a store, Sears I think it was, to do some shopping. I had just arrived from Rome, and I hadn't yet had time to unpack, so I was still in my suit and tie. As I was browsing around, a tall man in a Stetson hat, checked shirt and cowboy boots approached me, and asked me the price of a certain item he was looking at. I picked it up and told him '$39.99'. He then asked the price of another item on display nearby. Again, I looked at the price. 'It's a bit more expensive,' I said, '$45.59'. He picked up a third item and asked me the price. It didn't have a price tag, so I told him I didn't know.

'What kinda salesman are ya, anyhow, if ya don't know the price?'

'I'm afraid I'm not a salesman,' I told him, 'I'm a customer just like you.'

He apologised profusely. He said that he mistook me for a salesman because I was wearing a 'coat and tie'.* I have never

---

* Coat in the UK means overcoat, a long warm winter coat to be worn when one goes outside to confront the cold. In America it means a jacket. Hence, sports jacket in the UK, sports coat in the US, nowadays incorrectly and annoyingly referred to as a blazer.

worn a suit to go shopping again.

In the shopping heyday of sixties Britain, it was always easy to get a job in retail. I'd worked in a variety of jobs: a bookshop in Primrose Hill, a small men's outfitters in Bayswater, and selling vinyl long-playing records on Saturdays at a music shop on Finchley Road. I had once operated a lift in Selfridges, when I was really strapped for cash.

Sadly, Simpson closed its doors on 30 January 1999. Their tweedy and twinset styles had become an anomaly, and their loyal middle-aged customer base had long gone. They had already lost the younger set in the mid-sixties to Carnaby Street, a new shopping district less than a mile away, which had become the epicentre of a new fashion trend, exemplified by Mary Quant, the miniskirt designer; David Bailey, the trendy photographer; and Mick Jagger, London's favourite son of rock.

Simpson had failed to keep in touch with the onslaught of this new pop culture, and the musical and sartorial revolution that was a key part of it. British shoppers in the remaining decades of the last century were dominated by a totally different socio-demographic group: youthful, non-traditional and anti-establishment.

The iconic Art Deco glass and chrome building on Piccadilly where I worked in the summer of 1963 is now the flagship store of Waterstone's bookshop chain.

Looking back on my time at Simpson, I wish I had spent more time working there. Perhaps I could have even made a career in the retail business.

I have not worked in a store since.

CHAPTER EIGHT
ORIENTAL EXTRA

'Teddy Tai. Take one.'

'Action!'

'*Iarrgghh. Uurrgghh.*'

A few incoherent words from a short script sent to me the week before, which I had supposedly read and committed to memory, seemed to have spluttered out of my lips. Or didn't. I couldn't even claim to have fluffed my lines. All I remembered were a series of babbling sounds.

Then I froze.

'Cut!'

Here I was, Sound Stage 3, Shepperton Studios, standing in front of an enormous black movie camera, taking a screen test for a small role in *Lord Jim*. The bored old cameraman sighed. He was twiddling with his Arriflex 35, trying to focus his lens on me. A middle-aged lady and a crew of three technicians were patiently waiting for expressions of love, joy, fear, envy, passion, happiness, anger, sadness, surprise, excitement, elation and any other emotion that the script called for from my lips – together with a corresponding display from my eyes and my movements, both hands and body. It's called '*acting*'.

'Teddy Tai. Take two.'

'Action!'

I blinked and froze again.

'It's all right, dear! It 'appens to the best of us.' The assistant to the assistant to the assistant casting director, a motherly-looking woman of fifty, was trying, encouragingly, to coach me. She had a slight cockney twang. She was kind and patient.

'Even Sir Laurence Olivier gets stage fright once in a while. Why don't you go to the toilet for five minutes and pull yourself together! And then we can start all over again.'

I couldn't even see her face. The camera lights had temporarily blinded me. I raised my right hand to shield my eyes, and looked straight ahead into a dark void, desperately searching for a way out of this embarrassing situation.

'Madam, even two more hours in the loo isn't going to help,' I told her, blinking nervously. 'I now realise that I can't act at all and I'm sorry to have wasted your time. I'm going back to what I was doing before I came here. Thank you for being so patient.'

'It's all right luv! I fully understand. Don't forget to pick up your four guineas at the desk outside before you leave. By the way, what work do you do?' I told her I was a law student and hoping to get called to the Bar.

'If I was you, young man, I would go right back to what you was doing. And don't give up. Not many of us are so lucky. I wish my son 'ad the same opportunity as you.'

It was the best advice I ever had in my life. I hastily left the studios and took the next train back to London.

The last words I heard from her was 'Right, who's next?' As I left Sound Stage 3 and collected my 4 guineas, I saw a short line of Asian hopefuls waiting for an audition. I wished them luck.

It was February 1964.

★ ★ ★ ★

The idea of a film career had been floating in my mind for some time. Pondering in my bedsit in Onslow Gardens, alone and broke, I often wondered whether I had made the right decision. Was I really meant for the law? Until that seminal moment at Shepperton Studios when I discovered I couldn't act, I had often dreamt of the riches that could be earned as a film actor. These visions began when I was starting to get hired as a 'film extra', a fancy title to describe one of the many people engaged in a crowd scene of a film, as more new productions set in an Asian context and requiring 'Oriental' roles were being produced in the UK.

The money wasn't bad either. What I would earn in one day on a film set was as much as I earned in five and a half days in a department store. I was paid a basic four guineas for each day on the set, equivalent to around 100 UK pounds today, the highest paid job I had ever had. For 'special action' sequences, one could earn any amount between one and ten pounds extra, depending on the action. Carrying a tray with glasses and a bottle of Champagne as a waiter could earn an extra one pound, and another one pound if it involved serving the table where the actors were doing their scene. Carrying and running with a rifle and getting shot on the battlefield could earn as much as ten pounds extra. I know. I have done both.

The sixties were regarded as a period of change and transformation in the British film industry, when big budget Hollywood films were starting to be produced in the UK, replacing the local production of old black and white Ealing and J Arthur Rank comedies and war films, normally shot on a budget. But to me they remain the best of British cinema, still relevant today. Whilst I've already forgotten the 'blockbuster' I saw on Netflix last week, classics like *The Ladykillers, Kind Hearts and Coronets, The Dam Busters* and *The Third Man*, are indelibly fixed in my memory and form the basis of my film culture.

The transformation began in the fifties when American film directors flocked to England for inspiration and intellectual freedom, during the era of communist witch hunting, instigated by the mad senator, Joseph McCarthy, in America. Joseph Losey (*The Servant*), Stanley Kubrick (*Dr Strangelove*) and Richard Lester (*A Hard Day's Night*) were among them.

More importantly, there was an increased American involvement and funding in British film productions. Producers were discovering that British film production facilities were more economical than in America: to shoot a film in the Borehamwood, Elstree and Pinewood studios cost much less than in Hollywood. By 1967, nine out of ten British releases had been underwritten by American investors.

My first foray into the film industry was purely by accident. It was during the summer holidays of 1958. I was asked by a Chinese friend to take his place as a film extra on a movie that was being shot at Borehamwood studios, in Hertsfordshire. The film was the Twentieth Century Fox production of *The Inn of the Sixth Happiness*; the producers were looking for a great number of Asian extras to play Chinese peasants that were needed to populate a Chinese village built in the studio backlot.

At the end of three day's shooting, I collected my fee from Mrs Warran, an Indian lady, who was a casting agent for Asian film and theatre roles in Britain. She was beautifully turned out in colourful sari. Her job was to supply the production houses with the correct types (male, female, teens, seniors etc.) and the right numbers of Asian extras required for each production, and also to act as a talent scout. She ensured that each and every film extra under her charge – sometimes hundreds – was correctly paid, a challenging administrative task. She was also responsible for our well-being on set. Through her, we were all trade union members of the F.A.A, the Film Artistes' Association. Mrs Warran was good-natured, well spoken and a remarkably well-organised lady.

For the next ten years, through the good offices of Mrs Warran, I worked in 16 feature films, several television dramas, a number of film commercials, and once I even appeared on the London stage production of *Flower Drum Song*. Always, of course, as an extra – an Oriental face in a crowd. Among a great many typecast roles, I have played a coolie* (once), a terrorist (once), a soldier (once), a Native American (once), a waiter (twice), a mercenary (twice), a peasant (several times), a Chinese ambassador (only once), and even one of Chairman Mao Zedong's Red Guard revolutionaries. All these roles, without any acting talent whatsoever.

The only time I came remotely close to anything like acting was during one episode of the *Somerset Maugham Hour* series in 1962, based on his short stories, shot at Wembley Studios for ITV. Suitably outfitted in a sarong, I was cast as a Malay houseboy, and a brilliant British actor, whose name I have since forgotten and who was playing my colonial master (a rubber planter), started shouting. 'Where the devil is my gin and tonic?' When I appeared on the veranda, cowing, he continued his tirade: 'Where the hell have you been? You're never around when I need you!' He glared at me angrily. He looked as if he was going to hit me. I was terrified. It felt so real. I was not acting scared, *I really was scared.* When the scene was over he came up to me, all smiles and friendliness. 'I say old chap,' he said, shaking my hand, 'I'm sorry if I frightened you. I was only acting, you know.'

My film extra career, if we can call it that, mostly consisted of waiting around on the film set doing absolutely nothing until I was called to 'do' my role. It can be the most boring job in the world.

In the meantime, everyone else in the studio was working like mad to get the expensive film production moving ahead: carpenters busy erecting the stage; set designers ensuring the integrity of their

---

* Alec Guinness' very first acting role was in *Queer Cargo*, a drama in the Picadilly Theatre, in 1934. His part? A Chinese coolie. He admits that 'in my enthusiasm for appearing as a Chinese I shaved the top of my head; my hair never really recovered from the shock and now is lost forever.'

designs; prop guys getting the right props together; lighting crew checking to see that there was enough light; camera men setting up the right shooting angles; sound engineers preparing to record the soundtrack; wardrobe people making sure that we were all suitably dressed; make-up artists dabbing their Max Factor puffs on anyone who was in the shot; continuity and script girls (always girls, don't ask me why) checking and rechecking the script; assistants to the director running around to see that everything was happening; directors studying the script; and actors rehearsing, or, perfectly understandably in this chaos, having a tantrum. Not forgetting, of course, nervous producers hanging around to keep a tight rein on the budget. I had never seen so much mayhem in my life. It was far more chaotic than the winter sales at Harrods. At the end of the shoot, though, an extraordinary cinematic work of art would sometimes miraculously emerge from this apparent pandemonium. In most cases it was a total waste of time and human effort, not to mention money – what the film critics call a 'bomb'.

On the next few pages, then, are a few of the hits, and many more misses, that I have been involved in as a film extra, and a collection of anecdotal observations of my own:

THE INN OF THE SIXTH HAPPINESS
1958, Twentieth Century Fox, American

Loosely based on the true story of Gladys Aylward, a servant girl who became a brave English missionary and went to China at her own expense during the Sino-Japanese War in 1938, without official recognition from the London Missions Board. She was the Protestant version of Mother Teresa, who was also not recognized by the Vatican during her early years in Calcutta. Gladys famously led a hundred Chinese barefooted orphans away from the dangerous war front to safety across the mountains.

One of her many achievements was to successfully persuade the Chinese not to bind the feet of their little girls.

Tiny and diminutive, dark-haired and dark-eyed, Gladys was born in North London, and spoke with a cockney accent. She was virtuous and a virgin. Her biography, *The Small Woman* by Alan Burgess, was an inspirational story of faith and devotion to the call of God.

The Inn of the Sixth Happiness, however, was made into a romantic love story, and when the film came out, it was reported that Gladys was upset by the love scenes, saying that she had never kissed a man in her life.

The entire film was a miscasting disaster. Despite her moving performance in the portrayal of Gladys Aylward, the blue-eyed, blonde, five-foot-nine Ingrid Bergman, with her distinctive Swedish accent, was a physical and cultural mismatch. The Chinese mandarin in charge of the village was played unconvincingly by Robert Donat, an Oscar winning actor for his touching 1938 performance as the quintessential English schoolmaster in *Goodbye Mr Chips*. Sadly, *The Inn of The Sixth Happiness* was his last performance, and he died before the film was released. The biggest miscast of all was Curt Jurgens, a tall Austrian actor, who played the Eurasian Captain Lin Nan, Gladys', or rather, Ingrid's, love interest.

Hollywood not casting Asians to play Asians was as uncomfortable as the use of make-up to make their white actors' appearance more Asian. In this epic production of miscasts, a Swede plays an Englishwoman, an Englishman plays a Chinese and an Austrian plays a Eurasian.

As for myself, cast and clothed as a Chinese peasant, this film was an active three days' work, when I joined 60 other Asian extras to make the Chinese village of Wangcheng in the middle of Hertsfordshire actually *look* Chinese.

I asked Ingrid Bergman, the first film star I had ever seen

in the flesh, for her autograph on a white Benson & Hedges cigarette pack inner wrapper.

'I hope I'm not signing a cheque,' she said, smiling.

She was the most beautiful woman I have ever seen in my life.

THE WORLD OF SUZIE WONG
1960, Paramount, American

This love story between an artist living in Hong Kong and a woman who works as a Chinese prostitute, is based on a novel by British writer Richard Mason.

Here, again, we have the classic case of Hollywood fiddling around with the casting. Instead of an English artist, the film's struggling artist Robert Lomax was portrayed by an American, William Holden. Far too middle-aged and much too sophisticated – he wears a suit and tie for most of the film, even when he is painting – he looked more like a corporate executive than an artist. I would have preferred somebody like Terence Stamp, a bit more quirky, and certainly much more artistic looking. But in 1960, Stamp didn't have the box-office draw required for American audiences.

And here again, we have Hollywood stereotyping. Although the proud and illiterate prostitute is admirably played by Nancy Kwan, one still has the feeling that she is presented as an exotic and subservient Asian woman. Fellini's Italian prostitute, Cabiria, poignantly played by Giulietta Masina, had none of these traits. She was just a prostitute, period. Like Fellini, Richard Quine, the American director, had tried to be honest about the subject, but in 1960 US audiences weren't ready for stark reality, and the film degenerates into a happy-ending soap opera. Primal clichés on screen were easier for the audience to digest than human suffering.

The exterior scenes of *The World of Suzie Wong* were shot in Hong Kong, and what a valuable record of the sixties it is too. For old-timers like me who has worked in Hong Kong, it's worth seeing the film just for the locations alone. Tsim Sha Tsui, the Ladder Street in Central, Yau Ma Tei, Sai Ying Pun, Aberdeen and Telegraph Bay are seen in the film as they once were, before Hong Kong developed into a megacity of glass and steel high-rise office buildings, opulent shopping centres, and expensive apartment blocks.

When Chairod Mahadamrongkul, my flat mate, and I, were called to present our Oriental selves to the film's casting director, we donned our best mohair suits, ready to take on sophisticated roles like a hard-nosed banker or a businessman, or ballsy roles like a Hong Kong playboy or a suave Chinese gambler. We both looked like a million bucks.

At the studio just before the shoot, a man pointed us out from a crowd of extras. 'You two,' he said, looking straight at us, 'are perfect waiters.' Thus spoke the person who decides who is who in a film.

Without slipping on the carpet or dropping plates and glasses all over the floor like a Marx Brothers comedy, we played our roles waiting at tables in a Hong Kong restaurant reasonably well. We were positioned so far away from the camera that we were hardly recognizable on screen. We worked for two days in this posh restaurant film set, where Lomax takes Suzie out to dinner for the first time, only to discover that she is illiterate and can't read the menu. A touching scene.

Two weeks later, at least 200 Chinese-looking Asians were called, cast as slum dwellers in an outdoor night scene during a heavy typhoon storm. The slums of Kowloon's Walled City were rebuilt with incredible accuracy inside MGM's massive Borehamwood studio. The shanty town was a marvel of film set construction. Overhead, water sprinklers and shower heads covered the entire area, and created more rain than I have ever experienced in a real monsoon. At the high point of the film, Lomax braves the typhoon and hastily climbs up the slum's narrow streets to look for Suzie Wong, against the flow of fleeing slum dwellers (including my good self) rushing down to safety in the opposite direction. The climax of this scene is a dangerous mudslide when Suzie's shack slips down the hillside, and she is saved in time by our hero. It took a week to shoot this scene alone, and clothed in our peasant costumes, we were drenched to the skin every day. Although we were also paid danger money, many of us came down with a bad cold.

It was during the shoot of this scene that I caused the lighting crew to go on strike. A huge studio light had exploded overhead, sending shattered glass all over the wet floor where I was standing. I started carefully picking up some of the bigger pieces of broken glass, strewn across a tangled mess of thick electric cables. I was helped by some of the other Asian extras. With our flimsy peasant cotton shoes, it would have been dangerous to walk about on this flooded undergrowth of glass shards, not to mention the fear of getting electrocuted. Suddenly, all work stopped on the set. There was dead silence.

We had inadvertently caused a strike. The trade union rules were clear. We were not supposed to do other workers' jobs. The impasse was soon settled in a friendly discussion between the film artists' union and the lighting union. Suzie Wong was back on schedule.

'You bloody Chinese are trying to take away our jobs!' one of the lighting crew said to us jokingly.

I have always admired William Holden's performances. His portrayals in *Sunset Boulevard* and *The Bridge on the River Kwai* are heroic, not because he dies in both pictures but because *he simply doesn't want to die.* Unlike invincible Hollywood heroes like John Wayne and Errol Flynn, Holden was to die in five more films. He was a chain smoker of Salem cigarettes and a heavy drinker. He himself died before his time, aged only 63. Inebriated, he accidentally slipped on a rug, banging his head on a bedside table, and bled to death in his apartment in Santa Monica, California, in 1981. A sad end to one of Hollywood's greatest leading men.

ROAD TO HONG KONG
1961, United Artists, American

A tedious and final sequel to the totally forgettable Bing Crosby/ Bob Hope series of musical-comedy travel-romp films, with Dorothy Lamour on the distaff side. The series started in 1940 with the *Road to Singapore*, followed by other '*Road*' films: to Zanzibar in 1941, Morocco in 1942, Utopia in 1946, Rio in 1947 and Bali in 1952. By 1961, both Crosby and Hope were well past their prime, and their dialogue, songs and dance numbers were embarrassingly outmoded. James Agee, the American writer and film critic, commenting on the film, wrote that 'the American genius for movie comedy has disintegrated.'

The only memorable scene in the picture was Peter Sellers' hilarious performance as an incompetent Indian doctor, charged with curing Bob Hope's amnesia.*

---

* It is interesting to note that Bob Hope, that uberAmerican comedian and master of one-liners, was born in Eltham, not far from my school, and emigrated to America with his parents in 1908 when he was only five. Displaying a childhood talent for singing, dancing and comedy, he won a prize for an impersonation of Charlie Chaplin when he was 12. Between 1938 and 1990, he performed on stage, radio, film and TV, and he ended his lifetime contract with NBC at 93 because he wanted 'to become a free agent.' In 1998 he was awarded a British knighthood, and for the first time in his life he said he was 'speechless'. He lived to be 100, and when he was asked on his deathbed where he wanted to be buried, he told his wife Dolores 'Surprise me.'

I had one day's work in this film, as a spectator in a theatre in Hong Kong, constructed on the backlot of Shepperton studios. I was sad to see Dorothy Lamour, still looking fabulous at 47, reluctantly appearing in a cameo role as herself, and not in a starring role, as she had been in past *'Road'* movies. She was considered 'too old' by Bing Crosby who, much aged himself, chose Joan Collins instead.

During one of the breaks in the filming, there they were on the stage, all three of them, Bing Crosby and Bob Hope, with Dorothy in the middle, posing for the publicity stills. Not many people were taking notice of her. She was a has-been and clearly unhappy. Bob Hope was doing his best to console her. It was he who had insisted she have a role in the film.

'What the fuck am I doing here!' she shouted plaintively, more than once, not just to her two co-stars, but seemingly to anybody ready to listen to her.

It was the first time I heard the 'f' word uttered in public. I was shocked and embarrassed.

I also felt awfully sorry for Dorothy Lamour.

THE DEVIL NEVER SLEEPS
SATAN NEVER SLEEPS (US title)
1963, Twentieth Century Fox, American

Since *The Bridges at Toko Ri* in 1954, William Holden had been appearing regularly in a series of films shot on Asian locations with a Far Eastern theme: *Love is a Many Splendored Thing* in 1955, *The Bridge on the River Kwai* in 1957, and *The World of Suzie Wong* in 1960. *Satan Never Sleeps* was the latest.

Holden had developed an affinity for Asia, and for a while, he maintained an apartment in Hong Kong. He also acquired a substantial collection of Asian antiques, among them some valuable Lao and Vietnamese bronze rain drums. After his death, his Asian collection was donated to the Palm Springs Museum of Art. On a visit to Palm Springs in 1989, I was fortunate to visit the museum, which had a fascinating room devoted to Holden's Asian collection.

The script of *Satan Never Sleeps* was adapted from a story by Pearl Buck, about a pair of Catholic priests – Father Dovar, played by Clifton Webb, and Father O'Banion, played by Holden – struggling to maintain a mission in a remote outpost in China during Mao's Zedong's Communist revolution in 1949.

The bad guys, of course, were the People's Liberation Army* soldiers. I was one of them. For two full nights, all I had to do on 'action!' was to sit rigidly still with seven other mean looking Communist soldiers in the back of an army truck clutching our rifles, *doing absolutely nothing,* but looking mean. It was freezing cold.

So strong was the anti-Communist bias of this film that one would be forgiven for mistakenly believing that it was bankrolled by the CIA, and not by Twentieth Century Fox. Satan, of course, was meant to equate with the Communists.

The closest the production of this film ever got to China was the Chinese village in Hertsfordshire, left over from *The Inn of the Sixth Happiness.*

In a review from the *New York Post,* the film was described as 'embarrassingly predictable until it becomes so bad that you couldn't even imagine it.' This was not William Holden's finest hour. A British critic said that the audience would fall asleep long before Satan.

---

* The name given to the armed forces of the People's Republic of China and the armed wing of the Chinese Communist Party. Forty years on, the People's Liberation Army massacred their own people at Tiananmen Square in 1989, with at least 10,000 deaths, according to newly released documents in 2017 and reported by the BBC.

GOLDFINGER
1964, Eon Productions, British

After six decades since its production, it is a pleasure to reflect upon what many contemporary critics describe as the best James Bond film ever made, and to remember the scenes I worked in with delight, cast as one of Goldfinger's dangerous Korean mercenaries.

For readers who have not seen the film, or may have forgotten its storyline, here is a brief summary: Auric Goldfinger – brilliantly portrayed by Gert Frobe – is a villainous billionaire who has the largest gold reserves in the world. He wants to increase the value of his own gold holdings by rendering the United State's reserves in Fort Knox radioactive, and thus worthless. When British military intelligence suspects that Goldfinger is up to no good, 007 is sent to investigate him. Bond discovers that Goldfinger plans to detonate a nuclear device in Fort Knox and sets out to prevent this, but not before confronting Goldfinger's heavily armed Korean mercenary army, and his final duel with Oddjob, Goldfinger's fiendish right-hand man, whose weaponised, razor-concealing derby hat, when pitched like a frisbee, is capable of lopping a man's head off.

It saddens me that the most important actor in the 007 franchise passed away in 2020. I had been with Sean Connery, playing James Bond, every day for nearly a month, working on the final climax of the movie (there are many climaxes in Bond films). The action scenes took place in and around the Fort Knox film sets built at Pinewood studios. In fact, there were *two* sets: the *exterior*, a massive reproduction of the Fort Knox building erected in a huge field in Buckinghamshire, and the *interior*, a huge stage set on two floors, with gold bars piled up from floor to ceiling.

In blue uniforms and caps, with a yellow sash tied around the waist, Goldfinger's mercenary army looked like a horde of fearsome Taekwondo ninjas, but they (we) were no match for the heavily armed American troops that were eventually called in by James Bond to help out at the end of the film. (What would Hollywood do without the US Cavalry coming to the rescue?)

The battle of Fort Knox is about 20 minutes long on screen. The filming of the same battle in the surrounding English countryside took almost three weeks. It was dangerous work defending the Fort against the US Army. Although we were warned in advance *where* the explosives were placed at different locations in the field, we never knew *when* they were going to be detonated. Being too near the spot of the explosion could cause serious burns. There were English professional stuntmen in blue ninja wardrobes like us, whose job was to get blown up. It was terrifying. I was actually shot to death in one long sequence. I was only allowed to die once, though, just in case my face was recognized in the cutting room as having been shot *again*, in which case the whole scene – an expensive footage of film – would have had to be trashed. I remembered the day when one of the continuity staff shouted, 'Hey! You're already dead!' pointing out an extra who had been shot the day before in a close-up scene. He was sheepishly invited off the location. There goes the old myth that all Orientals look alike, I thought.

After several weeks of fighting for Goldfinger's armed force, I became battle weary, but at the end of the film shoot, I was able to earn a few hundred pounds, including an extra 10 pounds for getting killed!

Goldfinger was a seminal James Bond film. For the first time, Desmond Llewelyn's 'Q' introduced the inside of his secret weapons' laboratory, with his lethal pens, flame throwing gizmos and homing devices, not forgetting of course, his prized Aston Martin DB5. The gadget laden iconic car, with its bullet proof windshield, ejector seat, trailing smoke screens, oil slick, reversible number plates and mounted guns, was seen for the first time, and reappeared several times in subsequent 007 films, including *No Time to Die*, filmed in 2018 with a delayed release in 2021, due to the Corona virus pandemic. *Goldfinger* cost three million US dollars (about $25 million today) to produce, and grossed $125 million worldwide (a billion today).

I continued to work as one of Goldfinger's baddies in the interior scenes of Fort Knox, after so many of my fellow ninjas had been killed. I was a lucky survivor. There were fewer crowd scenes, so I was fortunate to observe the actors close up. I had never worked in a film with so much glossy violence, so much tension and so much fantasy, which is, of course, the stuff of cinema.

Even the ironic dialogue was unique. Goldfinger always addressed 007 as *'Mister* Bond'. Harold Sakata, an Olympic silver medalist weightlifter, who played Oddjob, a squat, slow moving gorilla of a man, would have killed James Bond, had he not been electrocuted. To me, it is one of the best *mano a mano* duels in any Bond film. So authentic was the fight, that Sean Connery had to be hospitalized with a back injury after shooting this scene.

Sakata was unfriendly and snobbish. Temporary stardom must have gone to his head. Sean, on the other hand, was cooperative, professional and courteous.

One evening after a late shoot, I was alone, waiting for a bus to take me to Uxbridge station, and from there, back home to Kensington on the Tube. A rather beat-up Jaguar saloon car stopped beside me. The window on the driver's side rolled down.

'Can I give you a lift?'

Sean Connery was offering me lift. I thanked him and told him I was going to Uxbridge station; he said he was sorry, but he was going in the opposite direction. Turning left, his car sped off.

I miss him still.

THE BEAUTY JUNGLE
CONTEST GIRL (U.S. title)
1964, The Rank Organisation, British

'Pinewood needs you to be a judge in an international beauty contest in Monte Carlo.'

When Mrs Warran, my agent, informed me of this new role, my first reaction was to pack my bags immediately and take the first train to Monaco. In those days, there weren't any direct flights.

But long before I stepped into the auditions office of Pinewood studios to report for duty, I knew that Monte Carlo was going to be right here in Buckinghamshire.

The assistant to the casting director briefed me on my role. I was to sit elegantly in my dinner jacket (I had been told to bring one along – an extra pound a day for that), in front of a raised platform, where the beauty contestants from various nations would be parading. I was to be one of the judges. For the next five days, I would be looking at bathing suit costumed contestants (the platform was built on a much higher level than the judge's seats below, a perfect angle for the camera, but hell for my neck), and behave as an impartial judge (whatever that meant) to decide who was going to be crowned the next 'Miss Globe'.

If the reader thinks that looking at leggy girls in swimsuits all day long is fun, think again. The platform was so high, I couldn't even see the contestant's faces. Craning my neck, looking up at a continuous parade of legs, trying to look like a professional judge for three full days, was much more challenging than running back and forth in a Chinese village escaping attacking Japanese aircraft, or waiting in a restaurant carrying a tray full of drinks and clearing tables, while avoiding to spill wine on customers.

On this particular shoot, I was one of only two Asians. The other was Miss China. The rest of the cast were all Europeans, supposedly French, this being Monte Carlo. Why was I chosen for this role, I asked Mrs Warran? This scene was meant to be an international event, she was told, and they were looking for a serious looking Asian. She sent them three photographs from her casting portfolio, and they selected mine. Apparently, with my horn-rimmed glasses, in their eyes I fitted their description of a 'serious' Asian. I was glad to get out of the typecast mold as an oriental peasant, waiter or soldier. How nice, I thought, to be perceived as a person with *gravitas* – my word, not hers.

The Beauty Jungle is a hackneyed story of a starry-eyed girl, a pretty typist from a small provincial town, played by Jeanette Scott, who graduates from local beauty pageants to winning the national 'Rose of England' beauty contest in London, and – surprise, surprise – loses her innocence along the way. The hustler who launches her is a journalist, who eventually falls in love with her. He is not very well portrayed by Ian Hendry.

The denouement ends up in Monte Carlo. So determined was she to win the Miss Globe crown, she invited one of the judges to her bedroom (not me, but Rex Carrick, a fading film star, who turns out to be gay, played well by Edmund Purdom), and then goes to bed with the contest's sponsor, the owner of a French cosmetics company.

In a supposedly tense moment, the votes are collected from the judges and given to me, and I then hand over the results to Edmund Purdom. But the contest is rigged and Miss Rose of England loses to Miss Peru. She returns to England, predictably world-weary and much disillusioned.

The *Radio Times* summed up *The Beauty Jungle* 'as a plot short on twists and real insight.' So much for the film that could have launched my film career, because I appeared on screen continuously for at least 15 minutes.

LORD JIM
1964, Columbia Pictures, Anglo-American

I was called up one morning by Mrs Warran who asked me if I would like to have a small acting role in a film, or a 'fillum', as she was in the habit of pronouncing it.

'Columbia is looking for a Southeast Asian actor, and seeing you come from that part of the world, I thought you might be interested,' she said, adding, 'the film is called *Lord Jim*, starring Peter O'Toole. They are going to shoot it on location, in Cambodia.'

This was a period in my life when I still fancied a career in the movies where the pay, I was told, was 'incredible'. The prospect of going to Cambodia was also exciting. I told her, that yes, I would very much like to work in a film as an actor rather than an extra, but how does one go about getting 'discovered', I asked.

That was when she arranged for me to have the screen test, on that disastrous day in February 1964 at Sound Stage 3, Shepperton Studios. I was so hopelessly naïve that I came up with a stage name, 'Teddy Tai', while dreaming of becoming a 'movie star'. The audition, if the reader recalls, was a total shambles. I discovered that I couldn't act to save my life. I instructed Mrs Warran never to use that name again. It was a formative moment for me when the assistant casting director told me to go back to my law studies.

The 'starring' role I missed out on being Waris (played by Juzo Itami, a famous Japanese actor) was an important character in the movie. Waris, the son of a tribal chief, becomes Lord Jim's (played by Peter O'Toole) best friend. Partly due to Jim's misjudgment, Waris gets killed during a skirmish with a band of white pirates, and Jim himself is executed by Waris' father.

The film is based on the novel by Joseph Conrad, about a disgraced sea captain, Lord Jim, accused of cowardice, who seeks to repair his damaged reputation by embarking on a perilous journey through the Far East, seeking redemption and salvation. The film turned out to be a vacuous adventure story.

According to a review by *The New York Times,* the film ' – misses out at being neither Conrad nor sheer entertainment cinema.'

Despite my screen test debacle, I still had a couple of day's work as an extra in *Lord Jim* on a studio backlot at Shepperton, cast as a half-naked Malay hawker on a small craft moored alongside Lord Jim's ship. I finally got to see Peter O'Toole in person. He looked down at me from the rails and his sky blue eyes held mine for a moment, as if to say: 'You missed out being my best friend Waris.'

WHERE THE SPIES ARE
1965, MGM, British

There is very little to relate about this insipid spy film, where I was cast as an Asian businessman waiting for my flight (to God knows where) at Orly airport in Paris (Elstree Studios).

I was the only Asian on the set. What I found interesting was that all the British extras, seasoned members of the Film Artistes' Association, had a strong dislike for the star of the film, David Niven. Some of them had worked with him in the past. I eavesdropped.

'He's the meanest man in the business.'
'Never lend him any money. He will never *pay you back.'*
'He has never offered anyone a cigarette or a cuppa tea.'
'He's bloody rude, a frigging snob, and …'

I had seen David Niven many times on the big screen since my childhood and had always enjoyed his stiff upper lip performances, so I was shocked by their comments. It was the first time I had ever heard an actor being openly criticised on the set. So much for British reserve.

Looking much aged and definitely past it, Niven played Dr Jason Love, who was recruited as a cold war spy to head a secret mission and penetrate Soviet operations in the Middle East. His mission was complicated by a female double agent, played by the beautiful French actress Francoise Dorleac, his 'sexy' love interest, here looking very much like his grand-daughter. Dorleac, sister of Catherine Deneuve, tragically died in a car accident on holiday in the Cote d'Azur in 1967, only 25 years old.

In my scene, both Niven and Dorleac are waiting to board their flight. Suddenly, an airplane on the tarmac is blown up by the bad guys (terrorists) and all the extras, including myself, were instructed to show signs of immediate shock, followed by sickening revulsion. Our cue for action was the sound of a mighty explosion.

Kaboom!

Thus ended another exciting day's work at Elstree.

YOU ONLY LIVE TWICE
1965, Eon Productions, British

Hoping to catch sight of Sean Connery in his fifth James Bond film, I was disappointed. I never saw him once.

I was required on the Pinewood set for only three days, cast as one of an army of Japanese mercenaries, dressed in yellow jump suits, operating an underground monorail hidden in a dormant volcano in Japan for Blofeld, the mad leader of SPECTRE, an evil organization, played by Donald Pleasence. This scarfaced tyrant was planning to start World War III from his volcano hideout in Japan, and almost succeeded, had it not been for the heroics of 007 who saved the world once again.

Except for the spectacular finale in a huge volcano crater set in Pinewood, the film was shot entirely in Japan. It was not Connery's best 007 film and he knew it, vowing never to play James Bond again.

The film was described by *The Chicago Sun* 'as heavy on gadgets, but weak on plotting,' and by *The New York Times* as 'shamelessly excessive'.

In all Bond films, the plumb roles go to the cunning villains, who are always trying to take over the world, and whose performances I enjoyed the most. Blofeld was one of my favourites.

A COUNTESS FROM HONG KONG
1966, Universal Studios, British

'All right, boys and girls,' shouted the assistant director in charge of the crowd scenes, 'you can all go home now!'

It was still the middle of the day, but the film's star, Marlon Brando, had unexpectedly walked off the set in a huff. He had just had a big argument with Charlie Chaplin, the film's original creator, script writer and director. Once 'Mr Brando walks', we were told, he's *gone* for the rest of the day.

It was such a crucial scene that the film could not be shot 'around' him, which is when an important actor, for one reason or another, is not present. As often happens in the movie business, shooting could continue in the absence of the star, but in this scene, no Brando, no film.

For the producers, tantrums from their big stars were not just expensive, but also upsetting for the co-stars, the directors and the crew. The shoot had been forced to come to a halt. I was sad to see Charlie Chaplin's crestfallen face. But for movie extras like us, it meant going home early and another day's work.

Unfeelingly, many British extras silently cheered Brando.

Mrs Warran had called a week earlier to offer me a job on this much awaited film. I had just sat my Criminal Law and Law of Tort exams, so the timing was perfect. She was putting together a team of Asian extras for a ship's crew and waiters, for a few weeks film shoot on board a liner (cruise ship) at Pinewood Studios, where half the story takes place. The movie was to star Oscar winners Marlon Brando and Sophia Loren, and would be directed by the legendary Charles Chaplin. Never before had Mrs Warran worked on a film with so much talent. Even the title, *A Countess from Hong Kong*, she said, was exciting.

The film turned out to be less than exciting. A countess (Sophia Loren) escapes Soviet Russia and winds up in Hong Kong as a penniless White Russian refugee, and is forced to become a dance-hall girl. Grabbing the chance to go to America, she stows away on a ship that is sailing for San Francisco. She hides in a suite occupied by an American diplomat (Marlon Brando).

The rest of the film was meant to be an amusing badinage between these two great actors. A weak script, an embarrassing attempt at bedroom farce, and an incongruous romantic story, could have conceivably been saved by Brando and Loren, had there been a grain of chemistry between them. There was none whatsoever.

It was reported that Marlon had said that he noticed black hairs growing out of Sophia's nose after their first kissing scene. Sophia, who loved her pasta, complained that all Signor Brando wanted to eat all day was ice-cream. Cast as a waiter (again!) in the ship's dining room where both stars were supposed to be having an intimate meal together, even I could clearly see that there was no rapport between them at all.

Sophia was stylish, cool and professional. During one break in the filming, she asked me for a light. Hands trembling, I clicked open my Zippo lighter and as I got close to her cigarette, she spread both hands around mine as if to protect the flame. It was a dramatically memorable moment for me. She had the longest fingers and the most beautiful hands I had ever seen. For her, it was simply getting her cigarette lit.

Marlon Brando was the most difficult actor I had ever worked with. He rudely ignored everyone around him. He never smiled and he never said thank you. In one scene, seated at the dining table with Sophia Loren, dressed in his black 'tuxedo', he must have taken umbrage at something Chaplin had said. He angrily threw down his napkin, rose from the table, and left abruptly. Sophia remained seated, calm and composed, without blinking an eyelid.

Despite Charlie Chaplin's calm professionalism, I could see that this film wasn't going to work. He was completely out of touch with modern reality. When the palm court orchestra struck up their ballroom number during the awkward dance scenes between Brando and Loren, Chaplin announced to no one in particular that the music reminded him of San Francisco in the Thirties.* But this was Britain 1966. All one heard in the streets of London were *'Eleanor Rigby', 'Day Tripper'* and *'I Can't Get No Satisfaction'.*

I liked Chaplin. He was just as much a great teacher as he was a film actor. When he saw us waiters with our trays of food and drink walking straight across the ship's ballroom, he called us over, grabbed a tray, and enthusiastically gave us a demonstration on how to sway back and forth uneasily across the deck's floor, teaching us how to keep our balance in the middle of a storm over the Pacific Ocean. Chaplin's style of direction was to act

---

* I could sense that Chaplin was homesick for America where he had happily lived and worked successfully for 40 years, before being cruelly informed by telegram in 1952 while he was on board a liner half way across the Atlantic, that his visa had not been renewed by the US government for being a communist sympathiser. He never returned, nor lived or worked there again, except briefly in 1972 to receive an Honorary Oscar award, which he accepted with tears in his eyes.

out each scene in great detail with his stars, down to their facial expressions and arm movements. This was the first time that a film director went out of his way to direct a lowly extra like myself. Marlon Brando, however, did not like to be taught.

I sympathized with Chaplin. He put his entire heart and soul into the production. He even cast himself in a cameo role as an old ship's steward. But the critics on both sides of the Atlantic agreed that the film was a sad failure. The picture that I worked in for more than a week, expecting it to be one of the greatest films of the decade, turned out to be a comedy without laughs, and a romance without feeling. *TIME* magazine unmercifully suggested that it was time for Chaplin to retire.

Implausibly, the film's theme music, '*This is My Song*', the instrumental backing to many of the romantic scenes, and a vocal rendition by Petula Clark as a pop single, became a global hit. Both song and lyrics were beautifully composed by Charles Chaplin.

THE NAKED RUNNER
1966, Warner Brothers, American

The first time I saw Frank Sinatra in the flesh was not on stage in a concert hall, like most of his fans. It was in the summer of 1966 on the film set of *The Naked Runner* in Pinewood Studios. His big hit that year was a corny song called '*Strangers in the Night*'. I saw him again in 1990, performing live at the London Arena, where he sang a selection of his best numbers. By popular demand, he also sang '*Strangers in the Night*', but not before commenting, 'Boy, do I hate this song!' I couldn't have agreed with him more.

I have to admit that I was somewhat star struck when I learned from Mrs Warran that Sinatra would be making a film in England. I was looking forward to seeing the pop music idol of my teens in person. During my Eltham College days, I use to sing along to his swinging numbers, like '*Anything Goes*' and '*You Make me Feel so Young*', on the radio. At the time, he was the epitome of cool, and no other popular singer could match his jaunty style of singing. A tuneful Cole Porter number, with a jazzy brass backing by Nelson Riddle, would always lift my spirits.

When I presented him with one of his music album sleeves for an autograph, he looked at me with his penetrating blue eyes, got out a cheap biro pen from his pocket, and signed it. He then said, 'Thank you, *sir*.' He was polite, gentlemanly, and did not act at all like the youthful swinger that used to get my fingers snapping at school. In his crisp grey suit, he looked more like a rich and successful middle-aged American businessman or politician, the kinds I used to serve at Simpson or meet at diplomatic cocktail parties.

The first thing that struck me when I first started work as a film extra was the familiar face of a film star that I'd seen on the screen so many times, larger than life, almost as if I knew that person already. Seeing Sinatra for the first time was one of those moments. 'Hi Frank, how've you been?' I felt like asking.

Sinatra was in town to star in a film about espionage, the movie flavour of the sixties, no doubt due to the worldwide appeal of James Bond. But *The Naked Runner* was not about fast cars, explosions and glamorous female spies. It was serious, but not serious enough. An American furniture designer (Sinatra) is on a business trip in Leipzig, East Germany, when his son is kidnapped. He is blackmailed into an assassination plot by MI6 to secure his son's freedom. It's old hat stuff. An honourable man is slowly being corrupted to perform a dastardly act.

Sinatra's performance was solid, and although he played his distraught role well, he looked old and tired, when he could have been a tad more heroic.

My role? An equally tired traveller at Leipzig airport.

NOBODY RUNS FOREVER
THE HIGH COMMISSIONER (US title)
1968, The Rank Organisation, British

Just in case the reader thinks that *Nobody Runs Forever* is a sequel to *The Naked Runner*, think again. The 'runner' in this film happened to be the Australian High Commissioner to the UK, played by Christopher Plummer, who is about to be arrested for murder. The cop, who has come all the way from Sydney, is played by Rod Taylor. But the tables are turned halfway through the story, and the Aussie cop becomes the bodyguard to the very man he was supposed to arrest. The film, a formulaic political thriller, has its fair share of assassination attempts, bomb explosions and mysterious intrigues, with the complicated participation of the High Commissioner's attractively mature wife (Lili Palmer), his pretty but not-so-efficient secretary (Camilla Sparv), and the needlessly sexy boss of an assassination ring (Daliah Lavi), all of whom are woven into the story to provide more sex scenes. To sum up, the film is a big ho-hum.

I was cast as the Chinese ambassador, attending a cocktail party on Australia Day, at the envoy's residence. A few days before the shoot, I was directed to Bermans, theatrical outfitters, in Soho, to get suitably kitted out. A grey Nehru suit was selected for me. Unfortunately, it was uncomfortably tight and extremely short in the legs, because it had recently been tailored for Woody Allen who had played the idiot son of James Bond in *Casino Royale*, a 007 send-up. Even though the suit was good enough for me as the movie ambassador, I didn't know if my father, who was the Thai ambassador to Italy at the time, would have approved.

Bermans intrigued me. Here were rows upon rows of clothes racks, with hundreds of costumes: for bandits, musketeers, soldiers, sailors, Elizabethan pirates, Arab sultans, Red Indians,

American cowboys, Roman soldiers, Nazi officers, RAF pilots, Spanish bullfighters, Chinese mandarins, Indian maharajas – you name it. That day, Dirk Bogarde was walking alongside one of the clothes racks, maybe three feet away from me, looking for a costume. Without even glancing up, he walked straight passed me, and theatrically pushed me aside with his delicate hand. Dirk Bogarde was doing his Marlon Brando bit.

With my Chinese ambassador's suit, I appeared on cue at the Australian diplomatic cocktail party, quite near Daliah Lavi, who swished passed me, in a close-up shot that lasted a few seconds, and then for another ten minutes, next to Christopher Plummer and Lilli Palmer, who were talking to each other. Although I was to work on a few more feature film productions in England, it was the last time I was recognisably visible on the big screen.

THE MOST DANGEROUS MAN IN THE WORLD
THE CHAIRMAN (US title)
1968, Twentieth Century Fox, American

Another cliché espionage film. Under pressure from the Pentagon, an American scientist, Dr Hathaway (Gregory Peck), is sent to Red China to steal the formula for a newly developed agricultural enzyme. He crosses into China from Hong Kong, and meets up with an old Chinese college friend, a scientist, who has developed this new formula and will help him take it out of the country for the 'benefit of mankind'. In the course of this dangerous mission, Hathaway is caught up with the Red Guards and the Cultural Revolution.

I was cast as one of hundreds of young Red Guard revolutionaries who were violently overtaking a village.

I asked Mrs Warran if my Italian wife, Manuela, could be in the film with me, since I learned it was going to be a huge crowd scene. When Mrs Warran agreed, Manuela was thrilled. She really wanted to see a film being shot. She dyed her hair jet black, and with heavy application of eye-liner, her brown eyes were made to look Oriental. Dressed in a Red Guard black cotton pajama suit complete with cloth cap and red star, and given her small stature and light olive-toned skin, she easily passed as Chinese in a crowd. On 'action!' we joined dozens and dozens of yelling Red Guard extras in the burning of books, by throwing them onto a huge bonfire in the village square. Manuela threw a book onto someone's head by mistake, but no-one seemed to notice. It was a night scene, and such was the melee, the wild mob were really getting into the swing of the action.

The scenes of violence went on for three days. It was during one of the tea breaks when a Chinese extra stared rudely at Manuela across the table.

'*You not look Chinese!*' he said.

'She's half Chinese, half *ang-moh*,' Cantonese for a white person. I lied to him, just to keep him quiet. I also told him to mind his own business.

But he wasn't convinced. '*I know you not Chinese!*' He repeated this several times.

We were called back on set and we never saw him again.

His comments made me think. Was he a racist trying to keep the Han race pure, or was he concerned about the integrity of the film? My conclusion was that he was just a jackass.

★ ★ ★ ★

It was the end of Trinity Term. I had just sat my Bar Final Exams, and was preparing to get called at Middle Temple on the last Thursday of July, 1968.

I informed Mrs Warran that on certain critical dates in 1968, (with a few exceptional windows for a one day shoot), I would not be able to accept any further commitments. I told her that

I was planning to return to Thailand in 1969, and thanked her for being my agent for the last ten years.

Thus in 1968 I ended up doing one day gigs in 3 British films: the first being in *The Virgin Soldiers,* starring Hywel Bennet and Lynn Redgrave. In it I played a Malay National Liberation Army freedom fighter, blowing up a train transporting British soldiers, during what the Colonial Office euphemistically called the 'Malayan Emergency', but was in fact Malaya's bloody war of independence in 1960. In the second film, *The Mind of Mr Soames,* starring Terence Stamp, I played a Japanese guest surgeon invited to attend a revolutionary brain operation, on a man who had been in a coma for 30 years.

The third – and the last – before departing Britain, the country where I had lived for 23 years, was *The Best House in London,* an allegorically fitting end to my life as a student and part-time worker in the city where I was born. My final role was a profligate Chinese customer, in a licensed brothel during the Victorian era, where I witnessed Joanna Petet's bare breasts.

CHAPTER NINE

GOODBYE JOBS, HELLO CAREER

'Isn't it about time you had a career?'

These were almost the first words my father said to me after we had not seen each other for almost four years. It was August 1969. I had just landed in Bangkok on a rather tiring flight from London. I couldn't tell my father that I was about to embark on *three* careers, because I didn't know that myself.

My First Career

My carefully edited papers were flying everywhere. Pages three to ten had just flown out of the window. I bolted down the stairs and into the street to retrieve them, but it was too late. My papers ended up lying in the wet gutter of Sanamchai Road, a soggy mess. It was my first experience with the monsoon rains after twenty years. It was also my first week at the press office, the Information Department of the foreign office, and my assignment was to edit and compile the foreign minister's speeches into a book for posterity.

I had followed my father's footsteps as a career diplomat

and I had just joined the Thai Ministry of Foreign Affairs as Third Secretary.

The press office was located in a huge high-ceilinged ballroom on the first floor of the Saranrom Palace, built in 1866 for King Rama V's family until 1885, when it was turned over to the Ministry of Foreign Affairs.*

The office space was surreal. Huge casement windows opened up to the ancient temples and pagodas of the Grand Palace across the road, with an ever changing vista of golden spires and carved finials, at times shimmering in the midday sun, at others in dramatic profile during a monsoon rainstorm. It was one of the most spectacular office views in Bangkok.

There were twenty to thirty heavy teak desks spread across this palatial space, with several huge ceiling fans spinning their large blades across the room, creating a force of wind that would have sent important documents flying out of the window, had they not been weighted down by large pebbles. The little stone that someone had kindly given me to hold down my work was a hopelessly inadequate paperweight. I was outdone by my co-workers who had bigger and better pebbles. The area was not air conditioned. Apart from the sound of the fan's swirling blades and the clickety-clack of typewriters, the office was eerily quiet, and the staff spoke to each other in low monotones. It was also very hot. There were no telephones on the desks. It didn't have the frenzy of activity that one would have associated with a press office.

A group of Third Secretary level officials were all busy at their assignments. I was surrounded by a bunch of highly qualified people. There was Dr Tej Bunnag, a PhD from Cambridge U., doing his own typing for most of the day; and then there was Nid

---

* Now located in a modern building complex in Sri Ayudhya Road since 1999.

Pibulsonggram, an Ivy League Masters Graduate in diplomacy from America, diligently pushing a pen; and many other great minds. Then there was me, with the equivalent to a lowly bachelor's degree. I was relegated to reading and editing, and was given a red pencil to do the job. For the first week I didn't even have my own desk.

It was not demanding in terms of what I had to do, but it was boring and badly paid. We were all overqualified and underpaid. My problem was exacerbated by the fact that my father was also everybody's boss; he held the ministry's highest non-political position, the Permanent Secretary at the time. I lasted less than 6 months.

I admired my colleagues' determination and persistence. I realised that I just didn't have what it took to become a professional Thai civil servant. Tej and Nid made brilliant careers in the ministry and both became Ambassadors and Permanent Secretaries. I needed work that grabbed me, not just intellectually, but also my heart and soul. This one didn't.*

Thus ended my first career.

My Second Career

My next career move surprised everyone, including myself.

Even though I had hardly ever lived in Thailand, I never stopped calling Thailand 'home'. It was where my family came from, it was the way I was brought up, and it was the criterion upon which I judged myself.

Yet I felt more English than Thai. My first language, my education, my taste in the arts and literature, my moral standards, my thought processes, even my wardrobe, and especially my

---

* I briefly returned to the ministry 38 years later, in 2007, as Nid's Media Adviser when he became Foreign Minister.

preference for thick cut orange marmalade on toast at breakfast, were English. *Twelve x twelve is one hundred forty-four.* I have no idea what the multiplication table is in Thai. The true test to find out a polyglot's first language is the language that he or she subconsciously and immediately blurts out to recite the multiplication table.

Imagine the pleasant surprise when I received a *telegram from an Englishman* requesting an interview, after I had sent in an application for a job in an advertising agency as an English language copywriter, placed in the classified section of the *Bangkok Post*. It felt like I was back in England again.

His name was David Lander. He was the manager of Diethelm Advertising, a subsidiary of a Swiss trading company, and at the time Thailand's largest distributor of imported brands. Long haired and granny glasses à la John Lennon, and dressed as if he had just stepped out of a man's shop on Carnaby Street, he gave me the wrong impression at first. I soon discovered that underneath his extraordinary suit, there was an intellectual, with a highly creative and slightly mad brain. And very simpatico. He had specialised in Icelandic language and literature at university, and had been trained in marketing by Unilever UK. After less than three years living in Thailand, he had learned to speak and write Thai fluently. He was the only *farang** who knew more Royal vocabulary than many Thais. Royal Thai is totally different from the language spoken by the masses. He was particularly proud of his knowledge of Royal words that describe the intimate parts of the body, which nobody knew, not even Royalty themselves.

David interviewed me over lunch at the An-An Club, and we hit it off immediately. He also offered me five times the salary

---

* Thai for a Westerner, from *ferenghi*, Farsi for a person from Europe, which in turn came from francais, the French, who were in Persia in the 17th century.

that I was earning at the Ministry. It was quite a punt really, considering I knew nothing about the advertising business. I admitted to him that I was a late comer, and that I was willing to put in long hours to learn the business. It didn't seem to matter to him that I didn't have a proper CV. He was more interested in my eclectic life experiences. The law taught me how to write, which in turn gave me the opportunity to work in the agency as a copywriter. That was fine. The fact that I had worked in various trades and professions in Britain, he assured me, would serve me well in the creative process required in advertising. 'All grist for the mill', he said.

David was also an excellent teacher and bless him, he had great faith in me. Within less than a year, thanks to him, I was able to hold my own in the dynamics of advertising. For years I had been adrift for too long in a sea of jobs; I finally found my moorings, with a career that was to continue for the next twenty four years, providing me with much needed psychological stability.

When I told my father that I was forsaking what (he had hoped) could have been a brilliant career in diplomacy, he was understandably disappointed, but he wished me well in my newly found *métier*. He was happy for me. He expressed a bit of concern though, when I joined an advertising agency by the name of Ling-McCann-Erickson a year later.

'Hmm, let me see now. A *Chinese-Scots-Swedish* joint-venture,' he said, looking at me quizzically, 'you'll never make any money with them.' He seemed a bit more relieved when I moved to another agency by the name of Ogilvy & Mather two years later.

'Only *one* Scotsman involved,' he said. 'Now, that's an improvement!'

★ ★ ★ ★

My career in advertising turned out to be an exciting journey. I started off as a junior copywriter, progressed to managing clients' brands, then went on to become creative director, and finally got kicked upstairs to run the company. The fun part of the business for me had been creating the ads, and the rewarding part was selling them successfully to a client. Now, running the company wasn't half as much fun.

'Are you the one that writes the ads?' was often asked of me by clients in my early days in advertising, when it was my turn to present the work as part of a team's presentation by the agency. After less than 10 years in the business, I owned my own advertising agency, doing precisely what I enjoyed doing most: creating the ads and selling them myself. On my business card I had the twin position of Managing Director and Creative Director.

Advertising can be a very stressful business. Its very existence lives and dies by the accounts the agency wins and loses. Win an important account in a competitive pitch and your reputation – your own *personal* one, as well as the agency's – rides high in the marketplace. Suddenly you're 'hot', as they say in the business; you find yourself on a roll and in demand. Lose an account, and it could snowball into a losing streak, when staff are laid off, followed by client defections, to the point of even spelling the death of the agency. There is always an inherent fear of losing a big account which can sometimes hang over the entire agency like a guillotine, seriously undermining staff morale.

An advertising career often meant changing agencies every two or three years, especially creative talent who were continually looking for fresher pastures, but once you reached top management, be prepared to spend long hours at the office. I often arrived home well after ten o'clock at night, when my little daughter was already fast asleep. At one point, I suffered from peptic ulcer, which turned out to be the *mildest* form of illness endemic in the business. An American study compared the health of executives in manufacturing, banking, and advertising and found that ad people showed up the worst, including 'high blood pressure, organic heart and prostate problems, and abnormal blood counts'.* Many senior ad executives quit under pressure long before they reach forty.

Advertising is a people business and as they say in America, its assets go up and down the elevators. An agency's stability depends not only on the people who run it but also on the people who deliver the ads. Lose your creative director, and like a restaurant that loses its chef, you lose your customers.

Only those in the business know how difficult it can be to produce an ad: the anguish of rejected ideas, the futility of burning the midnight oil, after it is discovered that the ad that had finally appeared in print or on TV has met with disapproval from the public, or from the brand's stockholders, or sometimes the press, and even the wife of the client's chairman, as happened to me once.

★ ★ ★ ★

There was another David who was to become a great influence in my career. I was proud to have worked for a good eight years for David Ogilvy, the doyen of advertising. For those who are not familiar with the ad business, David Ogilvy was a Brit who went over to America before the war and in 1948 founded Ogilvy & Mather, a stylish ad agency in New York. By the fifties he had become an advertising legend, and in this millennium he was described as the 'Original Mad Man'. When I joined his company in the seventies, his agency had become a powerhouse in the international world of advertising.

In his early days in Madison Avenue, he created print ads for classic British brands. Ogilvy's most famous headline in those days was for Rolls Royce: *At 60 miles an hour the loudest*

---

* *The Mirror Makers*, Stephen Fox, William Morrow, 1984, p209.

noise in this new Rolls Royce comes from the electric clock.' When the chief engineer at the Derby workshop read the ad, he said disappointingly, 'We've got to do something about that damned clock!' In another one of Ogilvy's headlines, he used the word *'obsolete'* and discovered 43 percent of consumers didn't understand what it meant, and in another headline he used the word *'ineffable'*, and admitted he didn't know what it meant himself! He made his reputation for being a creative genius and once measured his IQ; he expected a genius score of 145 and disappointingly discovered it was a low 96, appropriate, he said, for 'ditch diggers'.

David is full of amusing stories about his early days in advertising and the clients he worked for.*

I met David in April 1978 when he visited his agency in Bangkok where I was working at the time. In his 60s, he still retained his classic film-star-good-looks (Leslie Howard), and was very much the quintessential British patrician, with the right accent to match. I was charged with looking after his welfare – like making sure he was safe and sound back at his hotel every night – as well as for his social activities. I had arranged a traditional Thai dinner party for him in the tropical gardens of the Siam Society, and an important part of the evening was a classical Thai dance performance. When the music started, he started to nod off. As he was sitting in the front row, nobody noticed. He was fast asleep throughout the show; a combination of jet lag and the heat must have taken its toll. I offered to help him remove his jacket, but he refused. I later found out he was trying to hide a middle-aged paunch that he had developed over the years. Later, while we were having dinner, a group of fifteen young Thai girls in tight jeans and t-shirts filed past our tables,

---

* David has written many books on advertising. He presented me with a copy of his most recent book on his memoirs, *Blood, Brains & Beer*, on my birthday during his Thai visit.

thanking us and bidding their farewells with a graceful *wai,* the Thai way of greeting and saying goodbye, bowing slightly, with their palms together in a prayer-like gesture.

Now wide awake, David asked me enthusiastically, 'Teddy, who are these fantastic young women? Why didn't you introduce them to me earlier?'

I told him that indeed, I did introduce them to him at the very start of the evening while I was emceeing the event. 'They were the dancers that performed for you, but you were fast asleep,' I told him. In their richly decorated silk costumes and gold headdresses, and their heavy makeup and cake eyeliner, the girls who paraded in front of us now looked totally unrecognisable.

Although David was obviously not a devotee of Thai classical dance, he was a well-travelled sophisticate. When he showed interest in the Thai culture, I offered to accompany him and his delightful wife Herta on a day's trip to the ancient capital of Ayudhya. At one point during our stroll on the banks of the river just outside Ayudhya, we came upon a festive procession with the participation of the whole village, including saffron robed monks, rice farmers and their families, school children and their teachers; among the followers were some pretty teenaged girls dancing to the music of a small band that led the parade. This time David was fully awake. The monks blessed David and Herta as they passed us by. We had a memorable day together.

David had many questions to ask me about the Thai culture which I happily answered. He also had a curious habit of asking some questions that were difficult to answer because they had nothing whatsoever to do with what we had been talking about before then. One evening as I accompanied him back to his hotel in the back of the car after a dinner party, he wanted to know where I got the red silk tie I was wearing. Red was his favourite colour.

After he left Thailand, I never saw David again. A few years later he did call me from Touffou, his twelfth-century chateau in France where he had retired, to persuade me not to leave the company. He had heard that McCann-Erickson had been in touch with me. They were looking for a manager to run their Thai operation.

'I implore you not to leave us,' he said. 'McCann is a terrible agency. They have a poor creative reputation and they don't look after their people.'

I was deeply touched. Although he was no longer running Ogilvy & Mather, he became Worldwide Creative Head, and continued to be active in the councils of the company he founded, bombarding the management in New York with ideas and comments, as well as honouring his creative staff around the world with the David Ogilvy Award. I was one of the recipients.

In 1955 he had turned down an offer to merge with McCann Erickson, at a time when O & M was still a fledgling agency. I decided not to join McCann.

Sadly, I lost both of the Davids who had encouraged and mentored me so much in my second career. David Lander died in 1994, and David Ogilvy in 1999.

★ ★ ★ ★

In the early years of the eighties, a feeling of restlessness had begun to seep into my work. I was running a small company – admittedly my own – but I just couldn't make it into the big time. Only small accounts were being offered to the agency. As a 'boutique' shop – a polite word for small but creative – Meridian was never going to reach the heights of an international agency. It was fun winning some small products from the big players, but pitching for multinational brands against giants like JW Thompson, Saatchi & Saatchi, and Leo Burnett was difficult, as I had neither their competitive power nor their international cachet.

Meridian had a good creative reputation in the local market though. In 1981 we won the prestigious International Clio Award in New York (the ad industry's Oscar) for a print campaign for Jim Thompson Thai Silk. Our profile in the Thai media was also good. We were often mistaken for a big player by locals not involved in the business – 'Is Leo Burnett as big as Meridian?' a Thai politician once asked the manager of Leo Burnett, much to my delight and to the latter's chagrin, but the reality was that Leo Burnett – famous for its macho Marlboro cowboy cigarette campaign around the world – was a global giant headquartered in Chicago, while we were a small fish in what was already a small pond.

When Young & Rubicam, in early 1984 the largest advertising agency in the world, and Japan's giant Dentsu, the world's second largest, offered me the task of launching their new joint-venture called Dentsu Young & Rubicam (DYR) in Thailand, I leapt at this unique opportunity.

During the rest of that year, I was busy preparing for the December launch of the first global American-Japanese advertising agency in Bangkok. It involved three major operations: getting a local team together; becoming acquainted with the management of both the New York and the Tokyo head offices; and lastly, and most important of all, learning how to combine the working cultures of America and Thailand, which were known to me, with that of Japan, so far still unfamiliar.

Putting a local team together was the easy bit. The news that I was setting up a new multicultural agency had spread through the marketplace; I hired a core team of like-minded people who found the challenge equally inspiring. My most important appointment was Garry Cooper, a tall, highly artistic and sensitive Australian, and a tennis champ, as creative director. Like me, he was quite sanguine about DYR's chances of success. He shared my mission. We hit it off immediately. Nearly 40 years on, we are still in close contact with each other.

The next stage involved two months of travel. I was to meet the American CEO in New York and the Japanese *Daitoryo* in Tokyo. It would be interesting to observe the cultural differences between the two companies.

★ ★ ★ ★

My initiation into the corporate rituals, the professional disciplines and the creative skills of Madison Avenue started in 1976. It was my first visit to New York, at that time the Mecca of advertising, where I had attended an Ogilvy & Mather training program for young executives from the company's offices around the world. After many – or multiple, to use a more contemporary word – corporate visits to New York over the years, I had become an aficionado of this great city. On every visit since, I have been infected by its frenetic energy, Yankee dynamism and cultural diversity.

Arriving on a hot and humid July day, New York did not disappoint. *Just like the movies,* I thought to myself.

My first impression was its sheer *size*. Everything in New York is overpowering: the neck aching skyscrapers towering above the clouds; thousands of joggers, bicyclists and gas guzzlers fighting for space on the broad avenues; giant gantries stretching their cranes across acres of construction sites; Big Man's Shops for the oversized, and the super-sonic volume of noise. *King-size* and *queen-size*, I was to discover, are standard fare in America. The Grand Central Terminal really is *grand*, in fact the grandest train station in the world. And then there's Central Park, 843 acres of woods, conservatories and grassland, twice the size of Hyde Park, and six times the size of Monaco.

Whenever I needed to escape the chaos of Manhattan, I headed for the most imposing building on Fifth Avenue, the Beaux Arts New York Public Library, guarded by two giant stone lions. Its vast reading room is an oasis of calm, and many great writers sought refuge and conducted their research here, among them E.L. Doctorow, Tom Wolfe, Norman Mailer and John Updike. The Russian revolutionary Leon Trotsky, spent some time here before the Soviets took over his country in 1917. It must be the only public building in the United States that was open to Communists and Capitalists alike.

Like no other city on earth, there is the display of performing arts acted out on the streets of New York every day. Music, rock and classical, performed by virtuosos, trios and choirs. Dance, hip hop, bebop. Kilted Scots troubadours, cowboy hatted country guitarists and long haired violin soloists. Bach arias, Broadway hits and rhythmic salsa. They are all performed here, by ebullient musicians blowing, plucking, fiddling, grinding, stomping and belting their hearts out on the sidewalks. On my last visit, rap artistes attracted the biggest crowds. The gifted buskers of New York were seemingly playing for *pleasure,* as if being paid for their efforts was secondary.

On any given day in New York expect to run into Israeli jewellers, Hungarian waiters, Thai tattoo artists, Peruvian doormen, Russian ballet teachers, Vietnamese manicurists, and the occasional English lord. Taxi drivers in the 90s were newly arrived Afghans, and in 2014, Ukrainians who had arrived after the first Russian attack on their country. Now, in the 2020s, their younger brethren are back in the driving seats in larger numbers, happy to escape from the hardships of their war torn countries, and grateful to be gainfully employed in America.

Manhattan is a paradise for eavesdroppers. Each day was a field day for me.

'*La Quinta Strada. Che meraviglia!'* Italian tourists in awe of the 'marvels' of Fifth Avenue.

'*Do you really think that modern American culture depends on the vigour and drive of our youth…'* a long pause, '*… or is the* *basic architecture of American life based on the traditions of our forefathers?'* There is no shortage of intellectuals in New York.

Most eavesdrops were about personal problems, marital confidences, emotional outbursts, or just down-to-earth gossip.

'You're not gonna believe this but Maury told me the other day that…'

'Like, I like him, but, like, does he really like me?'

'So I said to her, do you really have to do this? I wouldn't, would you?'

On my first visit in the seventies, New York was bankrupt and in decline: potholed streets, panhandlers and pickpockets on every street corner; bums, drunks and acid-heads sprawled all over the sidewalks at night, and unsightly graffiti thickly sprayed on the buildings and subways. The high level of crime earned New York the moniker 'Fear City'. Then came the nineties, when New York regained its former glory of the fifties, thanks to the joint endeavours of its denizens, together with a determined local government and a series of shrewd mayors. The Big Apple was back, a cleaner and safer city, with renewed energy. And richer.

★ ★ ★ ★

It was a sunny autumnal day in September 1984 when I arrived in New York for my meetings with Young & Rubicam's top brass. I was put up at the Helmsley Palace Hotel (it has today become the Lotte New York Palace Hotel) for two weeks, a scenic walk to the Y & R head office on 285 Madison Avenue. Once I got past the brutally unwelcoming immigration and customs officials at JFK airport, every American I met after that was the friendliest 'folk' on earth. With one blatant exception though.

Every morning, as I was leaving the lobby of the hotel to proceed to the office, I rubbed shoulders with a heavily made-up lady of a certain age, who behaved as if she owned the place. Reeking of Chanel No. 5, she rudely brushed past me, and indeed every other guest who happened to be in her way, as she haughtily proceeded to her stretch Mercedes limo at the hotel's entrance. She gave the appearance of an aging movie star, à la Gloria Swanson, but was not half as attractive. I was told by Pierre, the affable concierge (all New York hotels' concierges seemed to be called 'Pierre') that her name was Leona, the wife of old Mr Harry Helmsley, and that she was very much *the owner of the hotel*. She was self-styled as the 'Queen of Helmsley Palace'.

What Pierre didn't tell me was that she was also known by New Yorkers as the 'Queen of Mean'. She was brutal to her staff and used to fire them right in front of guests. Infamous for saying 'Only the little people pay taxes,' she went to prison for federal income tax evasion in 1989.

Mary-Alice Kennedy was my delightful guide through the corridors of power at 285 Mad Ave, and attended to my every need. She warmly welcomed me to New York, part of which consisted of tickets to the Broadway show *Hurlyburly*.* She was head of personnel (today called 'human resources') and through her efficient office, she set up appointments for me to meet all the key players at Young & Rubicam.

'Momentarily', was Mary-Alice's favourite word, American for 'any time now', which she would declare as we got closer to the time for my next appointment. The first time she used this word with me, was when I looked out of her office window and saw a small bank of grey clouds ominously creeping across the Manhattan skyline. I had asked her whether it was going to rain or not.

I have always been entranced by the American language. Since my first visit to America ('*the States*') in 1976, I was slowly getting used to words that I hadn't heard since I left the Overseas

---

* A comedy on changing American social mores, starring Harvey Keitel, William Hurt and Sigourney Weaver, who stripped down to her waist in one scene.

School in Rome. Two of my *favourite* New York words: *'block'* and *'sidewalk'*. (*'Y & R is 10 blocks down Madison Avenue on the same sidewalk from your hotel'*, I was told, and what a great walk it was too!)

Words that *confuse*: *'bill'* means banknote, and at a restaurant when I asked for the bill, I should have said the *'check'*. Words that *amuse* and always get a laugh at car dealers: a car bonnet in American is a *'hood'*, a car boot a *'trunk'*, a car silencer is a *'muffler'*, a car wing is a *'fender'*, and you leave your car at the *'parking lot'*, not the car park. (*'Oh my, you British, you use such cute words for auto parts!'* So said a Ford car salesman to me once when I leased a Thunderbird.)

Another diverting American term, the *'body shop'*, has nothing to do with the human anatomy, nor a retailer of beauty care products, but a *garage* where repairs to the bodywork of cars are carried out.

My most important appointment was with Ed Ney, Chairman and CEO, an iconic name in Madison Avenue. I felt comfortable with him right away, even before we shook hands. He got up from his desk to greet me.

'I'm so pleased to meet our man in Thailand,' he said.

Elegantly suited, Ed was a tall, handsome Ivy League American gentleman, greying at the temples, with a smooth smoky voice. He seated me comfortably in a sofa, while he sat elegantly sideways across an antique Hepplewhite chair, his long legs draped across its arms. There was a French impressionist painting hanging in his oak panelled office. After two minutes of a very pleasant exchange of small talk, I could tell that here was a leader who was genuinely interested in other people. He had also done his homework. He wanted to know what it was like being an ambassador's son. He showed an inordinate interest in the diplomatic service. We talked about a large variety of subjects for an hour, including our common admiration for David Ogilvy, a business rival in the fifties who had now become his dear friend, and my former boss. Mary Alice, who was waiting outside, told me that the meeting was only meant to be a short fifteen-minute courtesy visit.

I walked out of his office fired up with enthusiasm and the determination to make a success of DYR. I was drawn to the magnetic charm of this legendary Mad Man. In 1989 Ed was appointed American ambassador to Canada by US president George Bush.

★ ★ ★ ★

The next stop on my American familiarisation tour was a successful visit to the new DYR office in Los Angeles. This was my first visit to LA and Dorothy Delano, the office manager, was assigned to take care of me. She had a bubbly personality, and had this delightful American way of talking with an upward lilt at the end of each sentence, making a statement sound like a question.

'We want to make sure that your trip to LA is great? One that you'll remember forever?'

Once again I was given the VIP treatment, and put up at the famous Beverly Wilshire Hotel, opposite Rodeo Drive. It was the location for many Hollywood films, among them *Pretty Woman*, and where Steve McQueen and Warren Beatty had a penthouse in the seventies. The only celebrity staying in the hotel during the week I was there was Jacques Cousteau, the French underwater explorer and filmmaker. Every morning in the Pink Turtle café at breakfast time, he would hold court with his fawning young team in the coffee shop at the top of his voice *in French*, much to the consternation of all the other guests. I eavesdropped. I heard a stream of *'moi, moi',* a never ending *'moi';* it was all about him. As I was admirer of his work, I could have happily gone to his table to tell him how much I enjoyed his film *The Silent World*, but I decided against it.

'Filipino sir?' asked a cheeky Asian porter as he took me up in the lift to my room after I had checked-in. When it was established that we were both Thai I discovered that there were two other Thais working with him in the hotel lobby. I was given the royal treatment throughout my stay. Every morning, my shoes were beautifully polished and the *New York Times* was delivered promptly to my room. My rental car, all spick and span, was waiting for me in front of the hotel's entrance, accompanied by fawning bows and salutes before I got into the driving seat and drove off to the office.

I ended up paying out more tips than I have ever done in any other hotel I've stayed in.

'Let us know if there is anything you need,' my humble compatriots told me, as they surrounded me in the lobby. *'Anything'*, Sombat (not his real name) repeated, with a mischievous glint in his eyes. I let that pass.

One evening, as I was working on the next day's presentation in my room, Sombat knocked on my door. He wanted to know if I had ever been to bed with a *'dara Hollywood'* – a Hollywood star – and was very kindly prepared to arrange one for me. When I told him that only Jacqueline Bisset would do, and if he couldn't get her, he would be in serious trouble, he looked crestfallen and said that she was regrettably 'not in town that night' but *'mai ben rai'* – not to worry, he would find me someone 'much younger and more attractive'. I then told him angrily that it was shameful that a Thai should comport himself in this way, and that I would report him to the hotel's management the very next day. I never did, of course. But that probably explained the even *better* service that I was already receiving from his team for the rest of my stay.

★ ★ ★ ★

One pleasurable routine of mine whenever I went on a business trip in a foreign city was to hit the streets on foot after a long working day, to explore and discover the neighbourhood, which I did, as always, on my own. Typically, as I would often get lost, I would hail a cab to take me back to my hotel. I found myself looking forward to walking the beautifully manicured grass and pristine white pavements of Beverly Hills, which I could see from the window of my hotel room.

On my walking tours, I have always tried to blend in with the locals and dress accordingly. Nowadays, all over the world, it is the ubiquitous denim jeans, worn with a woollen jacket for the cold of winter, or a t-shirt in the heat of summer, that work every time on my urban promenades. It is a tribute to my successful attempts at assimilation with the locals that on the streets of Hong Kong, for example, I was often taken for a Cantonese; in Manila I was addressed in Tagalog; and in Tokyo, I was pleasantly mistaken, with my dark colouring, for a well-heeled Japanese, who could afford to ski in winter and live the outdoor life in summer. In cosmopolitan New York, blending in with the locals was easy. *Everyone* is a New Yorker.*

At last, dressed appropriately, here I was, about to tramp the streets of LA, the city I had long wanted to visit.** In 1866, Los Angeles was transformed from a tiny Spanish pueblo founded by 44 settlers from Mexico in 1781 to a small American town. The original Spanish colonial name was *El Pueblo de Nuestra Senora la Reina de Los Angeles de Porciuncula*, today often referred to as '*The City of Angels*', '*Tinseltown*' or '*La-La Land*'.

In the new town of Los Angeles citrus fruits were its main

---

* On my first trip to New York in 1976, though, I was asked by the Red Cap porter who helped carry my luggage to the taxi at JFK, whether I could speak English.

** Manuela and I lived a few months a year in LA between 2001 and 2004, and stayed with our daughter Malina who was working there as an architect.

produce, beans were grown in the fields of Beverly Hills, and there were large tracts of fig orchards in Hollywood. It wasn't until the introduction of the tramway in 1874, followed by an electric train system in 1895, that LA started to become a city. The first silent moving picture was shot here in 1910, and in 1913 Cecil B. de Mille produced the first Hollywood movie. America's showbiz capital was born.

Today, the amorphous sprawl of LA covers a vast area of more than 1,300 square kilometres, governed by 88 municipalities and connected by an intricate network of freeways. Old Mexican settlements like Pasadena, Gardena, Santa Monica, La Habra, Palos Verdes and Encino, names that evoke its Spanish colonial origins, integrate seamlessly with modern Anglo purlieus – Century City, Inglewood, Westwood, Brentwood, Sherman Oaks and MacArthur Park – resulting in a prosperous metropolitan merger that could only flourish in California. Today, LA is America's second largest city, and the nation's largest container port.

I crossed Wilshire Boulevard.* I lingered awhile at the most expensive car dealership in America; parked on the lot were dozens of Testa Rossa Ferraris, surrounded by salivating young men ready to shift their testosterone gears into overdrive. Walking up Rodeo Drive, an ostentatious street of fashion boutiques, I brushed past a covey of beautiful wannabe starlets and their aged sugar-daddy producers. One of them, I mused, could easily have been one of Jacqueline Bisset's stand-ins that Sombat was proposing to arrange for me. I made a note to return the following day to Giorgio to buy a bottle of their signature

---

* Marlboro might be the American spelling of Marlborough, but Wilshire is *not* the local spelling of Wiltshire, a county in SW England. The boulevard was named after Henry Gaylord Wilshire, a millionaire developer in 1895. You can imagine American spellings for Scarborough, Peterborough and the Duke of Marlborough!

perfume for Manuela. Their haughty sales personnel reminded me of my time at the Harrods' fragrance counter in the sixties.

Leaving behind the beaten track of the mega-rich shopping sidewalks, I wandered into the iconic palm-tree-lined drives and avenues of Beverly Hills, and followed my nose aimlessly, marvelling at the grandest residences I have ever seen this side of Versailles: a Victorian mansion competing with a Spanish castle, a Palladian villa slotted in between French palaces and five million dollar English cottages. The only audible sounds I heard on my stroll were the gentle swishing of sprinklers on the immaculate flowering lawns, and the whacks of tennis balls and rackets echoing in the distance. Otherwise it was eerily quiet and totally deserted. The garages were resplendent with Jags, Mercs and Rolls.

The Californian sun was starting to set on this idyllic and surreal motion picture nirvana. It was getting chilly. I found my way back to the pavement of a wide boulevard (Wilshire? Sunset? Beverly?) hoping to hail a cab. There wasn't a soul in sight. I was alone and truly lost.

As I was waiting in vain for a taxi, I realised why the pavements were spotless. *Absolutely no one walks on them.* Nobody in his right mind, I was later told, would even dream of walking the streets of LA, especially after dark. The unused sidewalks were clean enough to eat off. Not a single blade of grass was out of place, there were no footprint marks on the white pavement, and there was a total absence of dog poop and chewing gum. I surmised that there must be heavy prison sentences for offending dog owners and gum chewers.

Then it hit me, a mite too late perhaps, that in this city of automobiles where no one walks, why on earth would a taxi be roaming the streets in search of a fare, especially at night? It was a rude awakening.

In desperation, I decided to thumb a lift. But nobody stopped.

The cars just swished silently by. I even tried to flag down an approaching car with winking red lights, but it didn't stop either and just drove on.

'Hey you!'

I spun around quickly. A navy-blue uniformed policeman, big and burly, was getting out of the same car that had just passed me by and was now parked on the kerb a few metres ahead of me. I recognised from the American films I had seen that it was a police car. Its lights were blinking like crazy. He walked towards me at a deliberate pace. A pistol was packed in a holster and a pair of handcuffs was dangling from his belt. I didn't know whether I should have been relieved or alarmed.

'Whaddya doin' out here at this time of night? Lemme see your ID!' he shouted.

For a terrifying moment I lost my tongue. When I didn't answer, he asked me if I could speak English.

'I'm lost and I don't have my passport with me. I'm trying to flag down a taxi,' I finally blurted out weakly.

'*Taxi?*' He looked at me as if I was some form of alien from Mars. It would have been easier for him if I actually *did* come from outer space. He probably would have simply shot me on the spot.

'*Taxi?*' he repeated, shaking his head in disbelief, not to me, but to his younger partner who had just joined him. They went into a huddle out of earshot, deciding what to do with me. I tried eavesdropping. The only words I could just make out were '… a likely story…'

'You'd better come with us to the station …' He started to unhook the handcuffs.

'Why are you arresting me?' I asked plaintively. 'I haven't done anything wrong!'

'You're a vagrant without ID. *It's the law!*' said his partner.

I told them, this time more forcefully, that I'm a visitor and *not* a vagrant, that I'd lost my way, and that I could produce identification once I was back in my hotel.

'Hotel?' He looked at me, with an incredulous look. *'Hotel? What hotel?'* He had the annoying habit of picking up the last word of what a person had just said, and keep on repeating it.

I was getting bored with his repetitive monosyllables and told them both that my 'temporary home in LA was the Beverly Wilshire.'

There was a sudden volte-face in both their tone and manner, followed by a profusion of 'Sirs' and much apologising, after they discovered where I was staying.

They explained that with all the illegal immigrants on the streets nowadays, you couldn't be too careful. They offered to take me back to my hotel (*sir*), but not before I promised them never to walk the streets of LA at night again (*more sirs*).

Nathan, the uniformed doorman of the Beverly Wilshire, was very impressed when he saw the police open the car door and politely let me out; he swung back the front portals of the hotel for me with a flourish and a salute. 'You're the first guest whose ever been driven back in a squad car,' he said to me respectfully, after I told him that I had lost my way.

Being taken for an illegal immigrant, and almost being arrested by the police for vagrancy, was not my idea of blending in with the locals.

At the office on the following day, Dorothy told me that I had been stopped by the famous 'Beverly Hills cops'. One of the world's wealthiest residential areas, Beverly Hills is patrolled by more policemen per capita than anywhere else in America. What a singular honour, I thought to myself!

★ ★ ★ ★

After my successful American tour, I travelled to Tokyo to meet the top brass of Dentsu. I had visited Japan on business many times before, and had always been struck by the Japanese paradox. Here was a country with the latest advances in automotive engineering, consumer electronics and scientific robotics, where the masses were obsessed with state-of-the art gadgets, yet underneath all that technology and modernity, every Japanese person I met was shaped by one of the strongest cultures of tradition in the world.

Welcoming foreign guests to their country was one of those proud traditions. I experienced Japan's famous hospitality as soon as I entered my room in the Okura Hotel. Placed on the table was a beautifully wrapped box of traditional confections from Dentsu. There was another gift box of sweets and savouries from the hotel.

The next day a certain Saito San was sent to accompany me to the head office, the Dentsu tower, located in Minato-ku. He was young, formal and eager to help me settle in. He was to be my minder and interpreter for the rest of my stay. On the pavement where our taxi deposited us, I could see the Japanese flag and the Thai flag hoisted side by side, gently flapping together in the autumnal breeze, on an upper floor above the tower's grand entrance. My father would have been proud.

The executive suite was quite different from an American one. The private offices of the directors and top managers were working rooms, and not designed to receive visitors. I was led into a well-appointed space, not unlike a conference room in a deluxe hotel. A senior executive greeted me in English and introduced himself as vice-president and interpreter, beckoning me to take a seat at the conference table. A white-coated waiter came in and poured us a cup of frothy *matcha* tea. We exchanged the usual platitudes about my hotel and the rather cold weather for the time of the year.

At the *exact moment* when the wall clock struck ten, a door opened and a distinguished gentleman in his late fifties entered the room, accompanied by his bespectacled (male) secretary. The interpreter got up and bowed. I followed his example. I was introduced to Umegaki San, the President of Dentsu. I was struck by his air of authority. Keen eyed and tough looking, he was dressed elegantly in a bespoke grey pinstriped suit.

He welcomed me through the interpreter and hoped that I was comfortable at the Okura. So there I was, supposedly having a tête-à-tête with the Japanese CEO, in the presence of two other people. Normally, I was told, a private meeting with Umegaki San would be with at least a dozen people. It was an essential part of the Japanese business culture that a meeting could be convened *only after* everyone present was in agreement, through the famous Japanese group-consensus. All disagreements had been settled well beforehand.

I came fully prepared for a formal meeting. I told Umegaki San that it was an honour that he had entrusted me with the running of his company. It was translated and he nodded. I went on to thank him for the honour he accorded me with the hoisting of the Thai flag to welcome me. He nodded again, this time with a smile, and said that the honour was his. The secretary was diligently taking notes. The word 'honour' must have been repeated a dozen times. In less than half-an-hour our meeting ended, not at his behest, but by a whispered reminder from his private secretary.

'It would honour me greatly if you could come to Thailand one day,' were my parting words, as I made my exit with a low bow.

Over the next four days, accompanied by my minder Saito San (who spoke appalling English), I was guided through Dentsu's four main engine rooms: the account management, creative, production and media departments. Apart from the creative floors, each department looked exactly the same: dozens of desks neatly lined up, row upon row, with glassed-walled rooms for meetings and for the supervisors at each end.

The desks were 'manned' – there were no women – by diligent executives in their ubiquitous dark suits, working like beavers in relative silence. I marvelled at their discipline. Contrary to my expectation, the ads that came out of this controlled environment were often more inventive and imaginative than in the West, where the creative people were given much more – one could even argue, too much – latitude.

Lunchtimes were always special. The head of each department and his team would host lunch at the best Japanese restaurants in Tokyo. On the third day I was disappointingly taken to a *gaigin* * restaurant. It was neither French nor Italian, but presumably European. The menu was a fine work of art deco, but full of spelling mistakes. To this day I still don't understand what *'peanus salad'* was all about, neither did I bother to find out. When asked for my preferences right from the start of my tour, I told them that I liked Japanese food most of all. Half way through the week Saito San had apparently reported to the management that I didn't like Japanese food very much. It later transpired that I ate 'very quietly', a sure sign that I didn't enjoy their cuisine. In total contrast to their culture of silence and their polite manners, my Japanese colleagues slurped and burped each bite with much noisy gusto during mealtime, their faces beaming in pure beatitude and enjoyment. It didn't take me long to learn the Japanese way of eating.

My learning curve in the ways of working with the Japanese went up dramatically over the next few years.

One cross-cultural story has become a DYR classic. In the early days of setting up the American-Japanese joint venture in the Tokyo office, David Tree, a talented British creative director from Y & R's London office, was sent to work at Dentsu's creative department. David was selected precisely for his ability to work with different

---

* Means 'outsider', and used to describe Western or Westerner.

cultures and his easy-going affability. To put everybody at ease when he arrived at the office, for example, he would greet his Japanese colleagues with a friendly 'Good morning chaps!' After three months, they were asked to evaluate his performance.

'Every day David San insult all Japanese people,' came the feedback. 'Every morning he say "good morning Japs" with big smile on face.'

The biggest insult to the Japanese people was to call them 'Japs'. The misunderstanding was soon resolved, but not without a lot of difficult explaining.

One aspect of the Japanese corporate culture that took a bit of getting used to was the office get-together in a drinking club after work. Santory whisky, their libation of choice, loosened their tongues and they would speak openly. Some would get drunk out of their minds,* accompanied with lots of back-slapping and risqué jokes. Even senior executives would occasionally let their hair down and reveal their most inner thoughts.

If we were in a karaoke club, my hosts would take turns to sing at the mike, according to seniority. It was a mark of honour (exactly *in whose*, I was never quite sure) for the guest from overseas to start off the evening with a song. I was not invited to do an encore.

On rare occasions, Dentsu's top brass, or a senior client, would join their younger executives in these sundown revelries. Every employee would be on their best behaviour, but that didn't seem to cut down on their alcohol intake. When their chief or their client had become sufficiently blotto, and finally announced his departure, they would dutifully line up in a straight row on the pavement outside the club to see him off, bowing profusely while bidding their goodnights – '*oyasumi*' – to

---

* Like many East Asians, yours truly included, the lack of the Aldehyde Dehydrogenase enzyme involved in the breakdown of alcohol in their systems causes alcohol intolerance, rapid inebriation and facial flushing.

their gaffer, as he woozily clambered into his chauffeured Toyota Crown limo. Too late to catch the last train home, the executives would spend the night in one of many of Tokyo's famed capsule hotels, a private pod-like compartment the size of a couchette in a railway carriage. It was not easy being a Japanese 'salaryman'.

The next morning back at the office, it was as if the night before never happened. Everyone was back to normal, formal and reserved.

The fact that I had worked in four other agencies before joining DYR came as quite a shock to my Japanese co-workers, who, as loyal 'salarymen', expected lifetime employment at Dentsu. How could I possibly be loyal to their company, they must have asked themselves, if I had already switched my loyalties *four* times before joining them? By the same token, big companies, Dentsu included, didn't freely buy and sell each other. Toyota would *never* make a takeover bid to buy Honda. Western style hostile bids were an anathema to them.

I learned a lot by simply being an observer at Japanese business meetings. In a room with ten executives in identical dark suits and white shirts, they would all rise to bow when a superior, similarly dressed in a dark suit, came in. As more men (never women in the eighties) joined the meeting, the room became a sea of dark suits. It was considered an insult not to follow this ultra male dress code.*

---

* In today's Japan, for the first time in history, women are starting to take up careers. As of 2018, in a complete turnaround from the traditional patriarchal society, a greater percentage of Japanese women (except those below the age of 24) than American women work outside of the home, and about 71 percent of working-age women are now gainfully employed, one of the highest proportions in the world. Japanese corporations are desperately seeking to fill vacancies due to population aging, which had shrunk the pool of qualified male workers. (Mauro F. Guillen, *2030,* St Martin's Press, NY, 2020). By default, the traditional Japanese glass ceiling is beginning to disappear, although there is still a large gap in remuneration between the sexes.

I was able to sense when a superior was flexing his muscles simply by his tone while he was talking at the head of the table. I could tell when he was giving an order, showing his displeasure, or even bawling them out. But it was done in a *modest* way. A slight raise of the voice, perhaps, but never a shout. A leader would never boast about his achievements either. The Japanese audience, masters at hiding their true feelings, would sit still, making sure not to express an opinion or ask any questions, for fear of making a mistake. Face was critical.

The most common gesture during a discussion was a long pause, followed by a sound of deep sucking through the mouth. It would either mean that he didn't know the answer, or, if called upon to speak English, he was trying to construct the sentence correctly.

Every culture has its own body language. What is considered polite in one society could be misconstrued as rude or insulting in another. In Thailand, for example, it would be the height of disrespect to use your feet to point at anything, or to place your feet at a higher level than another person's head. In Japan, pointing at people or things was also considered rude, making direct eye contact an act of aggression, and folding your arms in a certain way a hostile act. A common gesture was pointing to one's own nose, which means 'I' or 'me'. While on the subject of the nose, blowing one's nose or sneezing in public is rude, and coupled with the Japanese obsession with cleanliness and hygiene, surgical mask wearing in public areas had long been a Japanese practice, several decades before the Covid-19 pandemic. Handkerchiefs are not used, and carrying one filled with *hanakuso* – 'nose shit'– in your pocket is repulsive to them.

★ ★ ★ ★

In November 1984, I returned to Thailand, eager to establish the American-Japanese joint venture. A sad looking Teshigawara

San had arrived from Tokyo to become Deputy Managing Director. He didn't ask for the Bangkok posting, he was just assigned, and like a good soldier, he followed orders. True to form, Teshi, as we would call him, would always wear his suit, even when I invited him to stay at my beach house in Pattaya for the weekend.

Within a year, he soon acclimatised to Thailand's relaxed atmosphere, and was to contribute hugely to the success of DYR. Setsuko, his charming wife, who joined him later, didn't speak English, and had decided to learn Thai instead. Whenever Manuela, my Italian wife, got together with Setsuko, they spoke to each other in Thai, their lingua franca. It was a sad day for me when Teshi was reassigned back to head office in Tokyo. There were tears in his eyes. He had come to love Thailand.

I was deeply shocked to learn several years later, after we had both retired from the company, that the day before he left Tokyo for his new position in Thailand in 1984, his father had just died. He never told a soul, not even, I suspect, his superiors.

★ ★ ★ ★

Nearly ten years on, I was getting restless again. And very bored with running what had become a successful agency. It was at the company's international meeting in Sydney in March 1993, that I approached my new boss, Gary Burandt, with my plight. He had made a name for himself setting up Y & R in Soviet Russia, and he was now head of DYR worldwide in New York. He was one of those dependable types of mild-mannered Americans you could trust. He looked more like a naval commander than an adman. I wasn't surprised to learn that he was in charge of a minesweeper during the Vietnam War.

Gary was sympathetic and sensed that my heart was no longer with the company that I had helped to build. He promised me an honourable way out.

Could my sense of boredom have been put down to my past as a young man in London, when I never held a job long enough to get bored? Or was this a sign of a midlife career crisis, I wondered? A change in direction could be just what I needed.

Looking back, though, I did enjoy the ride in the ad business. I had worked with some wonderful people, and taken great pride in the creative campaigns that I had produced. The business also introduced me to many exciting destinations across the globe, including several month's work at the McCann-Erickson's office in Singapore and DYR's in Hong Kong, as well as annual visits to New York's Ogilvy & Mather's and Young & Rubicam's head offices in the seventies and eighties.

After almost two and a half pleasant decades in advertising, only two *uncomfortable* episodes stand out in my memory.

The most *controversial* brand I ever worked for was through a new client I picked up at a cocktail party. It was the Italian National Day celebration at the Oriental Hotel on 2 June 1972. We bumped into each other at the pasta table. After the usual introductions, he held out his hand: Vladimir Beketov, manager of Aeroflot Russian Airlines.

'Are you interested in doing the advertising for Aeroflot?' he asked me after I told him I was in the ad business. 'I have a budget of one and a half million baht.'

Would I say no to today's equivalent of an almost half a million US dollar account? I eagerly arranged a meeting the next day at Aeroflot's prestigious office on 1 Silom Road. This generous new client also paid upfront, the first and only time I have ever been paid in advance.

The creative team at Ling-McCann-Erickson were over the moon. A dream print campaign – featuring the halls of the Hermitage in Saint Petersburg, the ancient Silk Route, the fabled mosques of Samarkand, and other exciting destinations in Russia – was approved, although in reality travel across the

Soviet Union was, at that time, if not almost forbidden, certainly not easy.

Aeroflot's solution for the Bolshevik class struggle was simple: seat all élite Soviet officials and members of the Communist Party of Russia up front in first class, whilst poor bourgeois decadents (such as myself) and long-haired hippies and students on a budget from the West, would be put in the back of the plane. Economy class flights to Europe via Moscow were the cheapest in Asia.

Over time an unusual client-agency relationship developed between Aeroflot and myself. Normally it is the agency that entertains the client. On this occasion it was the opposite. Once a week without fail, Mr Beketov would invite me to lunch. We would start off discussing generalities, until one day he began to talk specifics in a direction I was beginning not to like.

'Would you be interested in becoming an honorary member of the Communist Party of Russia and be our representative in Thailand?' he asked me.

Here I was, sitting in a restaurant opposite a person whom I had for some time presumed to be a Soviet agent, and who was now apparently recruiting me to join his country's intelligence organisation over lunch. Mr Beketov was naïve in his approach and dangerous in his mission. My father would have been shocked. I recommended my agency *not* to renew our contract with Aeroflot.

Many years later I read in the *Wall Street Journal* (11 October 2018) that the airline was a front for Soviet security services, and that its global network of offices and air routes provided payroll for its agents around the world, as well as for shipping clandestine cargoes.

The most *unpleasant* experience in my years in advertising was with Greg Woodson, the newly appointed marketing manager of Colgate-Palmolive. He was one of those artless Americans who had never worked overseas. He had been sent to Thailand where there seemed to be a problem with the sales of their brands, and this was his chance to prove to his bosses that he could turn them around. DYR Thailand had just been appointed Colgate toothpaste's advertising agency under an agreement in New York in 1983.

Over a lunch to get to know each other, which I happily hosted, I was told by Greg that his policy when dealing with his ad agency was *'not to take any prisoners.'*

I told Greg that there was a professional code of conduct between agency and client, whereby we were supposed to be working together as partners, and not as adversaries. I certainly wasn't aware that we were at war with each other. Was he trained by the CIA, I wondered? Fortunately, he was recalled back to his head office before he could execute any of my staff. But he did manage to terrorize many of them to the point of tears.

I have an American wife and an American son-in-law. I have worked for many US companies and have always admired Yankee sincerity and enthusiasm. I have spent many happy times in the US, and over the years, I have made many American friends. This aggressive bully was not one of them.

Three *unwonted* episodes are worth recounting.

The first was for a wonderful Thai tea, harvested and picked in the hills of Chiang Mai. Raming Tea's aroma and colour was as good as any British brew. I had invited the beautiful socialite Princess Koko Na Chiang Mai, a descendant of northern Thai royalty, to be the brand's spokesperson. I came up with a slogan, 'The Pride of Chiang Mai', for her to present on film and in print. The elegant campaign caused quite a stir. It was the only time royalty had ever done this kind of work, and the first time a local tea had ever been advertised. A few months later, just as Raming's sales were picking up, taking market share away from Lipton, the brand leader, I was informed by the client that Meridian's services would no longer be required, and was instructed to pull the campaign. I was informed privately by the tea's distributor that the owner's wife was upset because the café society of Bangkok thought Princess Koko was the *owner* of the company.

The second episode was when I was working on the Singapore Airlines account. We had proposed the headline 'Ten times more SIN every week from BKK',* for a print campaign to advertise increased flights from Bangkok to Singapore. The 'More SIN' concept would be the campaign lead-in for announcing new routes and services to the island republic in the future. This witty campaign was not only rejected by the airline's management, but deemed insulting to the image of Singapore.

And then there was the one that got away.

Every agency has a story about their greatest campaign that never saw the light of day. In 1982 Siam Motors was considering selling Alfa Romeo in Thailand. Through my connections with the Thai-Italian Chamber of Commerce when I was its president, I was invited to submit a launch campaign for the new Alfetta, and proposed a TV commercial with a James Bond feel, ending with the line 'The four-door saloon that behaves like a racing car.' A gripping car chase was outlined, with the Alfetta going through all its exciting and daredevil paces on the most challenging terrain: rickety wooden bridges, dizzying hairpin bends, and roads that edged perilously on deep narrow gorges. At the end of the cliffhanging ride, a cool elegant man in a crisp dinner-jacket steps out of the car, takes a silk square from his breast pocket and proudly wipes the dust off the Alfa's badge on the front grille. We cut to the final scene where he enters a boardroom to take the chairman's seat at the head of the table, and calmly says 'Sorry

---

* Three-lettered airport abbreviations for Singapore (SIN) and Bangkok (BKK).

to keep you waiting,' after having bravely survived, thanks to the Alfetta, the most hair-raising drive of his life. The Alfa people from Milan* liked the campaign but it was turned down by the Thai management of Siam Motors, because they were afraid to sell a car that 'keeps you waiting'.

I had been writing ads for the automotive, electronic, chemical, construction, petroleum, financial, hospitality, household appliance, packaged food, pharmaceutical, personal care, retail, fashion, toiletry and travel industries for over two decades. An adman never stops learning. You get to know your product or service so well you could go out and be a salesman for your client. I had become a bit of an expert on almost every business that I had got involved with. I had become a Jack of all trades, and master of none.

It was definitely time to move on.

The telephone rang. It was Gary Burandt on the line from New York. 'How would you like to teach at the University of Missouri School of Journalism ?' he asked me.

---

* Alfa Romeo moved its head office to Turin in 1986, after it was acquired by the Fiat Group.

CHAPTER TEN
MY LAST JOB

Thus ended my career in advertising; from *running* the business, I was now going to *teach* the business. As a reward for building the Young & Rubicam agency in Thailand – thanks to the good offices of Gary Burandt – the company sponsored my appointment as Visiting Professor at the University of Missouri School of Journalism.

In August 1993, I started my third career.

The first American university west of the Mississippi River, the University of Missouri was founded in 1839. Its prestigious Missouri School of Journalism was founded in 1908, and is the world's first journalism school, known colloquially as the 'J-School'.

My main responsibility was to teach two basic advertising courses: Strategic Planning and Creative Thinking, and how they dovetail together to build a strong brand, based on consumer insights and needs, rather than a campaign that the manufacturer normally wants: a smiling consumer, the client's company logo, a huge product shot, mention of the brand name at least five times, a list of product benefits developed by their R & D people, and *in extremis* – particularly in developing markets – a picture of their beloved factory.

One of my dicta: If you don't know *why* people buy your product and how they *feel* about your brand, every penny you spend in marketing and sales is money down the drain.

★ ★ ★ ★

As a result of Dean Mills' enlightened policy since 1989 to make the J-School more international, I was asked to introduce a new course to the faculty along these lines. I developed the new subject of Global Marketing Communications, which was included on the syllabus for the first time at the university. It was the third subject that I would teach.

It was great fun teaching my undergrad students, all seniors. The feeling was mutual. For a neophyte, I was pleasantly surprised to learn that I performed well in class, judging by the students' formal evaluation of my teaching methods at the end of each academic year.

I scored particularly well in a number of the university's strict criteria: *'enjoys working with students'; 'discussed current developments'; 'willing to meet outside class'; 'gave clear explanations'; 'encouraged class discussion'* and *'would recommend teacher to a friend.'*

Two common themes from my student's individual handwritten evaluation forms were the fact that I offered *'first-hand knowledge rather than a textbook class'* and a *'fresh, international point of view.'* My favourites: *'a fun man to learn from'; 'his humor made the class enjoyable'; 'great to hear his opinions since he's such an expert'* and *'the most intriguing professor I've ever had, second to none.'*

I looked forward to these annual evaluations. My ego was suitably massaged for another year.

A particularly rewarding moment during my teaching experience was when almost the entire class raised their hands in unison to answer one of my questions. That pleasure was brought back to me the other day when I was watching the news on BBC and saw a classroom of eager teenage girls in Kabul do the same thing. They were impatient to learn and to participate, and like a murmuration of starlings, they all raised their hands and voices at the same time, in the joyous expectation that they had the right answer. I knew immediately that the class was cohesive in their desire for knowledge, and that the Afghan teacher was getting through to her flock.

An extracurricular activity I especially enjoyed was that of a careers consultant to the students I taught. I was happy to help them plan their future. I was familiar with their strengths and weaknesses, so I felt confident in pointing them in the right direction.

One particular student, Joe, an African-American, had a wonderful, friendly personality and a creative brain, but he didn't have the intellectual skills and the pushy character required for an investigative reporter. His parents wanted him to become a 'famous anchor person'.

This was still an era when there were very few coloured broadcasters on the news networks. I learned that live news broadcasting in the eighties and nineties was very much the preserve of white males, and I told him so. Barbara Walters, the broadcaster famous for her vigorous interviewing style, and Connie Chung, the first Asian and the first woman to co-host the CBS evening news show, came to mind as notable exceptions, but I couldn't think of any others. I told him that it would be tough for him to hack into a white man's world, and I presented myself as 'neither black nor white', but as an objective non-American observer of the American media employment scene. I told him that with his bright personality he would do well in sales. I met his parents on graduation day, and they thanked me for being 'truthful'.

Most of my students knew what they wanted in life, but

when asked as a class what they aspired to after graduation, the answer would often be *'a celebrity news anchor'*. I took great pains to explain that fame and fortune is earned, and not 'conferred' simply by dint of having a degree from the J-School. Celebrity status is a bonus, I added, a by-product of talent, hard work and sheer good luck. Little did I realise that two decades later, being a celebrity – the Kardashians come to mind – would actually become a profession, thanks to reality TV shows and social media.

I failed miserably in one area of my students' evaluation and that was 'political correctness'. Here I quote one student comment: *'A few sexist comments were made by the teacher, but they were not intended to be offensive. They were actually pretty funny.'*

I once had a small difference of opinion on a particular semantics of political correctness with the Dean himself. In general conversation, he'd heard that I had often referred to myself as an 'Oriental'.

'Noo,' said Dean Mills. 'It is demeaning to call yourself *Oriental. Asian* is the politically correct term.'

I told him that, yes, historically Asia had always started at the Bosphorus, which was considered the *continental boundary* between Europe and West Asia, that included Middle Eastern countries like Iraq and the Gulf States, Persia, Afghanistan, and South Asian countries north and south of the Indian subcontinent, as well as all the new former Soviet republics on the Silk Route. The inhabitants of the Middle East and West Asia are, for the most part, Semitic and Indo-Europeans, and many, like the Iranians, are Aryan, but *not* Oriental.

Geographically and ethnically, then, the Orient refers to the countries on the *Pacific Rim*, also referred to as the Far East, peopled *inter alia* by ethnic Mongolians, such as the Han, Japanese, Korean, and Tais, as well as Filipinos and Malays. Thus the names given to the Oriental Hotel in Bangkok, the School of

Oriental and African Studies in London, the Museum of Oriental Art in Turin, the Orient Express train service, and finally Oriental medicine in America, not to mention the now defunct Northwest Orient Airlines, with services in the seventies and eighties from America to the Far East (never to the Middle East) and for many years the fourth largest US inter-continental carrier.

'Of the Orient means *of the East*, as opposed to Occident, or *of the West*,' I painstakingly went on to explain. 'Furthermore, etymologically, *oriens* is Latin for that part of the horizon in which the sun first rises.' Dean Mills was not convinced. He winced when I told him that we Orientals were of the 'yellow race' and less hairy, physically quite different from Indo-Europeans and Semites. The Dean was one of those evangelistic Americans who believed that what was correct for America was correct for the rest of the world. We argued.

But in the end he won. In 2016, President Obama signed a new legislation prohibiting the use of 'Oriental' in everyday language. In future, the correct description of 'Orientals' in America would be *'Asian-Americans'*. In America I am Asian, but in the rest of the world I will continue to proudly call myself 'Oriental'.

Nowadays – if I may digress for a moment – in our society's well-intentioned need to be politically correct, we seem to have forgotten good manners and the simple act of being polite. Twitter, and other public spaces, have become platforms for everybody, from the extremists – allowing them to express their hostility and hatred – to the discontented and victimised, who have the legal right to be offended. Disingenuous politicians, with their continuous prattle of newspeak in the media, are very much to blame. Political correctness, yes, but not at the expense of common decency, good manners and old-fashioned civility. Enough said.

It was less fun getting involved with the politics on campus. I'd always heard that politics in academia were brutal, much more so than in business. It had all to do with tenure track politics, and partly ego. 'Tenure track' in academia is the professional pathway to promotion and long-term job security. It is a process by which an entry level *Assistant Professor* moves up to become an *Associate Professor*, before finally becoming a highly respected, full-fledged *Professor*, at the top of the faculty ladder. It's a tough political climb that produces a very ambitious community.

At the very bottom rung are lecturers, instructors and adjuncts, but they are not on the tenure track. To get onto it, they have to play their cards right.

As an outsider, I was fortunately not part of this process. I was given the honorary title of *'Visiting Professor'* which initially raised a few jealous eyebrows, especially after it was discovered that I was not, and had never been, a university professor, and had therefore never been required to work my way through the tenure track. My 'spurious' position was no longer a subject of envy when it was later revealed that the endowment for my services, paid for by the Hearst Foundation, and hence my title, was only for three years. Being a 'professor' was great for the ego while it lasted though.

★ ★ ★ ★

The University is located in Columbia,* a picturesque Middle Western town of 90,000, in the rural heart of Missouri, half way between St Louis and Kansas City. It was founded in 1821 by pioneers from Kentucky and Virginia, and its downtown was reminiscent of Norman Rockwell's illustrations of everyday life in 'heartland America' of idyllic forties and fifties, when front doors were never locked and everybody said hello to each other. And when children could play safely in the town square and everyone went to church on Sunday.

---

* In the late eighties, it was nominated the best place to live in the US by *Money Magazine*.

When I arrived in Columbia with my wife Manuela in 1994, the reality of the American dream was either life in the dull suburbs, or in an eerily deserted downtown at night. It was an era when town centres in America were being abandoned by the middle class for the suburbs and left neglected, although during the daytime downtown Columbia still retained the charms of the general stores and the drugstores of Main Street USA of times gone by.

We found a newly built one-storey house with three bedrooms and a garage for two cars in the friendly suburb of Broadway Farms, where we moved into only after we had negotiated for more trees and vegetation to be planted in what the owners kept calling the 'yard', which alarmed us somewhat. In England, a yard is a piece of uncultivated, enclosed ground next to a building, like a builder's yard. In America, it means a garden with a lawn. The difference in terminology initially caused a bit of misunderstanding.

Our new address, 604 Nancy (Sinatra? Reagan? Pelosi?) Drive, was located on a dead end street. I couldn't see the other 600 houses, because of course there weren't any; there were just twenty identical homes on this short, three hundred metre long cul-de-sac. Our house was the 4th house up the street, not the 604th, and the last house, the 20th, was number 620. I was puzzled.

'Whether they're sports scores, Dow Jones Industrial Averages, automobile power output or Bill Gates' net worth, Americans like big numbers,' explained fellow Professor Henry Hager with much regalement. I vaguely remembered frantically looking for number *10,347* Wilshire Boulevard, an address I had to check out in LA on my business trip there.

Henry had once worked as creative director in Y & R Detroit, and had become my cultural adviser on all things American, as well as a dear friend during my time in 'CoMo', the name the locals affectionately gave to Columbia Missouri, their hometown.

★　★　★　★

I arranged my classes so that they fell on Monday, Tuesday and Wednesday, allowing Manuela and me the freedom to discover other parts of America's vast continent from Thursday to Sunday. For longer trips, I was given the privilege of being able to rearrange the timetable of my classes, so that I could take the entire week off, a definite benefit of not being on the tenure track.

Once a month, we flew to New York and were guests of our dear friends Nid Pibulsonggram, an old chum from my foreign office days, who was now Thailand's Ambassador to the United Nations in New York, and his charming wife Patricia, at their official residence: a six storey classic townhouse bang next to the Metropolitan Museum of Art on East 82nd Street and built at the turn of the twentieth century. It was the swishiest place we had ever stayed at in America.

Our most memorable American trips were our skiing jaunts to the Rockies together with Nid and Pat. The quality of the snow is unique there: light, powdery and a delight to ski on. The best slopes were at Telluride, Colorado, an old mining town, made famous by Butch Cassidy and his gang, who robbed the local bank here in the 1889, and got away with $20,000. At other times we would take iconic American road trips on the wonderful Interstate Highways (HWY), built during President Eisenhower's time in the fifties, connecting every state of the union.

Columbia was on the Interstate 70 (I-70), the major east-west HWY that ran from Maryland to Utah, crossing ten states; we used to drive west to Kansas City and Denver, and east to St Louis, passing through the torpid towns of the Rust Belt that were even then in a state of decay and neglect, and on to Baltimore. From there we would then connect the I-95 to Boston.

On one memorable trip in autumn, we picked up our daughter Malina in Cambridge, Massachusetts, where she was studying architecture at MIT, and drove as far northeast as Vermont (from the French *vert mont* or green mountain) to admire the beauty of the fall foliage that gently fluttered down from noble North American trees – ash, maple and beech – and carpeted the forest ground like multi-coloured confetti.

Another one of our frequented routes was on the north-south I-55 axis, connecting the Gulf of Mexico with the Great Lakes. We were entranced by Chicago's spectacular skyline viewed from a tour boat on the river, and impressed by its towers of granite and power. I was tickled pink when the Leo Burnett ad agency steel and glass skyscraper – a well known landmark – was pointed out to me by our guide.

Our favourite drive to the south was to spend a few days in Memphis, Tennessee, where black rhythm and blues music morphed into white rock 'n' roll in the fifties, thanks to a young trucker, Elvis Presley, who had cut his first record there, and created a new genre of American pop music.

On one particular return trip from Memphis on the I-55 in May 1995, I was stopped by the Highway Patrol for speeding. The Interstate on this part of southeast Missouri was one of their long, straight-as-an-arrow highways that seemed to undulate forever, opening up to the wide-open, wide-screen American landscape that one sees in the movies, which stretch endlessly for miles toward the horizon. There was practically no traffic. As the locals would say, it was 'awesome'.

I was driving a leased Ford Thunderbird with the radio blasting local country and western at full volume; I got carried away and put my foot down on the gas pedal, and a sense of freedom and exhilaration that I had never felt before at the wheel overcame me. This must surely be the carefree Great American Road Trip come true, I mused.

In my rear view mirror, I saw a police car with flashing red lights catching up on us very quickly. 'Looks like we're going to witness a car chase,' I told Manuela, not realising that we were the ones being chased. The car came alongside and the driver made gestures for me to stop, almost forcing me onto the shoulder, before parking a few metres behind us.

I was half expecting Clint Eastwood to step out of the car. Instead, a beefy middle-aged police officer, his black peaked hat planted jauntily on his head, came up to the driver's side of my car and made a sign for me to roll down the window. 'Could you step into my car, please sir?'

The word 'POLICE' was emblazoned everywhere: all over the body of the patrol car, on metal badges of his peaked cap and on the chest of his uniform, on different areas of the dashboard, and just in case I didn't get the message, on epaulette patches on *both* sleeves. I was impressed. I was also in deep trouble.

The first question the officer – for that was how I now addressed him – asked me was about the ownership of the car I was driving. Apparently this was standard procedure in America. Car thefts in America are staggering. In the nineties, an average of 1.5 million cars were stolen every year, not to mention the number of crimes committed with stolen vehicles. Just one month before, Timothy McVeigh, the Oklahoma City bomber, had been arrested while driving away from the scene of his dastardly evil crime in a stolen pick-up truck, after he had caused the deaths of 168 people.

My answer baffled him. I told him it belonged to the Ford Motor Company. 'Whaddaya mean?' he said. Once it was established that I had leased the car from Ford and had not stolen it, he then asked me to produce my driving licence. Once again he was baffled, but this time, also highly embarrassed. He was leafing through a ten page, passport sized document in nine languages, the *International Driving Permit*, but he couldn't find my photo and ID. It was hidden behind a gatefold on the last page, with *'Indications relatives au conducteur'* ('Particulars concerning the Driver' written in French) next to the details of my identity. English was on page 4.

As he started to read the 'particulars', I started to read his lips. He was grappling with 'P-a-l-a-s-t-h-i-r-a, S-p-h-a'. When he read that my 'Place of birth' was the 'UK', in 1938, he started to look at me from head to toe for the first time. I was wearing a tweed jacket and corduroy trousers, with an old pair of brown brogues very much in keeping with my role of college professor. But to him, I was an alien being, yet to be treated with respect. It was the final straw when he finally read that my 'Permanent place of residence' was Bangkok, Thailand. He took off his cap and started scratching his (bald) head.

'Whatcha' doin' in Missouri?'

I told him that 'I was a guest of the State of Missouri and a visiting professor at the University.' Again, he looked me up and down. I was getting more respect by the minute. He was starting to get carried away from his duties as a cop and told me that his niece Tracy was studying at MU. I said I would look her up. He then asked me what they called me at school. When I said 'Teddy', there was a hint of a smile.

He suddenly remembered that I had exceeded the state's speed limit of 65 mph, at which point he reverted to being a cop again. He pointed to a number on the screen of his speed camera. It read 98 mph. This was still an era before advanced IT technology, when traffic violations were still written out by hand. He got out his citation book and started to write out my details, carefully copying my name from my International Driving Permit. I could see from the worried look on his face that this was going to be a long lasting bit of paperwork.

All at once, he closed the book and looked at me straight in the eye. 'Teddy, this time round I'm gonna let you off,

but promise me you will never exceed our speed limit again!'
I promised.

He looked ahead and saw Manuela looking at us from the
back window of our car, appearing terrified.

'Who's the passenger?' he asked me. 'My wife,' I said. 'Where's
she from?' When I told him she was Italian, he must have decided
that he didn't want to have anything more to do with me for a
long while.

'Have a nice day, perfesser Teddy !' he said laconically, before
driving off.

This was my second brush with the American constabulary. I
might not be so lucky the third time, so I promised Manuela not
to break any more laws in America.

★ ★ ★ ★

During the long holidays we used to return to Rome where we
had a home and where Manuela would often stay on. We would
take a direct flight from Lambert Airport in St Louis (STL), the
hub of the now defunct Trans World Airlines, which went belly
up a few months after we had achieved gold frequent flyer status.

On one occasion, we were sitting at a bar at STL waiting
for our flight. A clean-cut soldier in his crisp khaki uniform, a
young Brad Pitt* lookalike, came to sit next to us, and ordered
a Budweiser beer. He looked at me up and down, and asked me,
not unkindly, 'What are ya' selling?'

It was an era when Asians (Orientals) were coming to America
to sell all kinds of products, from cheap fashions to sophisticated
electronics. Most products on the shelves of Sears or Walmart
were either made in China or Vietnam. I was at a loss for words
but didn't want to disappoint him, so I told him 'knowledge'.

---

* Interestingly, Brad Pitt, a Missourian, studied advertising at the J-School
in 1982, but did not graduate. Other J-School alumni: Hollywood actors
George C. Scott and Jon Hamm *(Mad Man)*, and Tennessee Williams.

He looked around the feet of my bar stool and presumably found nothing to support what I had just said, apart from a well worn pair of brown brogues I was wearing, and a dirty old rucksack. Was he looking for a set of encyclopedias, I wondered? Or a case of product samples?

He started to ruminate for a while. After several sips of his 'Bud', he suddenly blurted out: 'Ya mean you're a perfessor?' I nodded in agreement.

When his flight was announced, he got up from his bar stool, stood erect and bade me goodbye with a respectful salute and a big smile that showed off his beautiful white teeth. 'Have a good day, sir!'

At that time, STL had only one immigration desk operated by one homeland officer, a bumptious African-American lady, who would greet me with a welcoming *'It's you again!'* every time I returned from a trip. After several encounters with her, she asked me why I didn't get a Green Card.

'That way, you can come and go without a visa, and eventually you can even apply for US citizenship,' she told me helpfully. What she didn't tell me was that I could also be subject to paying tax on my income to Uncle Sam, wherever it was earned in the world.

After I told her that I had no intention of becoming an American citizen, she looked a bit disappointed and very surprised. She was curious to know where I came from. When I told her I was Thai, she was even more surprised.

'Gee,' she said. 'You are the first Taiwanese I ever met who doesn't want to become American!'

In May 1996, my teaching career at the Missouri School of Journalism sadly came to an end.

It was the most enjoyable job I had ever had.

★ ★ ★ ★

I can now finally say that my peripatetic working life so far has been a full and rich one. I've been lucky. I can only quote Thomas Carlyle, the nineteenth century Scottish writer and teacher, who could not have described my fully occupied life more succinctly: 'Blessed is he who has found his work; let him ask no other blessedness.'

I've worked for money and I've worked for nothing; I've worked at learning and teaching; I've worked on boards and for committees; I've worked for governments and for commercial enterprises. I've had jobs in school rooms, shop floors, hotel suites, airport lounges, and on film sets; I've worked in public areas and in the fields, and from home. I still work *in* the home, helping out with the cleaning and the cooking. I will continue to work at *caring* for the people I love.

Wherever I happen to be in the world, I'll be writing for the rest of my working life. There are no more paid jobs for me to do, no bosses to report to, no customers to service, no clients to look after, and no students for me to teach. All I have to do is write, and until my editor and my publisher get to see my typescript, I am beholden to no one except myself. That's probably the most difficult job of all.

I have, however, been able to express the lifelong search for my identity by writing this book, and I have finally discovered what my life has been all about; it has been an enlightening experience and a long journey. After a hotchpotch of jobs and three careers, I am now a writer. Each book I write feels more like a job than a career. May it continue to be a lot of fun.

And, yes, I am still eavesdropping.

CHAPTER ELEVEN
JOBS UNKNOWN

When you grow up, you might not have a job.
Yuval Noah Harari, *21 LESSONS FOR THE 21ˢᵗ CENTURY*

Despite my varied experiences in many different jobs, I was brought up with the work ethic of my father's generation and the generation before him, namely that the right choice of career would guarantee 'a job for life'. Today, very few employees can expect to have the same job for the rest of their lives, and both narratives of 'career' and 'lifetime employment' have regrettably become throwbacks from the past.

As I write this book in the third decade of the 21st century, its theme is almost an anomaly. Rather than about jobs and their comparatively easy availability in the fifties and sixties, it's now 'jobs unknown', as the job market today is in a constant state of flux and the future of work is not completely settled.

Rather, my agenda in this short chapter is to make a few of my personal observations, some admittedly anecdotal, others rhetorical, neither of which are conclusive or exhaustive, and by any means quantifiable.

I will attempt to outline what work has now become, and the kind of jobs that may be available in the future, based on the technological, economic and environmental challenges that lay ahead for young people about to enter the work force. I will also comment on the effects of the Covid-19 pandemic that have disrupted the employment landscape, accelerating even more important changes in the workplace.

Here are some trends (rather than predictions) based on how the workplace looks like today.

Working At Home

For those lucky few who find a job they like, the Covid-19 pandemic has forced many to move from an already fragile employment economy to working remotely at home via the Internet. They have the ability to participate in virtual meetings and conferences through the convenience of Zoom, Google Meet and Microsoft Teams, augmented by the occasional visit to the office. This is the era of hybrid jobs, in which post-pandemic work from home has become normal business practice. The need to go to the office will probably be for either collaborative or brain-storming purposes only.

Already in America, one third of the nation's workforce which once commuted to the office have been working from home since the Covid-19 pandemic. Tata Consultancy Services, one of India's largest companies, announced that 75 percent of their global workforce of 450,000 employees will be working remotely by 2025.

According to a study by the McKinsey Global Institute in 2021, twenty to twenty-five percent of the workforce in advanced economies will be working from home, between 3 to 5 days a week.

Shorter Working Week

And then there is the growing popularity of the Icelandic model, now being adopted by Finland, of the four-day working week.

By reducing the number of working hours a week from 40 to 35, it was discovered that the level of productivity not only remained the same as the five day week, but actually improved. Workers had more time to pursue their own interests, and were thus more willing to work harder and longer over those four days.

Virtual Work Networking

The Internet has offered virtual work networks for everyone, an economical, fast and time-saving method of conducting business perhaps, but at a costly human price. It may be effective for those who seek less commitment, but for those who want to build human relationships, Internet networking is not quite the same as personal connections. I used to have twenty business associates whom I would meet frequently, and another thirty that I corresponded with regularly by telephone or by post. Today, I have three hundred names on my e-mail address file, a lot of electronic connections, but with very little social bonding. The decline of human bonding has been further exacerbated by the Covid-19 pandemic.

Even job interviews will no longer require human contact. Algorithms will evaluate job applications and be the final decision maker on whether a particular person will be hired for a particular job. Discrimination will no longer be an issue if the computer is programmed to ignore race, gender and age.

Outsourcing vs The Value of Personal Service

Corporations will no longer be committed to their brands and customers, and even less so to their diminishing number of employees. They will only be beholden to their shareholders. They have been outsourcing their daily management responsibilities like accounting, administration, purchasing, training, human resources and customer relations for several decades now, and the system has worked well. On the manufacturing side, outsourcing to trusted suppliers has been a successful cost-saving and efficient method of production since the last century.

Outsourcing production of your widget to a Chinese manufacturer, however, is one thing. But outsourcing sophisticated personal services such as sales demonstrations of high-end products like Lear Jets, extolling the unique pleasures and thrilling experiences of travelling on a spaceship to explore the cosmos, or advice on offshore investment management, is quite another.

Greater value will therefore be placed on jobs that provide essential personal services, such as healthcare assistance for the elderly and infirm, nannies to care for toddlers, and personal trainers, as well as spiritual and psychological therapists. There will be openings for IT experts and technicians, taxation consultants, financial planners and legal assistants in advisory roles. Older people will need secretarial services to help them with their online needs, and active seniors and wealthy retirees will open their doors to new types of specialists that can customise products and services for them.

Outsourcing customer service assistance can and often does work for many companies under one roof, just as a plant can assemble many brands of widgets on the same jig. They can operate from their home far from the company's headquarters, and even in another country entirely. They are not company employees, and are therefore not on salary, and are paid by the number of hours they work, or by the number of units they produce. Their only qualification is a basic knowledge of spoken and written English, the lingua franca of our modern planet's e-commerce business; all they need is a mobile phone, a desktop computer and a roof over their heads.

It is a lucky customer indeed who does get to talk to a real person, albeit at a call centre in Bangalore* or on the Isle of Man. But in many instances, especially government departments, like the British and American immigration offices and their overseas embassies' visa and immigration sections, the clerical work required to complete a visitor's visa or a residence permit application, which were once performed by government officers, has now been transferred online for applicants to complete themselves. The travel and hospitality industries have developed the same systems. When you book a place to stay for your holiday, or your next flight, you are in effect doing the job of a travel agent or an airline employee. *Letting the customer do all the work is outsourcing to the nth degree.*

The Digital World of AI, Automation and Robots

As Artificial Intelligence (AI) and automation increasingly take over more work functions – simple examples are drones and driverless cars – that outperform both humans and computers, many jobs will be irrelevant. Looking ahead in a purely robotic world, the biggest challenge will be the *kind* of jobs that will be available in the decades to come.

To build a car and manufacture motorbikes and refrigerators, or indeed any other machine produced item, a single robot can replace an average of five to ten workers. Between 1983 and 2015, 300,000 robots were installed in the US, doing the work of nearly 2 million people. As AI continues to get faster and smarter, workers who are replaced by robots will be required to

---

* For every 1000 jobs British Airways sent to India, the airline saved $23 million. Michael F. Corbett, *The Outsourcing Revolution*, (Dearborn 2004).

learn new skills and must be prepared to change their professions. In manufacturing plants, there will be more controllers and programmers than workers.*

There are already widespread skills shortages. The US Air Force, for example, is not looking for more pilots, but is in great need of drone operators and data analysts.

There will be a concurrent decline in traditional jobs in the retail, banking, hospitality and travel sectors. As well as the physical work – a modern euphemism for manual labour – the clerical and retail jobs I did in the sixties have largely disappeared. Strawberry picking has been performed by robots for quite some time now.

Even the film extra work I did in the sixties is no longer the same. Crowd scenes are now digitally recreated on film. Some of the roles I have had have been replaced by 'fake crowds'. The 1959 production of Ben Hur employed 10,000 extras. Ghandi, filmed in 1981, holds the Guinness World Record for the film with most extras: the funeral marching scene alone employed *300,000* people. Today, thousands of spectators in an empty stadium, and even actors who are no longer alive, can be digitally recreated, using CGI – Computer Generated Imagery – technology. This application of computer graphics can create any kind of image, from de-aging seventy-six year old Robert de Niro to a young man in his thirties, to creating giant prehistoric dinosaurs and mythical avatars. CGI technology has generated thousands of new jobs in the film industry. Next time you watch a major film production, take a look at the credit titles at the end: hundreds of names of computer graphic technicians, compared with only a dozen or so actors who actually appear in the film, are credited.

Since the Covid-19 pandemic, unwell people with minor complaints have been going to hospital or to the clinic with less

---

* Mauro F. Guillen, *2030*, St Martin's Press (New York 2020).

regularity, and doctors have increasingly been conducting medical examinations with their out-patients online. However, doctors may find it difficult to make a complete diagnosis from what they see on the screen, and consequently they will be less able to identify specific medical problems with complete accuracy, nor will they be able to discover illnesses that the patient has not yet noticed or complained about.

This trend may be symptomatic of how doctors and many other professionals will do their jobs in the future. GPs may be replaced by Artificial Intelligence doctors, in effect computers, working on a single integrated system, so that patients with the same illness wherever they are in the world will get the same medical treatment and prescription. A doctor's diagnosis is extrapolated from collecting, organising, and analysing information about their patients, a task that AI can perform not only much faster and more efficiently, but with greater accuracy.

Surgeons performing routine tasks, instructors conducting introductory lessons, and even lawyers taking a brief from their clients, can have their jobs easily replaced by intelligent machines.

We are entering a world of internet connections where billions of smart devices such as processors, sensors and communication hardware share, collect, send and act on data they acquire from their environments – the Internet of Things – like a giant robot.* The Internet of Things is able to control and run offices, factories, warehouses, ports, transportation, hospitals, and even individuals, without requiring human intervention. A huge number of jobs will be required to support this colossal infrastructure, and at the same time a great many more will be eliminated.

---

* A simple example is the tyre pressure of a car that is now displayed on the dashboard, without the driver or the petrol station attendant having to measure the pressure manually.

The Great Resignation

There is a segment of the population, previously employed in physical work, who have refused to return to the jobs that they held before the Covid-19 pandemic. Healthcare concerns, based on the fear of being infected by the new variants at their place of work – as well as child care responsibilities and unemployment benefits that have helped many workers rethink their future – are the main reasons people aren't going back to their old jobs. They have been given time to prioritize their mental and physical health, particularly in the hospitality, medical care and service industries. In the UK, the most common reason for leaving work permanently was either long-term illness or retirement.

There are now jobs galore, despite the International Labour Organisation's report of 114 million lost jobs as a result of the Covid-19 outbreak in 2020. By the end of 2021 there were roughly 4 million fewer workers in the US than there were before the pandemic. How did all these paradoxes happen?

It was discovered that money was no longer the sole reason – and only source of fulfilment – for a working person. People who had left their employ no longer wanted to spend the rest of their lives slogging from 9 to 5 at the same unfulfilling job, neither did they want to – as an old song goes – 'owe their souls to the company store.' They had the opportunity to reflect upon their lives and values. Nobody wanted to be a bank clerk for the rest of their days. Importantly, they realised that job satisfaction was just as rewarding, if not more so, than getting a pay cheque at the end of their workweek. They wanted to build a satisfactory balance between work and life.

There has been an increase of so-called job-to-job moves, where workers have left their job to find something better. This could also benefit employers, who can now engage workers who are truly committed to the organisation. But the employers themselves will need to attract the right kind of employees, with added perks and benefits, otherwise they will lose out to ambitious workers who are quite prepared to strike out on their own and engage in new activities. Companies will need to spend more time listening to their staff in order to give them a sense of fulfilment.

The Gig Economy

Yet finding a fulfilling job will become increasingly more difficult; being paid on a salaried basis in many companies has become the exception rather than the rule, and a career for both professionals and non-professionals has become a rarity. A viable job today may be an obsolete one tomorrow, and even qualified people must expect not to have the same job for the rest of their lives.

The employable middle class is shrinking in America and Europe, not only because they are losing well-paying jobs to global competition, but simply because there are fewer of those jobs (i.e. stable jobs) available. It will be much worse for new young job seekers, who will not be able to gain access to a stable job in the first place. They will need to develop new skills not taught at school or university, and will have to reposition their status, and may need quite some time to discover their 'work niche'. Meanwhile, they will be taking up jobs that are temporary, seasonal or only required for a one-off project. Welcome to the gig economy.

Typical workers in the gig economy are Uber drivers, Airbnb hosts, Instacart shoppers, TaskRabbit jobbers, Deliveroo food deliverers, and independent contractors who can freelance their services to the supply side of the marketplace. Importantly, they have the liberty to choose their own hours.

The Self-Employed and New Opportunities

An overabundance of information in today's digital world may well produce an increased number of specialised jobs for niche market demands, with more software developers and qualified people freelancing their creative skills, thereby increasing the ranks of the self-employed.

As AI technology gets ever more advanced, the digital world of the future will create totally new professions and job descriptions. Here are some examples: virtual-world designers; a plethora of jobs relating to data (like data sourcing, data annotating, data labelling) and even data broking (for people who own and sell data); AI engineers; IT facilitators; man-machine teaming managers who will help combine the strengths of AI and robots (such as computation and speed) with the strengths of humans (such as cognition, judgment and empathy), this latter, representing 'a new division of labour, with machines and humans each doing what they do best.'[*]

A new generation of jobs could also be developed from the environmental crisis. At the purely physical work level, scores of labourers will be needed to clean up the polluted rivers, beaches and seas, not unlike the street cleaners and rubbish collectors in our cities. Eventually, these tasks could very likely be performed by robots.

At the entrepreneurial level, innovative recycling technologies from plastic and CO_2 waste, and cutting edge inventions to develop emission-free energy, will produce a new breed of scientists, new job descriptions, and new kinds of end products.

Recent breakthroughs in nuclear fusion energy development

[*] Fareed Zakaria, *Ten Lessons for a Post-Pandemic World*, (Penguin Books 2021)

that produce carbon-free power will create a demand for a great many more nuclear fusion physicists.

There could be an opportunity for specialists to invent new jobs for themselves. A doctorate graduate in galactic rocket systems, for example, could create a series of lectures, programs and literature to prepare people for future space tourism, or become a guide on a spaceship itself. Want to know more about protection against cyber threats, or improved deep breathing during a corona virus pandemic, or raising beavers to save the planet? There will be specialists who will have answers to all these questions and be ready to work for you.

It may all come down to the new class of Generation Z creative professionals – newly qualified scientists, engineers, artists, architects and designers – who have grown up with the infinite possibilities afforded by the power of computing and networking since the day they were born (between 1997 and 2012).

This young generation of entrepreneurial minded people has been shaped by the economic crisis, the pandemic and climate change. They will be eager to start and grow their own business, and be their own boss. There have been successful cases of those who have started locally, initially providing a need in their own community, before expanding their business to a wider consumer base via the Internet. Many budding new entrepreneurs may have a main job, and an ancillary occupation that will allow them to pursue their true passion, an activity that will 'make their heart sing.' They are only waiting for the opportune time when they can test their new idea on social media.

There will be more startup businesses by talented GenZs who will fully embrace the digital tools that will make their service or product unique. Already in America, this creative class accounts for about one-third of the workforce.*

---

* Fareed Zakaria, *Ten Lessons for a Post-Pandemic World,* (Penguin Books 2021)

The New Normal

We are entering into a New World Order, with uncertain times ahead, particularly for the new generation of young hopefuls who may wake up to the reality that they could be worse off than their predecessors. They must be prepared to live through stagnant economic growth, declining wages, inflation, job insecurity, higher costs of energy and food, fractious supply chains, potential Russian threats on EU borders and the degradation of the planet's resources.

They will also need to get used to living with the very real possibility of new outbreaks of different variants of the corona virus for the rest of their lives, as my generation did when polio and AIDS were the big killers of the last century. So far the most chronic variant, the Covid-19 Omicron, has spread exponentially, and until the entire world is vaccinated, the virus, and its new sub-variants, will continue to mutate and transmit infection to greater numbers of the global population. The pandemic will stay with us and change the way we work and play.

Mandated lockdowns could very well be reinstated and force more people to work at home, bringing 9 to 5 protocols to an end. Hopefully, traffic rush hours could be a thing of the past.

Here then ends a short discourse on my points of view on the state of the globe for young people who have just entered the workforce. As time seems to be running out, the entire planet must start to work together, *immediately,* with the cooperation of all stakeholders – consumers, businesses and government entities. They must operate with complete transparency, to provide opportunities, education and dignity for the next generation of job seekers, and to this end policymakers must support the economies of their country by upgrading and enhancing its digital infrastructure. Jobs are increasingly being replaced by robots, and becoming irrelevant. The free accessibility to digital technology should be an inalienable right, available to everyone on the planet. We must ensure that healthcare services, especially vaccinations during pandemics, are freely available for every last person on every continent. Most important of all, we must prevent an ecological collapse by rebuilding a healthier planet with bluer skies, where the new generation of job seekers can safely live and work in the future.

The new mantra for governments should be to protect workers, *not* jobs. Every little bit will help.

ACKNOWLEDGEMENTS

This book has been locked in my memory, waiting to be written for a long time. It is not a life story, but an attempt to recount the variety of part-time jobs I had in the UK in the fifties and sixties, a follow-up to *Addresses*, memoirs that I wrote more than a decade ago about my childhood in wartorn Britain and post-war Europe. It also covers almost three decades of gainful employment between 1969 and 1996.

It needed the encouragement and the patience of my wife Patricia, as well as her helpful suggestions, and the ample free time that the Covid 19 lockdown has afforded me, to help bring this book to fruition. To Patricia, my deepest gratitude. To Covid, thanks but no thanks. I don't need any more lockdowns until my next book.

Huge thanks to my publisher Ian Pringle at Talisman Publishing for his support and guidance, and to Paul Haines for his advice and suggestions.

What would have I done without help from *Bryson's Dictionary for Writers and Editors*? Did you know that 'cockney' is written with a small 'c'? That there are apostrophes in Macy's and Levi's and none in Harrods and Sears? And what is the proper spelling for encyclopedia?

For the correct writing of English, *'What not to write'* by Kay Sayce was also invaluable.

My heartfelt thanks to Sarah Rooney for her creative input and encouragement, as well as her advice.

I am particularly indebted to my dear friend Axel Aylwen,

author and master of the English language, for his patience and help in copy-editing.

Gaps in memory of my Eltham College days were kindly filled in by school chums Robin Hay and Stephen Brown, and of my Middle Temple days by fellow barristers Anders Grundberg and again, by Robin, who also gave me sound advice on the thorny issues of political correctness, such as race, sexual orientation, agism, inclusivity, diversity etc, as well as on defamatory matters. Thank you both.

To my friends and family, wherever they are, who have given me their advice and much needed encouragement, among them Yvan Van Outrive, Nick Grossman, Dawn Rooney, Stephanie du Chatellier, Marion Burros, Avril Grundberg, Olga Maitland, Vivian and Louise Robinson, Malina and John - to them all I offer my deepest gratitude.

And last but not least, my thanks to Teerapong Hoonnirun for his layout design and artwork production.

My early writing has been pieced together entirely from scraps of memory without the benefit of notes or diaries, other than references to places of residences and dates officially recorded in my UK Aliens Registration Book, issued by the Home Office on 25 September 1954 when I returned to the UK as a boarder at Eltham College, and to a very old and tattered address-cum-autograph book that I have kept and saved over the years.

My later years that are described in chapters 9 and 10 were written with accurate references to business publications and books on advertising, as well as to my personal files and diaries, that line the shelves of my home office.